A Spring Fortnight in France

A Spring Fortnight in France

Josephine Tozier

Ross & Perry Inc.
Washington, D.C.

© Ross & Perry, Inc. 2001 All rights reserved.

No claim to U.S. government work contained throughout this book.

Protected under the Berne Convention. Published 2001

Printed in The United States of America
Ross & Perry, Inc. Publishers
717 Second St., N.E., Suite 200
Washington, D.C. 20002
Telephone (202) 675-8300
Facsimile (202) 675-8400
info@RossPerry.com

SAN 253-85551

Ross & Perry, Inc. Edition 2001

Library of Congress Control Number: 2001093109

http://www.GPOreprints.com

ISBN 1-931641-49-8

♾ The paper used in this publication meets the requirements for permanence established by the American National Standard for Information Sciences "Permanence of Paper for Printed Library Materials" (ANSI Z39.48-1984).

All rights reserved. No copyrighted part of this publication may be reproduced, stored in a retrieval system, or transmitted, in any form or by any means, electronic, photocopying, recording, or otherwise, without the prior written permission of the publisher.

CONTENTS

CHAPTER		PAGE
I	Le Mans	1
II	Angers	33
III	Saumur	65
IV	Poitiers	101
V	Argenton	142
VI	Brive	166
VII	Rocamadour	191
VIII	Albi	211
IX	Carcasonne	239
X	Arles	298
XI	Tarascon	330

ILLUSTRATIONS

The Village of Rocamadour (in colour)		*Frontispiece*
The Cathedral in Le Mans	Facing Page	16
House of Richard's Queen Berengaria, Le Mans	" "	30
Modern Angers—"Place de Ralliement"	" "	36
Old House and Church in Ronceray	" "	42
Old Angers		
Walls of the Château d'Angers and Market Gardens in the Moat	" "	60
Within the Château Enclosures. Twelfth Century Chapel and Birthplace of King René		60
In the Abbey of Fontevraud	" "	82
Effigies of the Kings Henry II., Richard II., and Queen Eleanor of Aquitaine, and Isabelle of Angoulême. Abbey of Fontevraud	" "	90
Saumur—Maison de la Reine de Sicile	" "	98
Rock Habitations and a Wanderer's Van	" "	98

x

List of Illustrations

A Glimpse of Montrieul-Bellay	*Facing Page*		98
In Poitiers			
As in the Middle Ages	"	"	110
A Fortified Doorway	"	"	110
On the Way to the Cathedral	"	"	110
A Paticut Poitevin	"	"	110
A Bit of Poitiers	"	"	118
Poitiers—An Ancient Dwelling			
The Door upon the Street	"	"	130
The Door within the Courtyard	"	"	130
On the Way to Argenton	"	"	140
Argenton—The Right and Left Bank of the River Creuse	"	"	146
A Ruined Château of Central France	"	"	168
Rocamadour from the Cahors Road	"	"	192
Rocamadour			
View of the Valley from a Rock Gallery	"	"	200
The Court of the Sanctuaries	"	"	200
The Pilgrim's Steps	"	"	200
The Crumbling Gateway of the Town	"	"	200
A Terrace 'Twixt Heaven and Earth	"	"	208
The Beggars of Rocamadour	"	"	208
The Valuable Truffle Hunters	"	"	208
In Central France			
A Château Fallen from its High Estate	"	"	212
A Stretch of Fertile Country	"	"	218
On His Way to Town	"	"	218
Old Château	"	"	218

List of Illustrations

BETWEEN ROCAMADOUR AND ALBI
- THE CITY OF CORDES . . . . . *Facing Page* 224
- A PEASANT OF LES CAUSES . . " " 224

IN CENTRAL FRANCE
- WHERE THE HILLS CLOSE IN . . " " 230
- HOUSES CLUSTERED ALONG THE BANK . . . . . . " " 230
- ALBI—THE VIEW ON THE BRIDGE . . " " 236

CARCASONNE—THE LOWER TOWN
- LES LICES . . . . " " 244
- A MAIN STREET . . . . . " " 244
- COURTYARD OF HÔTEL BERNARD . " " 244
- AN UNDECIDED VOTER . . . . " " 244

THE CITÉ OF CARCASONNE
- FROM THE BRIDGE . . . . . " " 260
- ON THE RAMPARTS . . . . . " " 260
- AT THE PORTE DE L'AUDE . . " " 260

CARCASONNE
- AN OLD COUPLE OF MARKET-FOLK " " 280
- A POLITICAL DISCUSSION . . . " " 280
- A PROUD DONKEY . . . . . " " 280

ARLES—A BULL FIGHT IN THE ARENA " " 300

ARLES—THE ALISCAMPS
- A GALLO-ROMAN SARCOPHAGUS . " " 308
- THE CHAPEL AT THE ENTRANCE . " " 308
- ALLÉE OF THE TOMBS . . . . " " 308

A CORNER IN ARLES . . . . . . " " 314
ARLES—THE CLOISTER OF ST. TROPHIME " " 320
THE RUINS OF MONT MAJOUR . . . " " 326

TARASCON
- THE DOMESTIC BOULEVARD . . " " 334
- THE MARKET PLACE . . . . " " 334

xii *List of Illustrations*

MARGOT AND ROBINSON ON THE QUAY	*Facing Page*	338
THE TARASQUE	" "	338
THE TARASQUE LED FORTH	" "	338
TARASCON FROM BEAUCAIRE	" "	338

Maps

FROM LE MANS TO ARGENTON	" "	34
ARGENTON TO ALBI	" "	142
FROM ALBI TO MARSEILLES	" "	240

A SPRING FORTNIGHT IN FRANCE

The interchange between dead memories and present life is the delight of travel.—T. A. SYMONDS

Chapter I

LE MANS

*A*NGELA VICTORIA sat in an apartment in Paris surrounded by open trunks, boxes, bags, and baskets, and all that paraphernalia known in the French shops as *articles de voyage*. Gowns, hats, shoes, and numerous accessories of toilet littered the chairs, overflowed from the half-open *armoire*, or lay where they had been carelessly dropped upon the floor.

Angela was evidently preparing for a journey. Her face wore a troubled look, as in jerky sentences she addressed her sister.

"Well, if you can't go with me, I won't go your way, so I suppose I must go alone! It is very inconsiderate of Aunt Victoria to require your attendance just when I want you! I don't see why she can't wait a few weeks!"

"Perhaps San Remo is losing its charm. Can't you travel down there with me, and, after I have comfortably settled her in whatever place she likes better, we could then take the journey you have planned, only in the contrary direction, working from the bottom of the page to the top?"

"No, I want to saunter from spring into summer, not from summer back into spring! If you choose, you may go your way and rush down to Italy and

Aunt Victoria by night and the *Rapide*. I will meet you there. At this season every bud, flower, and blade is fresh and young. There are no tourist parties wandering around; I have never seen central France in this month, so I would rather travel slowly on in solitude than hurry with you. Perhaps I shall pick up friends by the wayside."

Angela Victoria settled herself back in the deep chair with a look of determination on her face. Her sister, Georgina, stood in front of her gently waving a telegram she held in her hands. She wasn't listening at all, and went on saying, rather to herself " I can't help myself. Here are the stern commands. I must start on Monday." Then, turning to her sister, she asked:

" Are you still determined to leave to-morrow? "

Angela nodded.

Georgina lifted up her chin with a jerk; a habit she had a of showing displeasure.

" Very well, if you insist upon going alone, you fortunately speak the language, and have enough grey hairs to protect you," she added, with a tinge of malice.

Angela glanced rapidly with a light start into a mirror by her side. She expected to see her fifty grey hairs suddenly transformed to fifty thousand, but in spite of Georgina's contempt they were not more conspicuous than formerly among her wavy brown locks; whereupon her happy nature reasserted itself with a bound, and her face beamed with sunny smiles.

"I don't mind the grey hairs. I like them. I shall see that everyone calls me 'Madame.' Who knows! Some one of the friends I meet may bring me back to you riding in an automobile! I'm sure to have an enchanting journey! I'm glad I look old!"

Georgina shook her head gravely. Then she became emphatic.

"I can't imagine how you're going to travel without me! Of course you will forget your keys; mislay your tickets, always leave your umbrella behind, and lose time everywhere!"

But Angela's countenance did not lose its hopeful and sunny expression. She showed no sign of discouragement. Indeed, in her innermost soul she rejoiced at the chance to try emancipation from Georginia's cast-iron methods. Notwithstanding, she made a wry face.

"Even with all these pitfalls you describe, I must be brave and go, because——" Angela pointed impressively to her desk where pads, pencils, rubber, and note books were laid out with a careful precision in strong contrast to the confusion of her wardrobe scattered recklessly about the room.

Georgina smiled, a stern, incredulous smile.

"A book?" she asked solemnly.

Angela Victoria had been threatening to write a book ever since she had turned sixteen years. She was now, at thirty-six, no nearer her literary accomplishment than resulted from buying stores of stationery. For writing materials she had a mania, but as yet they had served no deeper purpose than for scribbling bright little notes to all her friends and acquaintances.

"Pray, what kind of a book is *this* to be?" ironically pursued her sister.

"A book of travel," complacently announced Angela.

Then Georgina laughed outright. She had a perfectly undisguised pity for Angela Victoria's methods of travel. She declared them to be only sentimental lingerings, and contended that all her ideas were influenced by her name. Angela Victoria was not responsible for her name. She had inherited it from the old aunt whose telegram was now summoning Georgina away from the self-imposed duty of guardian angel and personal conductor. We all enjoy having a scapegoat, some utterly irresponsible object on which we saddle all our weaknesses, though we continue to cling to them. Angela was not behind her sister in making her name an excuse for her foibles. Georgina, now, was practical, and Georgina was commonplace. Angela Victoria was neither. When Georgina travelled she saw everything the guidebook said should be seen; and saw it thoroughly in an incredibly short time. Whereas Angela Victoria journeyed through the world, moaning over every interesting old castle, and dreaming queer dreams about the hearts which had once beat within the ruined walls. Georgina would explore thoroughly every corner, state every date connected with the place, and have its history so firmly wedged in her mind that she could instruct her sister concerning minor details which Angela totally disregarded for hours after. And now it was this unsophisticated, impossible traveller who expected to write a book!

Georgina became condescending and sweet as sugar. "*Chère innocente!* A book! You will mention the sights nobody cares for but you, and forget all the important objects your readers ought to see! Now, if I were along, you might manage such a piece of literature! How can you do it without my aid?"

"I can try," modestly replied Angela slyly. Her self-reliance was increasing by leaps. She rose and shook out her skirts. "Since I must learn to be independent I will now go and get my tickets. I think I shall buy a *billet circulaire*, or whatever you call the thing. Then I can stop whenever I like."

Georgina sighed. She was resigned, but alarmed.

"Then I will stay and attend to your packing," she said, thinking if her sister insisted upon going, wandering off by herself, which was not such an eminently perilous experiment, considering that she was approaching middle age and had passed a good slice of her life in France, that the luggage should be of proper dimensions, and that not all the suitable clothing should be left at home while Angela stuffed her trunk with articles she would never need.

"All you possibly can require I will see put in your small trunk. I will drag the big one with me to Italy."

"Drag it! You won't have to drag it!" declared Angela, putting on her hat while she proudly delivered herself of some words of wisdom; "*voiture à gallerie* costs but three francs fifty, if you have but one trunk or ten. You will need to take one for your own baggage. You know I never object to paying the railway charges. When my trunk is once on the *Rapide* you never see it again until it's taken out at San Remo. Drag it! How recklessly you talk!"

She turned a mischievous face toward Georgina as she pulled on her gloves.

"Are you sure you know where you're going?" asked her sister, waving a pair of silk stockings she had picked up off the floor at Angela, as she was about to vanish out of the door.

"No," cried Angela, looking back. "I shall depend on my good friend, the ticket agent. There is a nice one at the American Express. He will plan for me. If you want to know all about it, meet me in an hour at Chiboust's for tea, and while we eat the best little cakes in Paris you shall hear what your dear sister is going to do."

Georgina shuddered at such inconsequence, then, her sister being gone, sat down for a minute. Her conscientious, orderly mind was really alarmed at Angela's foolish frivolity. But what could she do! Their rich old aunt, who had been wintering in Italy and whom she was bound to obey, had sent such a peremptory message to her to come and settle her, along with a useless but devoted tirewoman, at Italian springs she insisted would save her from death, that Georgina was forced to go. Angela had not been asked for, and as she had long planned to travel in Central France every argument her sister could devise to make

Le Mans

her give up the projected tour met with decided and obstinate resistance.

"Well," sighed Georgina, while endeavouring vigorously to straighten out the chaos of clothing in the chamber, "after a few days of solitude, when she finds she can't possibly see the cities without me, she will probably give up the trip and follow." Which observation proves that even our nearest and dearest do not always judge us correctly.

The next morning very early, with Georgina still in close attendance, Angela drove to the Gare St. Lazare. An open fiacre sufficed for the luggage, which, by Georgina's careful calculation, had been reduced to one useful cabin trunk, a hand-bag, a basket, and an umbrella.

Georgina looked dubious, like the sky, which was overcast. "It's going to rain all the time," she remarked, making a last effort at discouragement.

Little cared Angela Victoria for the dark Paris clouds. She beamed on the contrary. Rain never came when she wanted sunshine; even if the drops were actually falling, her optimistic mind prophesied the clearing.

"Will you ever be old enough to see things as they really are?" asked her sister as they drove along. With a temperament keen for enjoyment, she never could be old enough to expect sorrow hidden behind every cloud. "What is, is good," was her device, therefore the final wise warnings of her anxious sister were only half heard.

Away she rolled, leaning out smiling at Georgina, who stood on the platform still looking very dubious.

From Paris to Le Mans the distance by road is two hundred and eleven kilometres. The train, if it is a very fast one, takes about four hours. The highway is smooth as a floor and without dangerous places, running between waving trees and over pleasant streams, and is an irresistible temptation for those who ride in motor cars to put on full speed. Angela, having no motor car at her command, followed the habit of her mind and rejoiced exceedingly upon being mounted so high and comfortably in the train; she could look over the walls into the fresh spring gardens of Ville d'Avray and see the carpets of violets and tulips, and surprise the bourgeoise families all out that fine morning in their bedroom slippers for a walk on the pebbly paths. No auto scurrying along the *grande route* could enter so intimately into family life, nor could they yet see, as she did, the enchanting panorama from the height of the railway at Surrennes. From the top of the rise near this little railway station she looked down into the deep valley of the earth, shining in its fresh green dress; saw the stately city far over the plain, soft and mysterious in the hazy atmosphere, standing forth from a background of hills where they faded into the dull sky, and watched the broad river glistening and winding off into the far distance. Masses of lilacs and blossoming fruit trees covered the hill from the carriage window to the very bank of the stream.

"No! surely one could not see this from a low

Le Mans

motor car!" was Angela's involuntary exclamation. And it brought forth such immediate response from a delightful old lady, who was the only other occupant of the carriage, that a bond of sympathy at once united them. This swelled into confidence at Versailles. They were both enthusiastically revelling in the juicy young green leaves of the princely forest when blackness suddenly curtained the windows.

"They have tunnelled under the royal springtime," ejaculated Angela.

"The Republicans, of course! *Toujours la République!*" answered the old lady, as the daylight came back to show her energetically shrugging her shoulders.

"*Madame* is *Royaliste?*" Angela said gently.

"*Mais! La plus possible!*"

There can be no more delightful companion on any occasion, particularly when shut up in a railway carriage, than a charming French woman. Angela's new acquaintance richly deserved this title. She was as enchanted with the view they got of the palace at Versailles when they puffed out of the tunnel as was Angela, although they had both seen it before, countless times. She became fluent with anecdotes about young cadets, her grandchildren, as they rolled past St. Cyr. She chatted about the death of Francis I., and of the great literary gatherings, as they ambled by the Château of Ramboullier, as if the history of the Renaissance was but a thing of yesterday. She pointed out with interest the ex-royal forests stretching for leagues beside the train, and spoke pityingly of that impotent monarch, Louis XVI., who was hunting under these trees while the furies from Paris were marching on to Versailles.

"*Il etait notre Roi, mais je crains qu'il fut bien imbecile!*"

She was as gleeful as Angela herself at seeing the peasants when they jumped loutishly aside to avoid the motor cars which whizzed along the broad highway running beside the track; she became both excited and curious about the smoke which curled out of the cottage chimneys; she wondered what the peasants could be cooking at that time of day; she was inquisitive and anxious about the vegetables growing everywhere, under glass; she overflowed with conversation, she made Angela feel clever, and together they laughed heartily at that inevitable flat car-wheel always found on French carriages, which she declared sung the little tune, and Angela promptly translated it as "Get-a-bump, get-a-bump." The tender hues of spring were spread all over the land; the moss-grown, thatched roofs, now becoming rare, excited her regret.

"They may not be safe or healthy, that is the modern cry, but I love the thatch, and so does the peasant. It is warm in winter and cool in summer, and picturesque! picturesque! In my youth all the farm houses and cottages were thatched."

Near the track stood a rough, grey, stone cottage. A deep, soft, green thatched roof almost sweeping the ground covered its rude walls. Two nodding poplars guarded the entrance. Against the gable end was a huge mass of white and purple lilacs. A little peach tree that was putting forth its pinkest buds stood like a nosegay beside the low door.

"So they all looked! Ah! *que c'est beau, la campagne!*"

After they left Chaitres the rain came down in a sheet, sending the peasants plodding along with big cotton umbrellas raised, and causing the motorists to crawl into their shells, which looked to the contented occupants of the secure high-swung railroad carriage like ugly brown beetles scurrying off to shelter. But as the train rolled on the dark clouds went off in the direction of Paris, and the sky of Maine was clear and bright before they reached their destination.

Shut up in the limited space of a *compartiment pour dames seules*, congenial souls are apt to grow confidentially chatty. So it now happened. The old lady told her name, Madame de Grandmaison, and said she was on her way to visit a sister who lived in the old family home at Le Mans; then, without impertinent curiosity, rather with pleasing interest, she drew forth from Angela that her solitary journey was for pleasure, and that she had learned her French in the Rue de Varennes.

"Ah! Then you must have been at school with my sister's daughter, Marie de Lalorge! She would have been just your age had she lived. Poor girl! It is now two years since she was taken from us, leaving a devoted husband and two lovely children!"

How is it that in this contracted world by some magic we always come upon those who have some connection with our past?

Angela had not only known Marie at school, but remembered her with affection.

"Then you will not leave Le Mans without coming to see my sister. She is an invalid, or she would call upon you. Marie's children are now with her. Come for *goûter*. What you call 'the tea.'" Madame laughed at she pronounced the English words.

The cordial invitation was accepted with alacrity. The necessary directions were given, and Angela promised to come at five o'clock. What would Georgina have said if she suspected how quickly her sister would meet with friends!

The journey ended all too soon. To Angela it seemed as if they had scarcely left Paris before they arrived in the station at Le Mans.

"'Le Dauphin' is the best hotel," the old lady had said in answer to an inquiry. "Au revoir until five o'clock."

Angela found the 'bus, and as she mounted into it fondly imagined that the royalistic tendencies of her new friend might have influenced her in praise of the hotel. "Dear Madame La Baronne, there will never be a dauphin again," she sighed, as they drove up to the door, when behold, carved upon the face of the inn before which they stopped appeared two wriggling fishes. Royalty had nothing whatever to do with this matter. Although it was a blow to her romantic sentiment, she accepted calmly dolphins instead of a king's son, and trotted contentedly up the well-worn staircase, following the valet whom the smiling landlady delegated to conduct "Madame" to her room.

Le Mans

Angela's experience with hotels in small provincial towns was exceedingly meagre. She had spent many years of her life in Paris, both in and out of school; she had several times raced through the châteaux country with American friends, putting up at caravanseries especially adapted to the luxurious tastes of foreigners. She was prepared now for new experiences, but the shabby corridor, the stone stair covered with worn carpet, the ugly iron balustrade, and the generally inartistic air of the dull hallways depressed even her buoyant soul. Up to the door of the room which the servant threw open for her a single step led from the passageway. She followed the man, and at first glance her good spirits returned. An inlaid floor polished until it shone was under her feet. The room was furnished with beautiful mahogany of a colour that only age can give. Indeed, it was as ancient as the hotel itself, which began life as an inn just before the Revolution. A desk on one side of the room made Angela green with envy, and a touch of colour was supplied to the whole apartment by the yellow silk coverlid piled up on the high bed of a truly classic form.

"I hope Madame will be comfortable here," said the servant kindly, as he threw open the long windows leading to a balcony. "Madame desires nothing more?"

Madame desired nothing at all but to look out over the square. As he left her, she stepped out to gaze about. *La Place de la République* in Le Mans is surrounded by hotels and cafés; the usual prominent

Bureau des Postes et Telegraphes bobs up in one corner, a large building architecturally uninteresting; on one side of the square looms an old church tower, the only picturesque object in view. A few trees grow in turfless soil; a gay kiosk and tramway station adorned with motley posters in glaring colours is in the centre, while a paved roadway, broad and clean, surrounds the square. Angela looked down on a dull crowd of peasants lounging in the street and talking vociferously. A queer individual, who raced round and round the entire square coatless and hatless, carrying a small French flag on a long slender pole, excited but indifferent interest from the crowd. He may have been engaged in a walking match against time, or perhaps working out a wager. The valet, who arrived the second time with a pan of hot water, could tell her nothing. He only lifted his shoulders when Angela questioned him and said:

"There are people like that! '*Il y a des gens comme ça!*'"

Which either meant nothing, or a great deal.

Angela Victoria questioned no further. Georgina would have been more insistent. She would never have let such an incident escape her inquiring mind. Nobody seemed really interested in the man but two unwearied companions who kept him company in his trot. The uniforms of a few loose-trousered blue-and-red soldiers, with their hands as usual in their pockets, brightened the dull scene; they were the only gay-looking persons she gazed down upon, yet this quiet provincial *Place*, sleepy as it is, has had fearful dreams. The

Le Mans

last one was when, at the advance of the German army in 1871, a sanguinary, desperate fight was fought by the French defending the city. In the eighteenth century, when the Revolution was sweeping over all France, a still more terrible nightmare assailed it. Under the windows of this very hotel took place the horrible massacre of Vendeans; blood flowed like water where now the peasants gossipped in provincial idleness and frisking dogs gaily gambolled with one another.

Angela looked at her watch. She had four hours for sightseeing before tea time, for she and Madame had eaten their *déjeuner* in the swaying dining-car on their way from Paris. She went below to inquire at the window of the bureau the nearest way to the cathedral. "It is but around the corner," directed her pleasant hostess.

"Round the corner" proved to be around three corners. Therefore, just when the tourist was convinced of having lost her way, she came unexpectedly upon the great church lifted high up on its terraces over the *Place des Jacobins*. With that consciousness of the value of vista which amounts to genius with the French, the old monastery gardens once covering this ground were long ago cleared away, that nothing might distract the eye from the dignity and beauty of the splendid cathedral, built over what was once the Roman wall of the city. Out of a mass of delicate verdure, fresh April foliage, young and tender, among leaves that sparkled from the rain of that morning, rose the choir and flying buttresses.

Angela sank down on the first bench she found, entranced by the scene. How glad she was to be alone! She could sit as long as she chose; had her sister been with her, after one all-embracing glance, Georgina would have ordered: "Let us go inside! Don't sit here and stare! We have seen other cathedrals in France!" But to Angela each new object of beauty, no matter how many others she had seen before, was a surprise. She wanted to gaze long and lovingly. This noble edifice seemed to her fancy to stand there haughtily uplifted like some splendid, proud creature expecting admiration.

Across the square from where she sat broad steps cut through the old ramparts led from the Place below to the cathedral square above. They are divided at the bottom by the basin of a fountain, and unite again on a platform halfway up. They lead to the old Place of the château, on which the great portals of the cathedral open. The rough pavement has endured for centuries, and the ancient houses, silent and deserted, as befit so venerable a nook of the old world, cluster about the church as they did when Henry II., England's first Angevin king, was brought a babe in his mother's arms to be baptised. Nine centuries has the west façade looked out upon a changing world. William the Conqueror knew these towers. Geoffrey Plantagenet clattered in armour through the great door many times, passing in to be married, to hold his royal heir at the rude font, to sing *Te Deum* for cruel, bloody victories, and to be borne at last to his grave with mediæval pomp.

Grass now grows up between the pavement of the

THE CATHEDRAL IN LE MANS

perron. The carved stone balustrade is broken in many places, and the great doors of the nave firmly closed. The heroes of Angela's fondest historical phantasies, the knights of the race of Anjou, once strode boldly up these worn steps. So now she complacently trotted after them; several centuries after them, to be sure, but being on the ground made sacred by their footsteps denied the greater and more royal portal, she pushed her way through the little side door and stepped reverently into the dim, tender light of the cathedral.

Her ignorance on all the major and minor points of architecture was simply unparalleled, and, as she took no pains to conceal it, Georgina constantly deplored her unwillingness to learn the proper things to admire.

She knew where the dead memories lingered, and she cared for nothing else.

This great, solemn, silent temple, its long nave stretching away to where beyond the choir the bright light of the early afternoon shone through the glorious old glass of the windows in the apse until they glowed like rare jewels, was where unwilling young Geoffrey of Anjou, handsome Geoffrey with his sprig of sunny flowers, wedded the equally unwilling Matilda, daughter of Henry I. of England. The groom was sixteen, the bride was twenty-six, and widow of an emperor, whom she haughtily preferred to a good-looking youth of lesser rank. It was a marriage of policy forced by her father. Fierce quarrels and a speedy separation ensued, but the iron will of King Henry I. prevailed, and this ill-assorted pair became finally reconciled, so that the future great king, their son, was brought here to this cathedral to be received into the arms of the church. Later Geoffrey lay in death under the splendid tomb beneath these arches, and within these grey walls his grandson, England's weak young king, Henry Court-Mantel, rested from his stormy career, his body held by the determined citizens of Le Mans, who loved him so much that they would not allow the procession to proceed on its way to the tomb prepared for him at Rouen.

Angela knelt down on a low *prie-dieu*, and like a sorceress summoned up the shapes of the Angevin rulers for her pleasure. All the Plantagenets came, filling the naves with figures handsome and knightly, displaying in her imagination that power of fascination which even the most contemptible of the race possessed. Old Henry I. of England, his father the Conqueror, strode in with a band of bold Normans, while poor murdered little Arthur and his miserable uncle, John Lackland, both joined the ghostly throng. Richard, tall, noisy, rough, captivating Lion-heart, dominated the shadowy shapes.

One of the most brilliant and touching scenes these walls ever witnessed was when, at their consecration, Fulk, the father of Geoffrey Plantagenet, being finally reconciled to his numerous enemies, offered this building to God. He was on the point of departure for a pilgrimage to Jerusalem. Surrounded by a glittering host of nobles and clergy, and attended by the Duchess, who was a daughter of Duke Elias of Maine, he took

Le Mans

the little Geoffrey in his arms and placed him on the newly hallowed altar. Then he prayed aloud to the patron saint with tears running down his cheeks:

"Oh, holy Julian, to thee I commend my child and my land! Do thou defend them both!"

The vandals of the French Revolution, those ravaging fiends, who, while shouting their loudest for "*Liberté! Égalité! Fraternité!*" allowed no brotherhood with departed princes, nor would give their ashes rest or peace, destroyed and carried off every vestige of the splendid monuments which once embellished this cathedral. The tomb of Richard's queen, Berengaria, tucked away around the corner of the transcept up against the wall, for all the world like a bed, is the only one left. On her couch the noble queen lies, a figure of regal size and noble mien, resting peacefully after her unhappy life with that wild, stormy lord.

Part of the spoil of the monument erected to Geoffrey Plantagenet, his interesting portrait done in gold and jewels, is now in the museum at Le Mans. It is a valuable memoir of his features and the costume he wore, and was preserved by mere chance. The clever forethought of a revolutionary collector who bought relics for a song saved this treasure from destruction.

As Angela Victoria went out onto the porch by the door in the transcept she left the knightly company behind and plunged herself in the amusement awakened in her complex mind by the grotesque carving with which the arch is laden. She laughed with the grinning monks and enjoyed the impossible beasts until, looking through a narrow slit framed by the two walls of antique buildings, a bit of living, sunlit, happy nature attracted her eyes. Miles and miles of glowing country stretching away to shadowy hills was the picture she saw. On one side of the frame a delicious old château, built that infirm priests might spend their last days in peace, and which bore the doleful name of *La Grabatoire*, now looks very cheerful amidst flowers and trees of a little garden. The names "*Madame*" and "*Mademoiselle C.*" written on the doorpost awakened her envy. It was precisely the dwelling Angela was eminently fitted to enjoy. Built centuries ago, with tourelles and sharp gables, the casement windows looked on the front out upon the grass-grown square at the grand façade of the mediæval cathedral, and at the back a stretch of flowering country through which a river meanders, winding, twisting, and curling, until it loses itself among distant hills.

Angela gazed longingly at the house, and fancied herself blissfully installed among piles of literature, all bearing upon the Lion-hearted Richard, handsome Geoffrey, and the masterful monarch, Henry II.

The romance and rudeness, the charm and barbarity of the house of Anjou, had been the crowning factor in the trip Angela was now taking. While on a visit during the winter she had fallen upon some queer old books in the private library of a bibliophile, and all her visionary spirit for the past had been aroused by the romances on which she fed at that time.

Now she was here, happy and satisfied to be at lib-

Le Mans

erty, free from her matter-of-fact sister, free to moon and dream as she pleased, and to give her imagination full sway. A wise-looking parrot was apparently the only living thing about the little château. It sat solemnly in the window and screamed bitter defiance at the grinning gargoyles opposite, insulting the rooks who were circling around the towers of the great church by crying mocking " caw-caws " in its squeaky voice. Angela went down the slit between the two châteaux and followed a narrow steep-stepped way leading between high garden walls down to the bank of the river. She crossed the bridge at the foot of the stairs over the Sarthe, rushing, swift-flowing and full with the spring rains, between gardens rich in blossoming lilac bushes.

From the side of the stream she thus reached, all the quaint, ancient beauty of Le Mans crowded on the cliff, crowned by the cathedral, a jungle of deep purple slate roofs, old towers, bits of heavy ancient wall, and dainty tourelles; feathery trees waving amidst the mass of masonry; dashes of yellow, saffron, red, green, and dull violet, stood forth against the turquoise blue of the sky of Maine, from which the remaining clouds of an uncertain day were hurrying home.

Angela strolled along to a bridge lower down, and then up again into the city. It was nearly time to seek out her friend; she went by the *Rue des Trois Sonnettes*, a street which has made no weak concessions to the evanescent taste of passing centuries, steep and ill-paved, with tiny children playing fearlessly in the roadway, inaccessible for the dangerous automobile.

Laughing girls, flirting with gay little soldiers who lounged beneath the quaint deep windows, shot the same sort of glances from the same sort of bright, coquettish eyes which looked down in the twelfth century from these very casements on the men-at-arms of Richard Cœur de Lion.

The *Rue des Trois Sonnettes* turns into the *Rue de la Truie-qui-File*, delicious in name and in archæological interest. The heavy doors that once guarded the houses are now hanging by their loose hinges along this broken way, and they gape to reveal the many bits of lovely architecture forgotten by destructive time. Higher up, this street changes into *La Grande Rue*, where the still fine houses of the old nobility are carefully hidden behind high walls from the prying eyes of the curious.

Angela had reached her destination. The bell of a heavy solid oak doorway was answered promptly by a liveried servant, who admitted her into a paved courtyard. She saw a massive round tower in one corner near the street, and a low, long, slate-covered wing of the period of the Renaissance stretching out before her. The house was not large, but a gem of its kind; the window frames richly carved, and a dainty, slender tourelle in the opposite corner seemed to smile contemptuously across the court at the homely, sturdy old tower of the most ancient part of the building.

Madame la Baronne de Grandmaison, her travelling companion of the morning, met Angela and led her through the salon to a terrace where her sister, Madame de Lalorge, sat in a wheeled chair. The courteous

Le Mans

hostess endeavoured to rise, and, gracefully smiling, blamed her rheumatic limbs for not allowing her to come to meet the guest. She clasped both Angela's hands between her own and welcomed her daughter's friend with that delicious charm which reaches its highest perfection in the true French aristocrat. Two children, a boy of twelve and a girl of nine, stood beside their grandmother's chair. They likewise greeted the visitor with a gracefulness and simplicity of manner which won Angela's heart at once.

A great salver laden with priceless china and matchless silver of the seventeenth century was brought out by one of the footmen and placed on a table near Madame de Lalorge, while on another little stand were spread tempting cakes. Chocolate and tea, this last a special concession to Angela's supposed wants, were served while the party enjoyed the soft air of a garden with gravelled paths winding between beds full of violets and tulips, a little plot of ground so skilfully planned that an air of spaciousness was given to what in reality was a very small enclosure. Two great trees and masses of lilac bushes shaded the tiny walks, while beyond a low vine-grown wall ran the whole length of the back of the garden, showing above an unbroken view over the wide country shimmering with the silver-green tints of the spring. Behind this garden wall the ground fell away abruptly, like a small precipice, to the street below.

"*Ma foi!*" said the baronne, in reply to Angela's question about the age of the house. "We were all born here, and how many generations before us I don't know. What is left of the original château is only the tower and the tourelle; you perhaps know that a tourelle was the mark of a noble's residence in the old times. Our family goes back to the wild days of Maine. The house through which you passed was built in the time of the Bourbons. Much of the ancient part has been pulled down. One tale in its history my sister and myself heard many times in our youth when our brave grandmother was still alive. She was left a young widow at the end of the eighteenth century, and lived here with her two little sons all through the furious epoch of the Revolution; keeping in some mysterious manner her estate, and her head on her shoulders. She used to thrill us when she told us how, shut up within these old walls, she listened to the wild cries and to the bloody fights raging in the narrow streets. The terrified servants were forbidden to show their faces at the window, or to walk here in the garden. Never under any circumstances were they allowed to answer knockings at the gate. Provisions were sent up by night in a basket lowered over the wall here to a retainer, who was one of the revolutionary committee, and who lived in the house the roof of which you can see there just below the wall. Water has always been plentiful in that well there in the corner." The well, with its rich iron-work, had been wildly distracting to Angela since she first began to eat the tea and cakes.

"How old is that well?" she asked.

"It was built in the time of Adam," answered the little girl. Her grandmother and aunt laughed heartily.

Le Mans

"Who told you that, petite?"

"My nurse. She says she knows."

"Then it must be true," they ejaculated.

The little girl nodded triumphantly.

"Have you seen the tunnel?" asked the boy, anxious to do his part, too, and exalt the city.

The tunnel is a modern passage cut to facilitate traffic through the great sandstone cliff on which Le Mans is built. It was much more interesting to the lad than either the well or the old towers of his ancestral home. "You can see the *Pont en 'X.* from the wall here," he continued, moving forward to show it to her. Like all the citizens, he was very proud of this new and novel achievement in the way of a bridge built for the tramway. Angela followed him down the steps and through the little path and tried hard to admire, while her eyes and her enthusiasm were really all centred on the beautiful panorama stretching beyond the flower-carpeted garden. Madame la Baronne then suggested an expedition for the next morning, a *belle promenade à travers la ville,* to find not only the remains of the old city walls and bastions hidden away in courtyards and behind houses, but, likewise, the dwelling where Scarron, the poet, and his wife lived in the days before that noted woman became Madame de Maintenon, the guide, philosopher, and friend of Louis XIV. There was also the house where Queen Berangaria once lived. "If you are going to Angers, the afternoon train will be early enough for you to depart," and, there being no Georgina to force the plans, Angela at once changed the hour of her leaving, and agreed with enthusiasm to meet her new friends on the following morning. She parted regretfully from her hosts and the garden, and strolled slowly back to the hotel, through queer streets full of little flights of steps and abrupt corners. Dinner time found her seated in the restaurant near a window; nothing should escape her, although her sister's theory was that when travelling you should rest the mind and the eyes during a meal. Angela was having a glorious time being thoroughly intractable, and disobeying all the advice Georgina had given her. The holiday crowd of sober peasants, the seven-leagued pacemaker and his flag had alike vanished. There remained alone on the Place a row of six or more fiacres which the custom of Le Mans supports. All French fiacres belong to the same family, thought Angela, they must all be born of the same parents. A young or new fiacre no mortal has ever seen. Angela contemplated a row of these little vehicles. The drivers were dozing after a hard day's work, and the horses gleaning what meagre refreshment they could from their slenderly furnished nosebags. The jolliest, fattest coachman of them all had just retired into the interior of his small victoria and filled the whole back seat, had settled himself comfortably for a nap, still chuckling over some joke he had been cracking with his comrade just behind him. Angela turned her attention to the salad; a very good one it was, too! but cries of pleasure and surprise again distracted her. The nodding old man had been awakened by visitors. Two peasant women with their husbands, dressed in their best blouses, were leaning over him as he sat in his carriage, and

Le Mans

from his improvised throne on the back seat he was welcoming his guests with loud expressions of delight. Angela strained her ears to try and hear some of the wit which brought forth immoderate laughter from the visitors. But, as they were all talking together, she could hear nothing. When the preliminary greetings were over every inch of his possession, from the top of the thin, sleepy horse's nose to the hind wheel of the carriage, was thoroughly examined and admired. An extra feedbag was brought out from under the box and into its depths all four visitors peered with intense interest. He had evidently just bought a new outfit. The cushions and the worn rug were taken out to be admired, the hood of the carriage was raised and lowered amidst exclamations of profound approbation, and the man walked proudly round and round his property, pointing out all its beauties with a visible pride of ownership. "How deliciously French!" thought Angela to herself, "no wonder they are so gay; nothing is too meagre to interest these people." She did not realise how light her own disposition was. When they had sufficiently admired, the coachman mounted his box and invited his friends to ride. They accepted with glee. And merrily laughing and chattering all four climbed in. It was a full load for a small fiacre, but the bony horse gallantly galloped around the square. Luckily no careless bicyclist or unhappy dog lingered in the way of that dashing equipage, for the driver's eyes dwelt not upon his skinny steed, but were turned toward the interior of the carriage from whence sounds of merriment floating over the Place proclaimed that his witty tongue was galloping as fast as his nag. With a great flourish of whip and reins he skilfully brought his fiacre back into the space it had left in the line. The visit was ended, his guests climbed out, the men pretending to be cramped by the long ride; farewells were spoken, and while approving nods were thrown back at the horse and his owner, the peasants were off, shaking their legs and stretching, and the coachman returned to his slumber and Angela to her dinner.

The night had grown chilly, the bed was comfortable, the warmth from the down quilt grateful, and the temptingly convenient electric light beside the bed prompted her to improve her mind by dipping into the historical literature with which she had made her travelling bag so weighty. Georgina disapproved of reading in bed, so Angela smoothed down her conscience with the excuse: "If I am going to write a book of travel I must sprinkle history through the pages or no reviewer will seriously approve of me. If I don't read at night, when can I find out what I ought to know? I must spend the days more profitably." She began with a French paper-covered book she had bought at a shop that morning while drifting around those many corners in search of the cathedral. The pages were divided with much advertising matter; it both distracted and diverted her mind from the information sprinkled between. She managed to find out that Le Mans stood on a spur of red sandstone rising abruptly from the bank of the River Sarthe. It was a citadel in the time of the Romans and a stronghold of the Gauls.

Le Mans

After the Latins were driven forth by the Franks the early monarchs of the land built more extended walls of defence than those erected by their predecessors, and the city became of such importance that later in its history the rulers of Anjou, when they became a power, cast envious eyes upon the flourishing town and stretched out their grasping hands to seize the territory, just as William of Normandy, used to conquering, conceived the idea that he wanted it, too, and snatched both citadel and the country around. Between these two greedy neighbours the citizens of Le Mans suffered many an unhappy day. Their rulers were betrayed, imprisoned, murdered, first by one and then by the other of these foes, and they and their families were given over to fire and sword, until at last the union of Anjou and Normandy through the marriage of Geoffrey Plantagenet with Mathilda, daughter of Henry I., gave the burghers peace for a time and caused a lull in the storm. It was brief. Peace and prosperity could not long endure in this divided land. Although Le Mans might reasonably have expected quiet under Henry II., fruit of this union, the city became during his reign a scene of struggle between that king and his rebellious sons. Richard Cœur de Lion allied himself to Philip of France against his father, and together they stormed and burned the town, driving forth the English monarch. In this battle Richard was wildly pursuing his father's band of faithful knights and riding recklessly out into the country, now stretching so fruitful in full view of the cathedral, when he became separated from his followers and found himself confronted with a great English baron, William Marshall. "God's feet, Marshall!" cried the reckless young rebel, swearing his favourite oath, "spare me! I have no hauberk!"

Marshall rose in his saddle. "Spare you! That I will and leave you to the devil!"

Those times were rude, and religion primitive. King Henry in his despair looked back from the summit of an elevation as he was flying from his son's wrath and saw the burning city he loved, where he had been born and baptised. It was in the possession of his hated enemy and his no less hated son. The King shook his mailed fist at Heaven and blasphemed aloud: "O God, thou hast shamefully taken from me this day the place I love most on earth; the city in which I was born and bred; the city wherein lies the body of my father and that of his patron saint. I will revenge it on thee as best I can. I will withdraw from thee my soul; that thing in me for which thou carest most!"

Wretched John Lackland, of whom a contemporary writer solemnly avers that by his presence hell itself would be defiled, again swung the torch and battle-axe over Le Mans while in pursuit of his unhappy nephew, Arthur, as it rose painfully from the ruin his brother Richard had worked. Not until the fall of the Angevin kings did comparative peace settle over unhappy Maine. It was more or less of a battlefield until the centuries directly preceding the Revolution. Then again the Vendeans came and camped by thousands in the square below the cathedral and blood ran freely within the gates. Later, in our own times, the city

HOUSE OF RICHARD'S QUEEN BERENGARIA

Le Mans

garrison, during the Franco-Prussian War, fought desperately to resist the Germans on their way to Paris. Angela hated bloodshed; she closed her book suddenly, touched the button and extinguished the light by her side, and nestled down into the great square pillow. How comfortable she felt in the cool linen sheets! Assuredly the French understand how to pile up a luxurious bed! Through the wide open window doors the stars looked in upon her where she lay under the golden-hued coverlid. A feeling of delicious self-satisfaction possessed her. She had spent a whole day travelling without Georgina, and she had made no mistakes; at least none to which she confessed. Well-being stole over her soul and soothed her to sleep.

The next morning she was awakened betimes, served with coffee, and even partially dressed, by the valet-de-chambre, who did duty as chambermaid and every other kind of maid, and proved an adept at hooking up her gown. Then she sallied forth with Madame la Baronne and her small niece, who arrived early for the walk about the town. They went first where they could watch the peasants coming in to market. Seated on a bench in an alley beyond the cathedral where they could look up at that splendid structure, they watched the braying donkeys who strode by laden down with great baskets of bright blossoms and many-coloured vegetables; they wandered through the old streets, falling precipitously down the hill, and peered into odd corners to find bits of quaint architecture and sturdy old towers which once defended the city; they walked along the cobblestone streets, where the house in which Berengaria lived still stands. It has, like all ancient Angevin dwellings, a peep-hole over the entrance door, where the guard of the house looked carefully out before he admitted any swashbuckler who might be seeking entrance in the rude and rough times of Richard the Lion-hearted. This grated little window is now filled up with stones. The house is for sale, and the great door closed forever by massive oak timbers. Under the richly carved casement, out of which the Queen may have gazed many times while watching for her tall lord, is now a shop window, where cheese, eggs, and cream are displayed. In the old church of *La Couture,* la baronne and her little niece prayed, while Angela gazed reverently around at the ancient structure. It was nearly noon when they parted at the door of the hotel, with sincere regret, uttering fond hopes of speedy reunion.

Chapter II

ANGERS

FROM Le Mans to Angers is ninety-seven kilometres, but Angela, not at all interested in distances, and only desiring to reach Angers at an hour when a single female might with propriety arrive alone at a hotel, climbed into an express train, tripped on her skirt in so doing, and literally raised herself into the railway carriage by the straps of the door.

"No wonder the French always speak of mounting '*en waggon.*' If these steps were any higher I should need a porter to lift me in bodily, and porters are scarce in these provincial stations."

She settled her small luggage in a corner, and finding that she was quite alone in the compartment, she made herself comfortable, leaned back in the corner, and reflected upon her sojourn in Le Mans.

"Georgina might possibly have seen more than I did, but I doubt it. She would not have cared for the jolly coachman nor his friends, and would have found, without the aid of Madame la Baronne, that the queen of Richard the Lion-hearted was not really buried in Le Mans, but that her monument was brought there from Espan, where she was interred. Perhaps she never lived in the lovely old house and never looked out of the sculptured casements over the cheese shop, but I'm not going to doubt. I believe she watched her handsome, dashing, blond husband caracole through that badly paved street on a prancing Normandy stallion. He could curvet and wheel and entrance any woman's eyes out of her head, I'm sure. How I wish I might have seen him making his way to the Cathedral with his knights to sing a Te Deum for victory won."

With the impressions of the precipitous, twisting streets, down which her hero so often strode, still fresh in her mind, and convinced that as a would-be author it was highly important to record every important inspiration, she drew forth a dainty note book, but in the jigging, jumping train, as it bumped along its uneven way, her unsteady fingers were unable to form one legible letter. The sentences ran all over the page from top to bottom, and the writing was perfectly unintelligible, even to her. With a sigh for the highly interesting matter thus lost, she tucked away her note book in her coat pocket ready for a happier occasion, and resigned herself to dreams awakened by the landscape.

The clouds, which had been threatening all the morning, now began to float down in soft rain. The country between Le Mans and Angers is low, flat, and swampy. Every inch of it has been fought over in the far-off centuries by the rulers of Normandy, Maine, and Anjou, with France interfering wherever possible, and England occasionally taking a hand in the quarrel. The battle here that fired her love of romance most was one in which Fulk the Black, then a lad of but fourteen, led his troops to the encounter with his foe, Conan of Rennes. Rash and inexperienced, the boy allowed him-

Angers

self to be trapped into an ambush somewhere in this marshy country. The Breton troops had dug pitfalls into which the flower of the Angevin chivalry rode heedlessly and perished. Fulk was thrown from his steed, but such was his superhuman strength that he sprang up unaided, no easy feat in those days of clumsy armour. Furious with rage, in a voice of thunder, he rallied his flying forces so completely that he routed his foe.

Trying to imagine this scene Angela gazed upon the peaceful country where the poplar trees grow quite as contentedly out of the water as out of the turf, and where, that wet morning, a goose girl sat on a stool in a pool of water with her wooden-shod feet well tucked up, and placidly waved a long wand over her waddling subjects. A boy was leading a cow carefully by a string from one succulent tit-bit of spring grass to another, and watching the train from under his pointed hood. The peasants trudged to market under great umbrellas, and an occasional automobile skidded on the shining mud of the broad roadway running along between blossoming orchards. Whole families of birds, undisturbed by the showers, were nesting in the snowy whiteness of the flowering fruit trees. They sang loud and clear above the noise of the railroad, and nowhere in the scene was there any suggestion of war and its miseries.

The hotel at Angers proved more imposing than had the Dauphin at Le Mans, but it was equally dull at its entrance and along the corridors. The landlady welcomed Angela as warmly as though they had been friends for many years, and tried gently to force her

36 *A Spring Fortnight in France*

into the lift, although the guest infinitely preferred walking up stairs to mounting by one of those exceedingly deliberate and casual French elevators, which crawl two stories more slowly than any healthy mortal feet could ever possibly proceed. That all these hotels had been new some time in their existence, Angela decided while she looked about her very comfortable bedchamber. She wondered how old this one was. The furniture, the inlaid floors, the mantels and the mirrors, she gave to that period which preceded the date when Louis XVI. and Marie Antoinette lost their heads, figuratively and literally. The dressing-room was entirely modern. No eighteenth century traveller ever required as much water or as big a basin as that!

"I am an ignoramus," she mentally decided, "and I shall be obliged to look up all these facts before I write my book." She sat down at once to record her ideas, not in a book of travel, but in a pile of bright little notes she sent off to a host of acquaintances.

In the restaurant she again chose a table near the window, although there was no amusement to be found such as she had enjoyed when watching the friendly coachman the evening before. The *Place de Ralliement* was quite as tiresome, while much more pretentious than the *Place de la République*. The same style of kiosks were to be seen here, only a trifle more showy. The same tram cars ran tingling around the square, a trifle more noisy. The same cafés flared with light, and the equally convenient postoffice was in an equally convenient corner, only a little more impressive. Even the frisking, barking dogs were the same, but they were

MODERN ANGERS
PLACE DE RALLIEMENT

slightly more subdued, because here they were muzzled. She was served with a much more pretentious meal, although it was not any better, and she rejoiced greatly to find that in the provinces the German waiter of Paris, who pretends to be a native born, was here replaced by a genuine French *garçon*. The head waiter alone sported a dress suit, which was a trifle less elegant than those to be seen in Paris hotels; others wore the old-fashioned jackets with long aprons, a costume of which she highly approved.

The next morning when Angela started off on her explorations she neglected as usual to inquire in which direction she ought to turn to find the Château. With her faculty for invariably going in the wrong direction, she made her way promptly toward the newer part of the city instead of crossing the square and entering the old streets which possessed interest for her. Her indignation grew greater every moment as the whitewashed modern imitation Parisian houses dawned upon her indignant eyes. Had Angers been destroyed and rebuilt since her favourite histories were written? That she herself had gone wrong never entered her mind. She was about to turn and fly, first back to the big hotel, then from the town, when she was attracted to a building standing in a great courtyard by the crowd gathered outside the railing and the numbers of fine carriages waiting in the courtyard on either side of the entrance. She turned questioning to a little old man who was standing on the curbstone.

"*À ce qu'il paraît*, every young person in Angers is getting married this morning."

"And a few old ones, too," put in a woman standing next to him."

"Then this is the Hôtel de Ville?" asked Angela Victoria.

"*Mais, oui, Madame*, and here comes a bride!"

A vision of fleecy tulle and shining satin appeared at the entrance, attended by an insignificant looking man, who wore a dress suit, although it was but ten o'clock in the morning. Immediately on their appearance one of the smart equipages, the horses and driver decorated with immense bridal favours, dashed up to the door to receive the bride and groom. When they had been safely tucked inside, the coachman drove his horses to the centre of the quadrangle and stopped with a flourish. Here he waited patiently until all the carriages containing the wedding guests for that particular wedding had, by skilful flank movements, drawn up beside him. Then at a given signal the bridal coach started away at a gallop, followed in proper order of precedence by all the others.

"Now they will have the fine wedding breakfast," quoth the old man.

"*Et après du l'ennui*," ejaculated a woman, who must have been either a sour spinster or an unhappy wife.

Angela Victoria stood amused, interested, and absorbed, in the recurring spectacle of brides and grooms, who continued to come on the scene like the figures of the living pictures until she saw the fourth one lost to view in a cloud of dust, whereupon she managed to tear herself away from the fascination, and tried to find the Château she was looking for.

Angers

She then decided to go into a small shop and buy a map of the city, that she might not further justify Georgina's reproach of losing her way fully twice a day. But alas! the deciphering of railway time-tables, and the unravelling of guide-book maps was a talent poor Angela did not possess. She invariably got morning and evening trains mixed, and according to her reading of the heavens the sun set in the north and rose in the south. Such a misunderstanding of the points of the compass completely relieved the map of Angers of its usefulness. Starting out after consulting it, with the desire of making a short cut to the Château, she arrived instead at the bridge "De La Haute Chaine," a point quite in the opposite direction. Having got there, however, she consoled herself with the fact that the view was enchanting, and proceeded as far as the middle of the bridge, the better to look at the bank and find the object of her search. The waters of the River Maine, swollen and broadened by the rain, went hurrying along near the queer old low tower from which the chain across the river was hung in feudal times to prevent attacks by night, and the waters reflected the scudding clouds and the brilliant blue sky.

Nearly a mile down the stream appeared the heavy towers of the castle. The great fortress seen from this point, with the towers, which formerly stood high above the curtain wall, now razed to a level with the ramparts, conjured up a sturdy leader followed by a sturdy army all clad in mail, going forward to an assault. A row of modern houses at the foot of the black rock whereon the fortress and the old city were built many centuries ago, make but a white line in the picture, and are overshadowed by the huge towers with which the precipice is crowned. The blunt, round bastions, deprived of their pinnacle roofs, have a grim, brutal look. They crown the promontory at a point where it rises abruptly from the river bank. Angela gazed long at the interesting sight, then crossed the river by the bridge, and found herself in a turfless square, the Champ de Foire, in the suburb of Ronceray, in front of the hospital St. Jean, founded by Henry II., and once the favourite charity of that monarch, but now a museum containing a heterogeneous collection of curiosities. She entered and with delight gazed up at the fine vaulted ceiling. The old bits of stone and marble scattered about everywhere interested her but indifferently. Georgina, the ideal sightseer, would have begun her investigations at the entrance, and with the utmost precision and rapidity have gone through the entire collection, whereas her sister simply stared about in a vague, dreamy manner as if she were expecting to see the ghosts of the past appear at any moment.

The museum was deserted by everybody but the *gardien*. "Will not Madame examine this superb old chest?" he asked, trying to be very gracious, not only to earn his fee, but to indulge himself in a little conversation to break the tiresome silence that the poor man had kept since early morning.

"Did it belong to the Plantagenets?" she asked.

Quick to take a clue, the wise *gardien* replied:

"*Ma foi!* I know nothing! But they do say—"

Angers

he invented in haste—" King Henry kept his crown in it," King Henry being the only king of that entire race whose name the man knew, and the lock on the queer box, surely strong enough to inspire him with his sudden flight of imagination concerning the crown. Angela willingly accepted the explanation, but, at the same time, seeing nothing further pertaining to twelfth century knights excepting some archæological remains, she thanked the man graciously for his information, bestowed twenty-five centimes upon him, and departed, leaving him sad at heart at being deprived of such a sympathetic and credulous companion.

She then made her way to the old Abbey of Ronceray, of which very little now remains. It was founded by the wife of Fulk Nerra, and grew to be a splendid shrine, raised around a miraculous statue of the Virgin made by the angels, as were all the statues in the Middle Ages, if we believe the legends. The angels who made this statue of Ronceray had a genius for bronze casting; when it was achieved, they hid it away among some thorn bushes; hence the name of the abbey, *ronce* being the word for thorn in French. Here in its hiding place the little statue was discovered by some children. Miracles worked by the wholesale soon announced to the pious and superstitious folk of that period the heavenly origin of this small figure. It is still to be seen in the ancient crypt, which was part of the old shrine and above which an ugly modern church has been erected. The whole of this suburb is full of a quaint charm of antiquity. Henry II., Richard Cœur de Lion, and his brothers often abode in the town. Curious old façades remain of the antique mansions from which issued forth trains of mediæval knights, who escorted these royal pilgrims when they went to pray before the miraculous image, to beg pardon for their crimes in order that they might depart to commit others at their pleasure.

Angela, under the guidance of an enthusiastic old sacristan, whom she enchanted by her reverence, descended into the damp crypt, a relic of the old chapel, and gazed long and fondly at the miraculous statue, whose beauty was hidden by the bedizened robes with which it had been clad, until the man, enticed by a silver piece and the very evident admiration of his visitor, condescended to lift the spangled mantle to allow Angela to examine the skill and clever craftsmanship of angel fingers.

Following his directions, Angela turned the corner, after she left the church, to an art school, which now stands on the site of the former abbey. There is little left of the old nuns' convent of Ronceray except the chapel, repaired, restored, and sadly changed, which is now used by the students. By a plentiful use of more silver she induced the *concierge* of the establishment to permit her to enter the garden. There he left her to her own devices, and seating herself on a garden bench, where she could see the ruined arches telling of the former grandeur of the old church, she sunk herself in visions, and promptly went tumbling down through the ages into a bevy of white-robed nuns, and fancied herself the most prominent and important of the young sisters; she who was ordered to stand before

OLD HOUSES AND CHURCH IN RONCERAY

Angers

royalty and offer the cup to the Lion-hearted Prince. Her dreaming heart fluttered as the King, himself superstitious in his childlike credulity, humble and repentant, with his best foot well forward, became a suppliant for the prayers of the gentle nun, and begged her to intercede for him at her matins. At this proud moment of the vision the commonplace *concierge*, who failed to comprehend why anyone in their sober senses should pay a franc to sit in a garden, which looked to him just like any other garden, and then stare vacantly at an ancient ruin, which he thought not only useless but ugly, shattered her bliss by coming to tell her that she must leave, as it was time for him to go to his luncheon.

Picking her way through queer streets in which the houses cling like barnacles to the side of the church as though begging for the protection of the shrine, Angela came to the Pont du Centre, a bridge half way between those of the Upper and Lower Chain, spanning the river from Ronceray to the foot of the Rue Baudriere, an antique street, where the long paved steps of the Monte St. Maurice lead up to the front of the cathedral. The façade of this great church, adorned by a row of warlike looking statues intended for saints, was evidently sculptured to suit the stern taste of the early warriors of the House of Anjou. On that April morning the eyes of these knightly images were staring fiercely down upon a small regiment of stalwart sextons and ancient crones who were employed in the business of cleaning the church furniture in preparation for the feast day of some saint. Two of the men held firmly to

44   A Spring Fortnight in France

the edge of a huge rug, while a third beat it with a thick stick, in reality gathering much more dust by this process than he got rid of. Occasionally the trio gave the heavy carpet a shake, sending up the dust in clouds and gathering a fresh supply from the pavement. Several old women lounged indolently on the church steps, phlegmatically waving dusters, from time to time gently beating a cushion or two, and interlarding their labours with plenteous advice to the shakers of the carpet, who received their wisdom with indifference. The whole party chatted merrily about matters which were much more entertaining to them than the subject of church cleaning; and they were joined by an audience of school boys who wore long belted aprons, and by a few market women carrying baskets laden with fresh, dewy lettuce, bright radishes, and dull, olive-hued artichokes. The scene was picturesque, the grey cathedral making a background for the fine old hues of the rug; the vivid colours of the women's clothing; the boys, and the motley market women.

Angela passed with a greeting which was cordially returned, and entered the cathedral.

She found the great church of Geoffrey, of Henry, of Richard, and of King Réné, was in the hands of the ecclesiastical decorators. The pious citizens of Angers, like the cleaners, were preparing for the fête, and, with more zeal than good taste, were busily engaged in winding the dark red marble columns that support the baldaquin over the high altar with blue and white paper scrolls purposed to imitate mosaic.

The superb tapestries and pictures in the transept

Angers

were being hidden behind yards and yards of light blue curtain material, trimmed with a hideous bright gilt fringe. Angela tried to forget the barbarity of this decoration by lifting her eyes above it to the fine colours of the glorious old windows, but her endeavour was in vain. Their beauty was destroyed by the foreground of ugly, crude colour. The solemnity, all the dignity, of this splendid old edifice was obliterated by the tawdry and theatrical embellishment placed here to adorn a religious fête.

The tombs of the former rulers of Anjou, fine remembrances of a great race, have vanished. It was not the vandals of the Revolution who were to blame for this outrage. The canons of St. Maurice deliberately destroyed every trace of the splendid effigies to make way for carved stalls in the choir.

Angela left the church disheartened and disgusted, and quite by chance turned into the Rue St. Evroult, thus stumbling inadvertently onto the most direct way to the Château. Previous to this she had carefully but unconsciously each time selected the longest way to her destination and then endeavoured to console herself for the additional steps and the time lost by rejoicing over the items she thus could gather for her intended book.

The Castle of Angers is typical of the House of Anjou. It rises so strong, so forbidding, out of the black slate rock imbedded deep in the bosom of the earth along the bank of the river, that if in Walhalla Fulk the Black was looking down when St. Louis erected this present massive pile, he must have nodded stern approval. It stands on the edge and the point of a spur of slate rock, which makes a promontory rising abruptly from the bank of the stream. Fulk's old, rude fortress stood on this same spot, but the palace in which he lived adjoined the cathedral. A broad boulevard skirts the foundations of the Château leading up from the river to a point where the wall of the moat begins and there turns, and a second time following this same wall makes another curve onto a terrace called "Le Bout du Mond," from which a splendid view of the surrounding country and the lower lying portions of the town is visible. Within the tall enclosure, with its blunt towers, nothing remains of the time when the Angevin kings flourished but an old chapel and a bit of an ancient sandstone hall. The moat is dry and now given over to flourishing market gardens and peaceful chicken yards. Fluffy little pullets peck at dainty morsels near the base of the thick walls where once the river water defended the garrison from all possible attack. Fulk the Black and his race are no more, but out of the ruined crevices filling broken balconies shines with living, glowing beauty the plant his descendant, Geoffrey, loved, a wealth of gleaming blossoms hanging gracefully in clusters over the wall, pushing out boldly a single flower through the paw of a headless beast or gilding with living glory a broken escutcheon.

Dead princes and ever-living nature!

Angela loved them both. She wondered why warriors should die when flowers came again each returning spring! It was a question on which she pondered frequently. It seemed impossible to her that the souls

Angers

of her heroes should not in some form return to the scene of their exploits when flowers and birds came back constantly to their birthplace and to the trees they loved. She seated herself beside the castle and looked out from the "End of the World" onto the landscape before her. The rain clouds were still fighting for a chance to fall, but they had had their play the night before and now drifted along high in the blue sky. The tender green of the country glittered with moisture, the vines hanging from the castle wall shook off diamond drops into the moat below, and in the far distance beyond the river she saw the windmills against the horizon twirling their sails as though they were doing a rushing business.

As she sat on her bench trying to make up her mind to visit the castle, a small party of evident sightseers, two gentlemen accompanied by a jolly fox terrier, sauntered over the bridge spanning the moat to the gateway of the castle. As they stopped to speak to the sentinel at the entrance Angela gathered courage and joined them. The dog sprang forward to meet her, decided at once she was a friend, and by attaching himself to her unceremoniously caused his master to smile and bow. All through their wanderings about the castle and ramparts the friendly dog continued to bring offerings of sticks and stones wherever he could find them to the lady he admired. Once, on the very tiptop of the highest tower, with the intention of showing how great a hunter he was, he attempted the life of a tiny mouse who chanced to put his nose out of a hole. Mousey escaped his giant foe, who then with many wags from his stump of a tail, apologising for his awkwardness, fetched Angela a harmless pebble instead.

There is little for the ordinary sightseer to enjoy within the castle enclosure. The guide, like all of his kind, had a lesson which he recited. He had surely never learned it from the sources of Angela's information concerning Angers. But the gentlemen who accompanied her, less learned, pretended to be deeply impressed by his knowledge of history. Angela became a trifle suspicious of their sincerity when the guide took them into a very cheerful donjon and then declared that here the ubiquitous Cardinal Ballou had hung in his cage for many years. One of them slyly remarked: "This poor prisoner must have been kept by Louis XI. travelling around like a prize dog going to a show all for the sake of future tourists. There is not a donjon on the Loire Cardinal Ballou and his cage did not inhabit for many a long year."

"He must have been at least two centuries old when he died, the wretched prisoner!"

"*Monsieur a raison!*" laughed the guide, not in the least disturbed by the incredulity of his listeners.

The master of the dog peered out at the landscape from between the wide bars. "If Monsieur le Cardinal was hung here, he could at least amuse himself with this fine view out of the window."

The guide's sense of humour came readily to his aid. "*Eh, quoi!*" he exclaimed. "The King, of course, hung up a curtain to shut out the view."

Seen from the ramparts directly over this dungeon,

Angers

the tortuous streets of the city look like furrows in a cliff, cut down between grim buildings with dark, deep roofs, rescued from gloom by clinging lichens of yellow, brown, and green; the majestic tower of St. Aubin, a relic of the Middle Ages, and the cathedral towers, soar above the dark army of dwellings on the rocky steep, while below the abrupt town and far over the river lies *la riant campagne*, sweeping off to where the hills rise blue and faint in the hazy atmosphere; a fair country smiling through tears watered by glittering streams.

At the most telling point of his story concerning Anjou and its potentates, the guide suddenly made the discovery that he had served when a soldier in a regiment of which one of the visiting gentlemen was an officer. Whereupon he promptly shoved history and his carefully learned lesson into the background and devoted himself to military gossip. The master of the dog and Angela, glad to be relieved from his chatter, wandered about at will undisturbed and indulged in their own speculations concerning the grass-grown space inside the fortification. The little pinnacled château in which King Réné was born was the most picturesque object they saw within the great grass-grown space. The chapel adjoining it belongs to the twelfth century, but as materials of war are now stored in both of these buildings, they are closed to visitors. In one corner stand the remains of the old sandstone hall to which Geoffrey Plantagenet brought home his rebellious bride after the marriage ceremony in Le Mans. Having been an empress, Matilda undoubtedly said very cutting things about this simple domicile, which, considering that she got with it a handsome husband some ten years younger than herself, was not a very gracious thing for her to do. It is no wonder they quarrelled.

The gentleman pointed out his *pays* to Angela among a grove of trees in the distant country. She saw only the chimneys and pointed roof of what seemed to be a charming little château. Being a native of Anjou, he could likewise indicate all of the points of interest much better than the guide, who was still absorbed in regimental gossip. He advised her to take a trip to the Ponts de Cé, a queer little town which in olden times Henry II. had bestowed as a gift on the Abbey of Fontevraud. "The tramway will take you there, and the road leads over seven bridges, a most interesting and charming little excursion."

Angela, glowing with enthusiasm, at once confided to the gentleman that her deep interest in Anjou and its rulers had brought her here on her travels and that she proposed going to Fontevraud the next day.

"Ah! Then I am indeed glad that I recommended you to see that little town over there in the marchland," he said.

The guide stopped once on his way through the entire regiment to give an account in vivid terms of the " frightful tornado " with which they had been visited in Angers a year or two previously. The gentlemen, with many French ejaculations, took his description quite seriously. When he pointed out a tall, thin chimney and a shallow roof on a garden hut, which he said the gale had carried nearly across the enclosure, An-

Angers

gela tried hard to feel impressed, but, *que voulez vous!* she was an American, and in the United States the word tornado does not mean merely a high wind.

Market gardening and flourishing fruit trees were as much an industry inside the castle walls as in the depths of the castle moat. The party could scarcely tear itself away nor the guide allow them to depart while he waxed eloquent on the subject of his industry and gain in this direction. They bade good-bye at the castle gate. Such chance meetings are so pleasant, thought Angela, as she went over the drawbridge, casting one lingering look back at the little gem of architecture in which poetic King Réné was born; King Réné of Anjou, poet and painter, but indifferent ruler, who left his country to become Duke of Lorraine and King of Sicily. After his elder brother's death gave him the succession to this marchland, he returned to Angers and married as his second wife Jeanne de Laval. There were great doings then in the city. His people revelled in gaiety and song; here his two daughters were married off, and one of them, the unfortunate Margaret of Anjou, became Queen of England, and after the stormy wars and final battle of Tewkesbury, returned to her father's province to die. Impractical Réné was completely deceived by crafty Louis XI., who envied him his fair province of Anjou; for a time the Duke was benefited by the alliance, but finally Louis sent him off to Provence with his books and his pictures, completely usurping the field.

On coming out of the château the *Rue Donadieu de Pulcharie* attracted Angela Victoria to exploration.

52 A Spring Fortnight in France

It is a narrow lane lined with high garden walls, with an old-time gutter sunk in the centre of the cobblestone way. After strolling down the tortuous little street for a short distance and finding nothing to look at but a boy sweeping the pavement, she returned to the bench on the terrace to gaze once more at the splendid panorama spread out before her. It was slightly past noon, and the birds were flying about among the tufts of golden plantagenet overflowing a broken balustrade and balcony that still clung to the rugged castle wall. The broad land was full of music and colour, the feathery trees swayed and bowed above the wide river, and a blue mist marked its course far off to the base of the shadowy hills outlined faintly on the blue horizon.

No wonder Fulk the Black craved all France to satisfy his ambition, when here it lies so smiling and tempting, spread out where his eyes must each day have been provoked to desire!

It always blows a gale on the terrace at the "End of the World." Where better can the four winds meet? They played with Angela's flimsy veil, gently at first, then suddenly with ruthless force snatched it from the carelessly put in pins. The long cloud of chiffon was torn from its fastening, and would have sailed down onto the moss-grown housetops far beneath the wall had not a lady who was seated beside Angela made a quick motion and caught the long streamer in its flight. When she returned it to its owner, Angela looked up with a grateful smile and saw traces of tears on the face before her. Impulsive and tender, she at once made her sympathy evident, not in words, but by the warmth of

Angers

her glance. The lady smiled back responsively into her eyes and then explained ingenuously:

"I have just left my two little ones at the convent school," she said; "I am feeling very homesick for them. I live over there in the country about two hours' distant from here, and I cannot get a train for some time."

"So you came to the 'End of the World' to be alone with your heart?"

"*Au contraire*," said the lady softly, "I think I wanted company, and seeing you sitting here alone, I came to join you."

Angela Victoria looked pleased. She was always ready to welcome companionship.

"Perhaps you can tell me where to find a good restaurant for *déjeuner*," said the lady. "Though I live so near, I am a stranger in Angers."

"*Déjeuner!*" Angela laughed aloud, to the lady's surprise. "I had forgotten to go to *déjeuner*," she explained, "but I am a stranger, too, and alone. Perhaps we can go find some place together."

The lady gaily assented, and together they soon managed to discover an inviting little café where tables were spread outside under an awning.

It was almost empty, for the hour was long past that when the provincial eats *déjeuner*. One gentleman sat on the other side, smoking and drinking his coffee. As Angela took the table facing him, she glanced at his face and felt a curious attraction, which need surprise no one, for the man, although no longer young, was very good-looking, and Angela liked good-looking men.

She forgot him in the serious task of ordering. And before the omelet was brought she had completely put him out of her mind, although he watched with interest the animated face she showed while listening to the mother who talked in lively fashion about the doings and sayings of little Annette and Lucille, sent to-day to school for the first time. When breakfast was ended, Angela insisted on paying the bill. "You have given me sauce to my meat," she said, when her companion with a smile objected in true continental fashion to being under any obligation. But as Angela was very persistent, the guest accepted with grace. The check was brought and Angela opened her purse. Horror and mortification! She had not money enough to fee the waiter. The lady laughed merrily and immediately drew forth some coin, but just at that moment Angela discovered a ten-franc piece she had overlooked. In her confusion she had looked rapidly toward the stranger and saw that his eyes twinkled with merriment. "He is laughing at me," she thought indignantly. "I don't see anything very amusing in being short of money!" Which was the reason for a slightly ostentatious manner as she put the small gold piece down on the waiter's plate.

"The gentleman looks like a foreigner to me," said the lady softly, after they had left the restaurant. Angela did not answer. She was too indignant to give him any further thought.

After parting with her new friend and promising faithfully to visit her some day at her château of Les Sables, Angela sauntered slowly back in the direction

Angers

of her hotel, gazing into the shop windows as she went with the intention and desire of purchasing some present her sister would consider useful. She stopped before a display of queer old brass, attracted by a card whereon stood printed with a pen in large and irregular letters:

"NO MORE THIEVES! THE ROGUES LOSE THE GAME!! RASCALS CONFOUNDED!!! APPARATUS AGAINST BURGLARS."

This strongly recommended invention was nothing more nor less than a simple device by means of which a bell rang when a key was turned in a lock. Angela concluded that in Angers burglars always entered by the door, if this device could deliver householders from such scoundrels. Her attention was absorbed by this fact when the barking of a very small woolly dog almost at her feet supplanted burglars in her mind. It had apparently been helping a very fat man to draw a barrow of flowers up the hill. The man stopped to pant and to mop his brow, the dog to sit down and gaze lovingly at his master.

"Does that little animal help you pull that heavy cart?" asked Angela, horrified.

Over the man's face broke a huge smile.

"*Mon Dieu, non!*" he said, as he stuffed his dingy red handkerchief inside his blue blouse. "*C'est mon petit camerade.* The law requires a dog to be leashed or wear a muzzle, so I tie him to the cart. *Voyez!*" He pointed as example to a butcher's shop kept by one who bore the suggestive Angevin name of *l'Anglais.* And there before the door solemnly sat two dachshunds, arm in arm, otherwise leashed together with muzzles as big as fruit baskets covering their long, pointed noses. Angela and the flower pedlar laughed in sympathy at the ludicrous sight, and she patted the wriggling *petit camerade*, who waved his funny bushy little tail in response. The man picked from among his wares a carnation of great beauty: "If Madame will accept—from Milord."

"So he was a little lord, the dog comrade?"

"*Mais, certainement, Madame!* Who more so?"

Angela accepted the gift with many thanks, then purchased a great bunch of tulips and lilacs, and left him with her arms full of spicy fragrance. Boys were coming home from school laughing and romping.

One of them looked merrily into her face, peeping around behind the flowers. "Oh, Madame! Will you buy me? I am cheap!" he cried, whirling around. On his back hung a large card, which the mischievous lad had snatched from some shop and whereon was printed in mammoth figures and pricemark:

"6 frc. 50."

"You are too dear. I must wait for another day," replied Angela.

"Another day I shall increase in price," he shouted, running away, crying all the way down the street, "Who will buy, who will buy? Only six francs fifty!"

A youthful crowd followed the funmaker until he disappeared down the ancient street, where overhanging galleries of mediæval slate and timbered houses nod condescendingly at the follies of youth. How many generations of happy boyhood they had seen! Within

Angers

their walls joyous lads had grown to stern manhood, and at their deep doors many had fallen, bathed in their own blood, fighting for the loved ones sheltered beneath those dipping roofs.

She went by the *Rue du Basse Figuier* and stopped long before the little jewel of a hotel built in the time of the Renaissance, once known as the Hôtel d'Anjou, but now called the Hôtel de Pince. It is one of the most charming bits of antiquity left in Angers, and shares that reputation with the Hôtel Barrault, another gem of Angevin architecture, now converted into a museum.

As Angela passed into the hotel she stopped for a word with Madame, her landlady, and to pet Madame's favourite dog, thereby winning an additionally warm greeting for herself and another invitation to ride in the sluggish elevator, which she refused and mounted the broad steps to her room, to instal herself in a comfortable chair, and, while she rested, penetrate the secrets of the House of Anjou through the medium of an entertaining history written by Miss Kate Norgate.

The natural advantages of the point of slate rock rising sheer above the broad River Maine, on which Angers is built, were not neglected by Gaul, Roman or Franc. When the adventurous Tortulf, the founder of Anjou, half bandit, half hunter, was put to guard France against the marauders from the north, the bold Norman pirates, he took up his position on this impregnable promontory, and won by his guardianship the approval of his master, Charles the Bold. Here he founded a race which was eventually to spread its dominion all over Southern France, to reign in Sicily and the Holy Land, and to swing itself up to the English throne.

The men of the House of Anjou had those qualities which insure great success in all ages and all positions of the world. Ambitious, far-seeing, unscrupulous, persistent, determined, they were gifted with shrewdness of mind and a fascination of manner few mortals could resist. The first Count of Anjou, Ingelger, so won the favour of the childless Countess of Gatinois by this charm that she made him her heir. Women were important factors in the fortunes of Anjou. His descendants furthered their aims by constantly making successful and rich marriages. One of them took to wife, says the chronicle, a lovely creature who brought the evil into the character of these princes. As the tale goes, this enchanting creature had but one fault: she objected to assisting at the consecration of the Host during Mass. To quiet the rumours poured into his ears by the courtiers of her strange origin, her husband resolved to detain her forcibly while the mystery of the Mass was being accomplished. Therefore, one day, when, as usual, she was about to retire gracefully from the chapel, her lord laid hold of her mantle. With a quick motion she loosened it angrily from her shoulders and, to the amazement of everyone present, rose in the air and sailed out of the window, never more to return. By her side her two children had been standing, but their father quickly seized them by their arms and they lived to continue the race and transmit to their progeny the violence and deviltry of their mysterious mother.

Angers

Richard Cœur de Lion was wont to make this lady the excuse for his own wild nature, saying: "From the devil we came, and to the devil we will return."

Tourists in the château country hear constantly the name Fulk Nerra, who laid the foundation of nearly every keep pointed out to them along the Loire.

This great prince was the most perfect example of the Angevin type. His character was a mixture of strange contrasts. Sometimes cool and calculating, at other moments shaken with furious bursts of rage; full of keen perception and stubborn perseverance; perfectly lacking in any sense of right and wrong, and committing without hesitation any crime which furthered his ambitious ends; intensely superstitious, but never understanding what real repentance meant. Once he caused himself to be dragged around the streets of Jerusalem by a rope fastened around his neck, crying all the time aloud to God to have mercy on his perjured soul, but almost immediately after this strange penance was consummated and he had got safe home again, he proceeded wantonly to steal and cruelly slay whoever stood in his path to the glory of Anjou.

In spite of his false nature, a nature which constantly took advantage of the weakness of his friends as well as that of his foes, the fascination Fulk exerted at will drew around him powerful followers closely attached to his interests.

He reigned fifty-three years, and during that time extended the power of Anjou on every side. He craftily profited by the superstition of the age to become one of the greatest castle builders in history, for it so

60 *A Spring Fortnight in France*

happened that at the height of his power all Christendom was agitated by a fear that the world was coming to an end with the tenth century. In France King Robert had been excommunicated by the Pope because he refused to submit to papal authority and discard his beloved wife Bertha. His kingdom was therefore plunged in darkness and misery, and the people deprived of the comforts of religion and what meagre instruction they got from the church. The world appeared to stop for everyone but Fulk Nerra. Superstitious though he might be about himself, he never permitted bigotry to interfere with business. He took prompt advantage of the fears of others and acquired territorry right and left, by fair means or foul.

Along the length of the Loire and the adjacent rivers there arose in quick succession the frowning fortresses of Loches, Amboise, Chinon, Langaies, Monrichard, Monbazon and the many gloomy keeps whose ruins still dot the heights of Touraine.

After him came a succession of clever, ambitious, grasping descendants. Fulk V., although surnamed The Good, who was the father of Geoffrey Plantagenet, and who by marriage with the heiress of Maine added that province to his realm, quarrelled bloodily with Henry I., Norman King of England. After horrible cruelties on both sides Fulk was forced to submit, and he gave his daughter as bride to William Aethling, that heir to England's throne who went down with his wild companions in the White Ship. Again united with England by the alliance of his son Geoffrey with Matilda, Anjou spread its hand over all France, and by

OLD ANGERS
WALLS OF THE CHÂTEAU D'ANGERS AND MARKET GARDENS IN THE MOAT
WITHIN THE CHÂTEAU ENCLOSURES, TWELFTH CENTURY CHAPEL
AND BIRTHPLACE OF KING RÉNÉ

Angers

the marriage of their son, Henry II., with Eleanor of Aquitaine, the crowning point of its prosperity was reached.

It was nearly five o'clock when Angela decided to go to the Ponts de Cé, remembering the seven bridges and the gift to Fontevraud. The tramway started from the Place de Ralliement. The landlady had assured her that there was ample time to take the excursion before the long twilight closed and that she could still have dinner on her return.

The roomy front platform of the electric car, on which six persons can comfortably stand without crowding, was so popular that a few extra centimes were charged for the privilege of riding there next to the motorman. This worthy, jauntily clad in a leather automobile coat, rushed his car like a true sport at a high rate of speed along the boulevard and out onto the country road, flinging witticisms right and left at all the friends he passed by the way. Outside the gates another driver changed places with him. They likewise exchanged amenities:

"The good are taken," said he who retired.

"And the evil remain," gravely replied his substitute.

"Therefore you are left behind."

The country, low-lying as it is, had been flooded by the rains. It was scented with the fragrance of violet and thorn. Clumps of iris, making great blotches of royal purple, hung over the meandering streams, under the many bridges. The rippling waters were green with the reflection of a peculiar afternoon sky. Along the dusty road a wild flower garden, shining with intensified colour in the misty light of the setting sun, grew luxuriantly. That orb, hanging low on the horizon, seemed undecided about making its appearance on the morrow. Patches of pink showed on the purple grey clouds massed heavily about the disappearing sun, behind the new, fresh green of the bending, bowing poplars. The sky made no promise of fair weather for the morning, and slowly the intense colour faded into soft, jade-like tints of green and peachblow.

The car went flying on over the seven bridges as far as the Pont de Cé, but the platform ride proved too exciting to leave, so Angela went on as far as the end of the line and climbed down at the village of Erigne, near a little inn, *À la descente des Pecheurs*. One lone fisherman sat drinking a sirop at a table in the dusty street before the inn. Angela longed to inquire his luck. The waiting motorman forestalled her:

"*Hé? quoi?* Not one fat frog?" he inquired laconically.

"*Rien, rien,* I must try again when the floods are not so high."

The motorman held out his arms with his hands spread wide. His sympathy for the disappointed sportsman found expression in a prolonged "*A-a-h! O-o-h!*"

The car was to return in half an hour, so Angela left the fisherman and the motorman to their gossip and strolled away up a deep-cut village street, over which hung rude plaster cottages inclosed in charming little gardens. Against the whitewashed walls the blossoms of the peach trees, the great bunches of luxuriant lilacs, and masses of yellow spring flowers, made

Angers

pictures well worth coming over seven bridges to see, were it not that the passion for huge advertisements, rampant in France, had disfigured these otherwise delicious little cabins with huge posters in blue, yellow, and red, whereon the shops of Angers invited custom.

In the open country beyond the hamlet some children were trimming a wayside cross with vines and flowers in honour of the coming month of May. Angela sat down and watched them, letting her eye wander over the road she had come, through the glistening marshland to the towers of the city, rising abruptly against a background of sky changed now to deep purple.

The long twilight was not yet ended when she reached the hotel an hour later.

Angela was fairly off on her travels; she had seen two cities without Georgina's aid and was starting for a third. She had not yet felt those pangs of solitude which Georgina had so feelingly prophesied the last evening they sat together. She had enjoyed her day in Angers. She had not accomplished all a really conscientious traveller on mind improvement bent should have done, but she had enjoyed herself perfectly in her own peculiar way. The inside and outside of the Musée Darrault and the other buildings of the town she had sufficiently impressed upon her imagination to furnish rich backgrounds for any romances she would invent for her own entertainment in future hours of leisure. The readers of her book-to-be were quite forgotten, as was the accuracy needed for such a work. To tell the truth, the book itself had gone quite out of her mind.

64   *A Spring Fortnight in France*

Before dinner she sent a postal crad to Georgina. She selected a picture of the solemn, gloomy château. The space for correspondence surrounding the view was limited, therefore she only wrote:

"I have had an enchanting day and met lots of friends." There was still a line remaining blank, so she scribbled: "One of them seemed amused at nothing."

It was the first news Georgina got from her sister after reaching San Remo. She was naturally somewhat puzzled by its ambiguous character.

Chapter III

SAUMUR

A NGELA had awakened on the next morning to find that a cold rain was coming steadily down, and cowering under the downy quilt she found herself a kindred spirit to those French *grandes dames* of the eighteenth century who spent most of their time in bed. She jumped up to close the long window which had been letting in the rain and the damp air, and the polished floor was as chilly to the touch as a street sidewalk.

"*Décidément*, the bed is a good place," she exclaimed, as she leaped back into its warm shelter and drank her coffee. She settled herself among the pillows, wrote a few postal cards to send to the United States, counted her money, darned a hole in her stocking, consulted the time-table. Then the valet knocked to say her bath was ready.

With that adaptability to surroundings which in reality made Angela a much better traveller than the wise Georgina, she had come in four days to forget that such a servant as a chambermaid ever existed. The *valet-de-chambre*, in his picturesque, striped waistcoat, had brought up her coffee every morning to her bed, had hooked up her complicated bodice where her own experienced fingers could not reach, and had even suggested that her gown was not put on as straight as it should be. With the sole exception of that reigning power, the landlady, French country inns harbour few female servants.

Her next stopping place was Saumur, chosen not only because it was closely associated with one of Fulk the Black's choicest exploits, but because it was in the close vicinity of Fontevraud, that last resting place of Richard Cœur de Lion and his father, Henry II. Having visited the nest wherein the eagles of Anjou were hatched, she wished to follow them to the spot where they lay buried.

Saumur is not many leagues removed from Angers. The ambling train travels there in one hour's time, so there was no need of hurrying. She would take an early *déjeuner* here in Angers and go at her leisure. When Angela Victoria was finally ready for her last look at the town she discovered that her sister's dark prophecy concerning the weather, and likewise that one concerning her own carelessness, had been fulfilled. Where was her umbrella? She needed it now for the first time, and it was missing. She searched the room and the anxious valet crawled under the bed and explored the most inaccessible corners without result. She made a rapid and mental review of all the trains, cabs, omnibuses and hotels she had been in since she began her short journey, but her memory refused to discern the umbrella.

It was pouring steadily; she must have protection, so, borrowing for the moment of her hostess, she sallied forth to a " *grand bazar* " near by, there to replace the very necessary article she had so soon mislaid.

One of the late modern achievements in every French

Saumur

provincial town is the department store. These are usually entitled "Le Grand Bazar," "Le Petit Bazar," "Au Paradis des Marchands," and other enticing names. They are most tempting to travellers like Angela Victoria. From seductive stationery and postal cards at lowest possible rates, the gamut mounted to baby carriages, perfumery, photographic supplies, *articles de voyage, mercerie*, china, choice bric-a-brac and irresistible souvenirs. Angela left the particular bazaar she visited with the indispensable umbrella, costing two francs, fifty centimes, pronounced *bien solide* by the clerk, and with five francs' worth of unnecessary stationery.

"If I ever get time to write my book, I may be unable to buy good paper as cheap as this is."

The two fox terriers and curly spaniel who helped to keep the "Grand Hotel" defied the weather and, probably in grateful remembrance of several lumps of sugar surreptitiously distributed among them by Angela, braved the wet and accompanied her to the door of the omnibus as she was leaving. The dogs would have gone to the station if not restrained by their mistress, who reminded them that they were unmuzzled, and in the same breath wished the guest an "*au revoir*" which was as hearty as if her stay had lasted months instead of hours.

The drive to the station was through a dull part of the town not improved by the storm.

Beyond the city limits piles of broken slate like that on which the town was erected were lying by the track. Angela laughed quietly to herself at the sight of the shiny black slabs. Her mind jumped back to the days when her passion for a glistening, clean slate was indulged at the expense of strictly sanitary methods and frequently brought down the wrath of her meek teacher upon her offending mouth. "If I could have trimmed the frame with yellow wreaths as these great slates are decorated, I am sure she would have let me spit on it all I chose," murmured Angela, half aloud, filled with admiration at the artistic effect of the great bunches of golden genet gleaming like sunshine around the tablets of black rock.

In the carriage was an old curé who industriously read his breviary, and a farmer who eyed the gentle old man with modern French suspicion. They remained with her as far as *Les Rosiers*, a charming little town where a statue commemorates the gay Jeanne de Laval, the beloved second wife of good King Réné.

The skies ceased to weep, but still looked very sulky. The dark slate and its yellow flowers had given place to widely cultivated fields which rolled away in fertile furrows until the great yellow castle of Saumur, square and turreted, loomed high on the horizon above a small town stretched along the opposite bank of the Loire.

The inhospitality of the weather made Angela's hospitable reception at the "Hotel Budan" doubly acceptable. The traveller fell in love at once with her amiable, elderly hosts and their friendly dachshund, who came forth in their company to meet her with fawning politeness. She felt at home at once. No *ascenseur* was needed here. The broad, low, curving staircase led

Saumur

by easy steps to the cosy room on the first landing offered for her inspection.

Angela pulled back the curtain of her long window and looked out on the rushing Loire.

There are compensations to be found by optimistic minds in all trying circumstances. Angela Victoria now rejoiced greatly to see for the first time the Loire worthy of its title, a great river. On her various and many expeditions a-touring in Touraine, the River Loire had always presented itself as a capricious little stream trickling through sandbars. The body of water racing and running at high speed under the long bridge just outside the hotel was a phase of its being she never had witnessed. The valet, Jean, lit a crackling little fire, cackling pleasantly to himself the while, and bustling about he pushed an armchair up to the window, saying:

" Madame can amuse herself for a while, I am sure. The showers will not last. Such pelting *averses* soon pass over Saumur. There are always the donkeys and the market women passing over the bridge to see, as well as the fine cavalrymen from the school and the omnibus of the " Hotel Budan ! "

" The omnibus? " she inquired, not quite understanding.

" *Mais bien sûr!* It passes at every moment. There are so many trains. Saumur is a great junction," he said proudly.

The bridge was a tossing sea of big umbrellas and pointed hoods. Angela decided then and there to purchase immediately one of those useful capes which these hoods adorn, for no waterproof of her experience seemed to protect so thoroughly against the weather. "Then it will not matter whether I lose my umbrella or not," she concluded, desperately. When the entertainment from the crowd ceased to interest her, Angela sent her fancy floating off down the rushing waves of the historic river to the country where the kings she was following to their burial place had wrought so many deeds, knightly, heroic, and romantic. About three o'clock she was overcome by a gnawing desire for *goûter*. There was sure to be a cake shop near, and she had eaten nothing since her *déjeuner* at eleven o'clock. The rain looked inclined to stop, but it was still drizzling sufficiently to force her to unfurl her cheap new umbrella, which she admired hugely. She walked quite a distance up the broad street, around the corner from the hotel, before she saw any cakes which were dainty enough to suit her palate. There were *pâtisseries* in plenty, but the wares they displayed did not tempt her. When she finally found a most attractive shop the spitting rain again came down in a pelting shower and lasted long enough to nearly cause her to ruin her digestion by tasting every cake in the shop. The clouds luckily exhausted themselves before all her appetite for dinner was hopelessly gone, and when they scurried away, leaving a bit of blue sky, Angela entered a narrow street, too narrow and slanting for the boldest motor car to attempt, and climbed the steep, roughly paved way, neglecting the queer old twelfth century church, until on up over the grass-grown cobbles, through the silent, winding lanes, under overhanging gables and unexpected tourelles, which cling

Saumur

like dovecotes to the ancient houses, she came to the topmost point of the hill, where a cone-shaped mound girt with trees stands above the castle. She went over the drawbridge, and rang at the massive door in the castle wall.

The stronghold was garrisoned by a feeble old woman and a tiny little girl, who with one arm swung back the heavy portal and with the other clasped a mutilated doll.

"Oh, dear!" exclaimed Angela, who expected at least a warder with huge keys to admit her to such an imposing entrance. The old woman was washing clothes at an ancient well and silently waved permission for the visitor to wander where she pleased. There was not another living being visible. The great castle loomed up across the vast courtyard, its octagonal towers rising on the edge of a precipice against the cloudy sky. The intervening space, which, perchance, was formerly the knights' tilting ground, was carpeted with coarse turf. This mediæval stronghold is now an arsenal, and the open towers of former times have been covered with shallow roofs. Angela strolled across the quadrangle and, leaning over a wall, looked at the deserted old château. Although on the verge of a cliff, a deep moat ran between the place where she stood and the castle foundations. A pretty garden, with blossoming peach trees, occupied the deep, wide trench, a graceful bit of colour against the ochre of the walls. The outworks of this strong castle were dug in the rock and then strengthened by walls raised on these solid foundations. The commanding position it occupies was early seized upon by the Romans; they built here one of their first citadels when they came to dominate Gaul; after they had left the country, the Tour du Tronc, which may have been the remains of the Roman keep, served as a refuge for the peasants when they fled from the Norman pirates who swept down the Loire.

Later, the monks of St. Florence built, adjoining the keep, a fortified monastery, in which to protect the relics of their patron saint. The sanctuary was made nearly impregnable, and Fulk of Anjou, who had tried at various times to assail it, only succeeded when Gelduin, lord of this country, and called the " Devil of Saumur, of whom the Devil of Anjou was afraid," incautiously left his home. Then Fulk descended rapidly by night on Saumur. Although the loyal citizens burned their town rather than deliver it into his hands, they could not save the castle from his rapacious might. The monks of St. Florence marched out of the citadel bearing the relics of their patron. Their conqueror stood in full armour watching them, and cried out to the saint:

" Let the ruins burn, Holy Florence; I will give thee a much better home in Angers! "

The saint, in spite of these fine promises, objected to leaving the territory of Saumur. The boat containing his relics stuck on the sandbars of the Loire, and though Fulk swore he was " an impious rustic who would not allow himself to be well treated," the monks could make the boat move no further. Fulk finally allowed the saint to land at that spot and built an

Saumur

abbey there, after possessing himself of the Castle of Saumur.

Angela, peering over the wall above the garden moat, saw in the inner court graceful windows and carved balconies, now falling into decay, recalling King René and the days when he came to Saumur and made it gay with the life his daughters and his wife Jeanne brought to the old castle. Ruined though they be, these delicate stone traceries still remain, and in fancy Angela pictured Margaret of Anjou, not then England's unhappy Queen, in gay flowing robes, surrounded by her ladies, leaning over the stone balustrades to watch the pages and the dashing squires play in this inner court. How forlorn it must have been without sunlight; in this forbidding stronghold few are the windows looking out upon the splendid view above the river. All the casements were on this dull court, which, lovely as its stone work appears, must have been dark and dreary. Angela shuddered in the damp air and thought of a life without hot water and rooms with stone floors and draughts everywhere. How cold and uncomfortable a castle must have been as a dwelling place! She greatly preferred the "Hotel Budan" and Jean's little fire. The clouds flying away over the broad country, the blue reflected here and there in the far-winding river, an undecided rainbow climbing up out of the feathery, green swaying poplars in the distance, all seemed to promise a fair morrow. On the cliff stretching along beyond the castle wall, windmills were waving their huge arms desperately about, hard at work in the driving wind.

A Spring Fortnight in France

Angela likewise waved a farewell to the ghosts gathered in the darkening windows and left hurriedly.

The small warder got a few pennies to buy a new arm and leg for her doll. The old grandmother, now hanging out clothes on the side of a bastion, waved a greeting, and when the great gate was swung silently into place Angela made her descent by a narrow flight of stone steps lying between high garden walls, over which floated the scent of freshly watered shrubbery. The stairs were wet, and it was with peril she reached the lower street, which came out below the narrow way close upon *Notre Dame de Nantilly*, the quaintest and most delightful church in Saumur. It was built in instalments, added from the sixth to the twelfth century. Réné of Anjou, the poetic King of the Two Sicilies, loved Saumur and this queer old church. He placed on one of the columns here a tenderly grateful epitaph to the memory of his old nurse, Thiephaine:

> La nourrice Thiephaine
> La magine qui de grant paine
> Nourrir de let en enfance
> Marie d'Anjou, royne de France
> Duc d'Anjou et depuis nomme
> Et après son frère Réné
> Comme encor est
> Roi de Sicile.

The rough old walls are hung with rich tapestries of great antiquity. The wear and tear of centuries have failed to dull the brilliant hues of the red and green costumes worn in these hangings by the Roman soldiers, who are represented as storming the walls of Jeru-

Saumur

salem with primitive firearms, very like giant peashooters. The walls of the Holy City are so low that any one of the attacking warriors could easily step over them, if he happened to think about it. Another delightful bit of the same handiwork pictures the Adoration of the Shepherds and the expressive countenances bestowed by the artist on the ox and the ass is worth a journey to see. In the background of this needlework landscape are farms, castles, most wonderful trees and such precipitous meadows that the shepherds playing on pipes appear to be seated comfortably in the air. Nor are these works of art the only deliciously humorous touches about the walls of Notre Dame. The free fancy of the stone carvers exceeded even that of the makers of the tapestries. The capitals of the pillars supporting the arches are wrought with fishes bearing ludicrous human faces; with a whole community of grotesque monks walking in single file and with monkeys biting at the wings of impossible creatures who seem to be half swans and half dachshunds; on another is St. George, with his head twisted around, trying to kill a mild-looking dragon, who does not resist his fate. Every sort of absurdity suggested by the weird imaginations of the Middle Ages; that sense of humour and love of caricature latent in human nature, which at that early period had no other outlet, found expression in the decorations of churches.

It had grown cold; it was dreary walking back to the hotel, but Jean again built a quick, jolly little fire of small sticks in the grate, and it soon gave forth a grateful heat. The dining-room was cheerful and warm, and a most attentive waiter served Angela with an appetising dinner, and her host assured her that she was quite right in her belief that the sun would shine next day. She was happy and content. After dreaming an hour or two before the cheerful little grate, her mind distracted from the necessity of doing any writing by the thought of black Fulk and his wickedness, varied by a contemplation of the absorbing question as to why all men chambermaids were named Jean, she got into the bed, piled fully half way up to the ceiling with springy mattresses, by mounting a chair and jumping into the downy heap, and was soon off fast on her way to the land of rest, lulled by the sound of the dropping rain.

FONTEVRAUD

Having mooned over the birthplace and lost her way in the ancestral home of the greatest of the Angevin kings, Angela Victoria prepared herself to visit his burial place, the great Abbey of Fontevraud, which is but nine miles from Saumur, whether you take them by tramway or by motor car.

The former was the sole conveyance possible for a solitary woman, and under the circumstances by far the most amusing. A small train of three cars starts from the very door of the Hotel Budan; for the weighty sum of fifty centimes she occupied the entire first-class section and amused herself in looking through a glass door into the second-class compartment, where jolly peasant women pretended to be very much alarmed at every flap of the live fowls they were carrying home

Saumur

in their baskets. The tram follows the river as far as the old Château of Montsoreau, then strikes back through a vine-clad valley until the line reaches the foot of the long hill crowned by the great Abbey Church. There it stops.

The doubtful rainbow of the evening before had fulfilled its promise: the day was glowing with sunshine. Angela started on her expedition as soon as she had finished an early luncheon. The woods between the white road and the river were full of the tenderness expressed by groves of young trees just flaunting their new-born leaves when glistening water forms the background of the picture. When the tramway left the river to roll along between the banks of richly cultivated country Angela looked about, hoping to find some remains of the dense woods in which Robert d'Abrissel, the Breton priest, and his pious pilgrim followers established themselves at the end of the eleventh century. The territory then belonged to the lords of Montrieul-Bellay. In the beginning the réligieuse lived in grottoes cut out of the tufa rock and in small cabins which they built for themselves. It was a unique community composed of men and women, in which eventually the women were to take the chief place. Robert d'Abrissel, a preacher of the Crusades whose eloquence had gathered about him a motley crew of both sexes of every age and degree, an ill-assorted multitude of good and bad who dogged his footsteps everywhere, finding these crowds hard to manage, came to this valley, and obtaining permission of the seigneur, he stopped here with his company.

The men and the women he divided into two communities, separated by a deep ditch and a high hedge. All he required of the women was to sing the praises of God and the Virgin; the men conducted the spiritual exercises and took upon their shoulders the burden of the hardest labour. Everyone who came was admitted to the fold: old and young, sick and well, rich and poor; even the lepers were not rejected. Before long monastery buildings were erected; one for the men and three for the women. Le Grand Moutier, for virgins and widows; St. Lazare, for the sick and leprous, while La Madelaine harboured the sinners. The men's monastery was dedicated to St. John the Evangelist.

The vast abbey grew and spread, favoured by the nobles and the potentates of the surrounding provinces. Both the male and female réligieuse were under the direction of an abbess appointed by Robert d'Abrissel. A near relative of the Count of Anjou, Herlande de Champagne, the widow of the Sieur de Montsoreau, was the first to whom this honour was tendered. The founder himself submitted to the judgment of this lady, and later, the Pope, influenced by Robert, who understood the value of powerful patronage, ordained that the Abbess of Fontevraud should always be selected from among women who had occupied a high social position in the world, giving as a reason that such women knew better how to conduct themselves with dignity and calmness than the recluse, who, reared in a convent, was only wise in spiritual matters.

There were very strict rules enforced concerning the separation of the sexes, and the use of wine was unconditionally prohibited. The dress of the nuns consisted of a long white robe with a black cowl and a twisted girdle or black belt. They wore a pleated *fichu* of batiste, white shoes and stockings and a black veil. When they left the monastery they covered their habit with a long, soft mantle of black. The men wore a black tunic and black girdle, with a large capuchin hood and cape. On the front and the back of their costume two long pieces of cloth about the width of a hand, called *roberts*, fell nearly to the edge of their gown.

The House of Anjou was associated with the Abbey from the first day of its organisation. Its destiny became linked with that of the kings of England still more firmly when Matilda, widow of the Atheling, sister of Geoffrey Plantagenet, retired to its famous enclosure and became for a time its abbess. Eleanor of Guyenne, the wife of Henry II., lived some years in the monastery and built the walls surrounding it. Her daughter Joan was educated there, who after the death of her husband, Raymond of Toulouse, King of Sicily, took the veil, dying there the same year which witnessed the burial of her brother, Richard Cœur de Lion. The criticism of contemporaries that the Fontevrists were " under the rule of the distaff " was answered by the assertion that the church was under the dominion of the Blessed Virgin. It was an enormously rich order. Sixteen royal princesses figured among its abbesses, and the daughters of the French kings were sent there to be educated.

The Abbey endured until the time of the Revolution,

growing constantly wealthier and more arrogant. Its aristocratic tendencies and the royal blood of the abbess of that period, who was a great-granddaughter of Madame de Montespan, brought down upon the monastery the fury of the "Reds of Saumur." A hooting mob burst into the enclosure, doing wild violence to all it contained, and after working fearful havoc fled, yelling as it went: "The royal Abbey is fallen!"

Some years after the Revolution this regal Abbey became a penal institution. The splendid church was at one time divided into four floors and used as dormitories, but is now being rapidly restored to its original condition as a *monument historique.*

The present town of Fontevraud, full of shabby relics of the priories which constituted its glory in the past, is now somewhat squalid. Angela walked slowly up the long, sloping, country road leading from the tramway station to the Abbey gates, looking as she went at the immense slate roof of the great church showing above the wall; she followed along the line of the enclosure of the Abbey, through muddy lanes and out into open fields, to catch a glimpse from time to time, when the ground was high enough, of beautifully ornamented gables and façades in the inner courts of the prison, shut away from visitors' eyes.

When, after her long walk, she reached the abbey entrance gate, a gentleman was standing there, who, with that perfect confidence in the universal knowledge of his language which distinguishes the Anglo-Saxon, said to her calmly, as he saw her about to grasp the long handle which sounded the bell:

Saumur 81

"I have just rung."

"An American," she thought to herself. Looking up to thank him, she saw a face which seemed familiar to her. Where she had seen it she could not recall. Then he smiled.

"The man at Anjou!" she said to herself. "How could I forget his face!" He was a tall man, with clear-cut features, blue eyes, and hair originally blond, but now turning grey at the temples. He might have been thirty-five, he might have been fifty. Angela was not a good judge of a man's age. Actually this man had just completed his forty-third year on earth.

A porter opened the door to admit them. Their ring had evidently disturbed his luncheon hour, for he held what the boys of the United States would call a hunk of bread in one hand, while in the other he brandished a knife. He laughingly excused his appearance when he saw who the visitors were, and smilingly conducted them across an outer court, directing their attention to the carved façade of a charming little house he said had once been a dwelling of the abbess, turning them over to the care of a dapper little soldier dangling a huge bunch of keys, who led them under an archway through a smaller court, where he unlocked a massive door and ushered them into the superb cloisters adjoining the church.

Some prisoners neatly clad in brown scurried through and entered what the guide said had formerly been the refectory of the abbess. Luckily, the heavy oak door through which they went did not close until the visitors got a good look at the fine stone vaulting and carved walls within. The ancient chapter room, at present in process of restoration, opens upon these cloisters. The fine twelfth century archway of the great portal is heavily carved.

They entered the church through a small side door, coming directly upon the nave, where a large corps of workmen were busy repairing the fearful damages done by ruthless hands during the last century. In less than five years, the guide declared, English visitors will find these lofty aisles restored to the grandeur they possessed when Richard Cœur de Lion strode down them to stand beside his royal father's bier before the high altar. Climbing over building stones and the débris scattered about by the workmen, Angela and her companion at last stood in the choir. There the guide skipped nimbly along on top of the long benches without backs, whereon the prisoners sit when they come to hear Mass, and beckoned to the visitors to follow him. As gracefully as possible Angela pursued the perilous path and finally arrived at the grating of a small rough chapel, quite in keeping with its *environs*, where, low on the stone floor, their former altar pediments gone the sad way of so many French monuments, are placed the noble effigies of Henry II., of Eleanor of Aquitaine, of Richard Cœur de Lion, and of Isabelle of Angoulome, the beautiful and wicked wife of King John.

These fine statues, which have had a most uneasy history since they originally were placed by one of the pillars in the choir or under the central tower, are in a good state of preservation. They have been some-

IN THE ABBEY OF FONTEVRAUD

Saumur

what restored, but the rich colour still lingers on the garments and they have a rare artistic, as well as deeply romantic, interest for all who are of Anglo-Saxon birth. The effigies of Richard and his father and that of his mother are carved in stone. The statue of Isabelle is of wood. How they chanced to escape the revolutionary mob which destroyed the monuments of the Queen of Sicily and her husband, Raymond of Toulouse, is unknown.

When the Abbey fell into decay these statues were put into the queer old Tour d'Evrault, once the kitchen of the Abbey. There they remained for eighteen years, until removed to a damp cellar where the prisoners went to draw water. An Englishman who came to Fontevraud at this period saw them in this latter place, degraded and chipped in places by their careless guardians. They once got as far as Versailles on their way to England, which had petitioned France to restore them, but a storm of indignation which was aroused in Anjou caused them to be brought back to their present resting place.

After all, were not these potentates more French than English? And they had elected to rest after death at Fontevraud.

The guide stood patiently aside and waited while Angela and her companion peered through the bars at the interesting effigies. The two kings are represented lying on draped biers, such as those on which they reposed when placed before the high altar.

Angela glanced furtively at her companion, fancying that she detected a resemblance in his countenance to that of Cœur de Lion. The brow and the straight nose were very like, but the dead monarch wore a short-cropped beard which masked the mouth and chin. She couldn't decide about the likeness there.

She was startled from her short reverie by her companion's voice:

"They were kingly looking men, were they not? Richard was one of my boyhood heroes! The hours I spent in his adventurous company when I should have been at more serious tasks is what has brought me here to-day."

"So poetic, so reckless, so courageous, so full of mastery!" she said, excitedly. "He had the true making of a hero."

"Yet the tradition-breakers of to-day, the really, truly, sober, practical history makers of this century, don't think much of that big fellow down there. They say he was a bad husband, a worse son, and a king who bled his wretched English subjects both financially and physically to further his craze for crusading. I don't care a bit for his sins, when I remember the way I used to go about and storm around the backyard in imitation of the manner in which he cleft a whole army of Saracens' heads with his battle-axe, as my thumb-worn romantic history vividly described. I refuse to believe any of the truths concerning him."

Angela glowed: "I know he must have been a great-hearted, whole-souled, fascinating, fearless creature. Don't you believe his father and his brothers treated him outrageously?"

The gentleman smiled incredulously. "Perhaps

Saumur

they did; but he paid them back every time in hard cash for all he owed them. That is sure enough."

The guide moved impatiently forward over the benches, went toward the altar and out again under the arch of the nave, until he led to where Henry II., broken with age, sorrow and disease, lay after death in state before the high altar. He had died at his favourite castle of Chinon, confessing his sins aloud before the altar of the chapel there. No sooner was the breath out of his body than his servants stripped him naked. One faithful knight alone remained to cover the body with his cloak, until Geoffrey, his natural son, who alone of all the children loved the King, came to clothe the dead form in what regal splendour he could gather together. A train of knights then conveyed the body of the deceased monarch to Fontevraud, where his bier rested among the praying nuns in the church that the prophecy might be fulfilled that in death " he should lie shrouded among shrouded women."

In the nave of this church took place the terrible scenes so graphically described by Kate Norgate in the " Angevin Kings ": " To the dead sovereign came the new king, Richard, making the echoes of this ancient fane ring with the clatter of his heavy mailed tread. The rebellious son stood beside the dead father and looked down on the severe, frigid countenance whereon was stamped the passions and sorrows of an eventful life. As he gazed a dark stream of blood trickled from the nostrils of the corpse, a phenomenon which, natural though it was, struck horror into the superstitious soul of his son and of the watching courtiers. Richard, overcome with terror, sank on his knees and prayed. Then he arose and vowed to seek pardon by a crusade to the Holy Land "—a kind of penance he thoroughly enjoyed, but which caused the kingdom he had inherited untold misery.

As the regulations of the prison forbid visitors penetrating further into the precincts of the former abbey, the guide could show them no more. Angela and her companion loitered in the cloisters and in the inner court, trying to recall vividly the former life in this great monastery.

"There must have been frequently great doings in this old place," he said, "if we can believe the chronicles. I like to think of the kings who came here to be entertained in splendid fashion, with their trains of gay court ladies."

"Oh, how I wish I could have seen the pride just one such gathering!" she exclaimed.

He laughed: "Except for the fact that men no longer go about in gaudy garments and with waving feathers, I fancy you could see just as much finery today in London, New York or Paris as ever came to Fontevraud."

"Oh, do you think so?" Her tone was one of bitter disappointment. "I never could believe that any modern assemblage could be half as splendid as when the last abbess came riding in to take possession of her office, with hautboys, flutes and trumpets, escorted by a gaudy band of carabineers and a host of magnificently attired friends from the court!"

"And she died on a miserable straw pallet in a

Saumur

Paris hospital, luckily escaping the guillotine. I got my learning from T. A. Cook in 'Old Touraine.' Where did you get yours?"

Angela laughingly confessed to the same source of wisdom. They parted from their dapper little guide in the court near the residence of the abbess. He refused the fee offered with becoming dignity.

"By George! This is a new experience!" exclaimed the gentleman, whom Angela Victoria secretly dubbed "Cœur de Lion," through that fancied resemblance she had discovered. They both thanked the man in their best manner, she in French and he in English.

"I felt like shaking hands with him," he laughed.

A file of prisoners came out of the gateway they had just left.

"The poor devils have a mighty fine place to live in. I am not sure I shouldn't enjoy it myself. This is what might be called being confined to artistic surroundings."

The porter who admitted them again swung back the great door of the fortified gateway to allow them to pass. He had finished the big piece of bread while they were in the presence of the kings, and ushered them out into the dreary street. Angela looked with regret after the tall figure, as, raising his hat ceremoniously, the gentleman strode off down one of the decayed avenues of the town. He seemed thoroughly in keeping with the place. She secretly wished he would go back on the tram with her. Looking about for a little shop where post cards were sold, she spied one across the muddy street. The entrance was blocked by a young soldier, who leaned against the doorpost, and in spite of his martial attire was frankly and ingenuously crying. Great tears rolled out of his blue eyes and down the rosy red cheeks of his boyish face. He made way for Angela to pass, and then went off slowly down the street. She stood for a moment staring after him, overcome by the spectacle. Then she went into the shop, which had as promiscuous a lot of goods to sell as any country store in an out-of-the-way American town. " Why was that soldier weeping? " she asked the woman behind the counter.

" He has been ordered to Paris," the shopkeeper explained, sympathetically. " He does not want to go."

" Not want to go to Paris!" cried Angela. " I thought Paris was the Mecca of all Frenchmen. But *pourquoi donc?* What is the reason?"

" Ah, *nous autre!*—we are peasants! *Ce petit soldat* "—pointing with his thumb at the weeping warrior going slowly away—" he, too, is the son of a peasant. He is afraid of Paris. It is said that some who go there are never seen again. I have been once to Paris. *C'est superbe, la grande ville, sans doute!* But for me, I find Saumur fine enough!"

"*Ah, dam!*" put in his wife, who was picking out the cards for Angela. " It is those English who have courage! They come so far. Every day in summer we have them here! Some cannot speak the language. Some do not even know the money. Ah, they have a courage!"

Then, while Angela bought post cards at a franc the dozen, the old woman gave her a graphic descrip-

Saumur

tion, interlarded with ejaculations from her husband, who did not wish to be left out of the conversation, of an Englishman who once left behind on the counter a gold sovereign to pay for only two francs' worth of post cards. At first the old woman did not recognise the foreign gold piece; when she discovered what it was, she, with her daughter, afraid they might be accused of robbery, ran breathlessly to the bottom of the hill after the man, trying to return the change.

"But he was in a big auto and we caught nothing but the dust."

"And the smell!" jeered the merry old husband.

"Has Madame travelled far?" his wife said quickly, changing the subject.

Madame confessed to having travelled as far as the United States.

"Ah, well," said the woman, determined to undo her sneers concerning foreigners, "that is not so bad, since they all speak French there!" Angela wickedly concealed the fact that some of the benighted Americans preferred on all occasions to use the Anglo-Saxon tongue.

Nothing would she have enjoyed more than gossiping away a long hour with these naïve and amusing shopkeepers. But the man, who was leaning against the doorpost, with his hands in his pockets, suddenly took them out, and letting his trig blue blouse fall about his hips, pointed excitedly down the hill at the engine of the small tram, which was getting up steam for its return to town.

"Madame must hurry if she would get back to

Saumur to-night. It is with great regret we see her go, but alas! this is the last tram." He smiled and bowed as gracefully as a courtier, and his good wife came out from behind the counter to say heartily, "*Au revoir.*"

Angela took a last look at the great gate of the Abbey and the old tower of its church, and left her new acquaintances as regretfully as they expressed themselves in parting with her. The companion of her afternoon visit to the Abbey did not appear. She made the journey back to Saumur alone, save for a fat, loud-voiced countryman, who kept up a running conversation with the conductor on the platform about the crops. The car slid down the flourishing valley between the Abbey and the river, and there on the bank they waited at a switch. Angela got out, and the conductor courteously promised to call her in ample time if she desired to walk a few steps beyond where they were waiting to a point where she could get a better view of the rugged Château of Montsoreau. This fine old specimen of a feudal dwelling was the home of the heroine of Dumas' thrilling novel, " Diane de Montsoreau." Here she dwelt with her stern husband, Jean de Chambes, although the noted fight and assassination of her valiant lover, Bussy d'Amboise, so vividly described by Dumas, really took place at the Château of Coutancière, which is not far from Saumur, but in another direction.

The base of the towers of Montsoreau formerly rose from the waters of the Loire, but now a road passes between the castle and the river. At the time

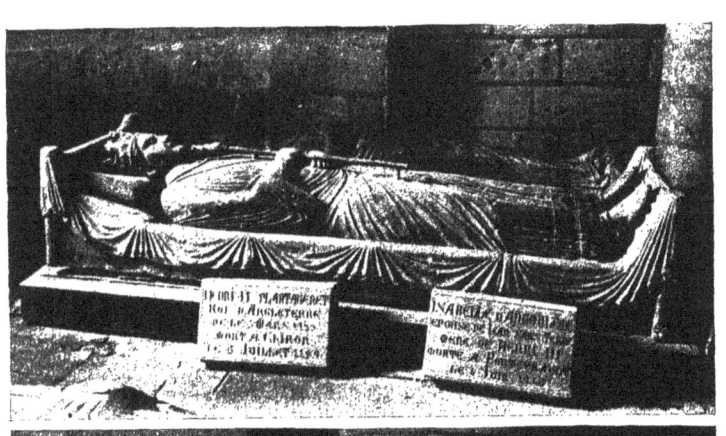
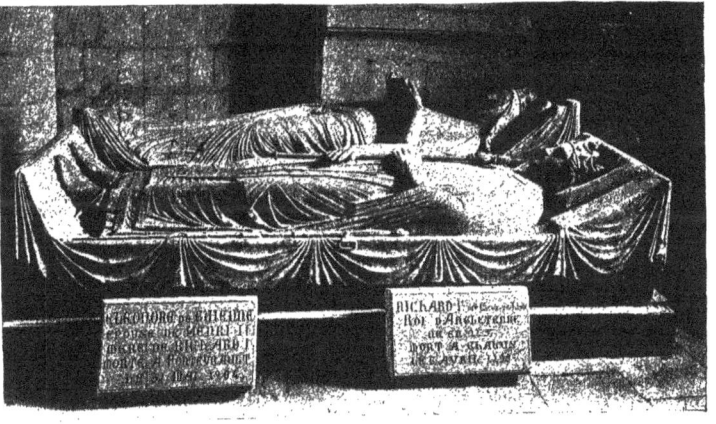

ABBEY OF FONTEVRAUD

EFFIGIES OF THE ANGEVIN KINGS HENRY II, RICHARD I, AND QUEEN
ELEANOR OF AQUITAINE AND ISABELLE OF ANGOULÊME

Saumur

of the Revolution this old structure fell somewhat into decay; not many years ago it was occupied as a tenement by labourers' families, but it has been restored by its present owners.

The tramway passes near another dainty and well-preserved little château at Dampierre, which has sad historic interest. It belonged formerly to François Vignolles, a Chancellor of King Réné, who put it at the disposal of the unhappy Margaret of Anjou, wife of Henry VI. of England. There she passed the last miserable years of her existence, after she finally returned from her captivity in England to die of grief and disappointment in the land of her father, King Réné. The statue of this sad mother and unhappy queen, with one arm thrown about her unfortunate little son, who perished so cruelly on the field of Tewkesbury, adorns the entrance hall of this château.

Between Montsoreau and Saumur the highway is but a long street, the tree-girt Loire on one side, while on the other village after village join each other in an uninspiring succession of utterly commonplace, whitewashed houses, with plastered walls decorated by huge posters, inviting the thirsty, in yellow, red and green colours, to drink Cusenier's liqueurs and recommending the hungry, in bright blue and white, to eat only Chocolat Menier.

Behind this long, ugly succession of village streets rises a picturesque cliff, wherein, dug out of the soft freestone, are dwellings of all sizes and kinds. Some are simply caves, innocent of windows or doors, their entrances protected with the drapery of heavy green, hung there by that most perfect of gardeners—free, wild nature. Others pretend to be villas of one or two stories in height, and have shallow fronts of brick, with curtained windows and terraced entrances clinging to the rock, in which are concealed the cave-like chambers of these houses. Angela's imagination pictured the whole façade of one of these sham dwellings coming off at a strong pull, like a doll's house which had once been her pride and delight, and ruthlessly revealing the private lives of such households, just as she was wont to display the secrecy of her dollies to her admiring friends. The most picturesque among these cave dwellings have window frames elaborately carved from the solid rock in which they are built, in the style of the Renaissance, and lofty flights of steps lead up to imposing doorways. The cave-dwellers in many cases had used such a rich fancy in embellishing their strange habitations that Angela gazed upon them with envious wonder.

She fancied how little the residents of such unconvenient domiciles could ever be at a loss for room; the wife, for instance, need only say to her husband: " Mother is coming to stay awhile next week; please dig her out a good-sized bedroom," or " The children seem to be growing up; can't you enlarge the kitchen? " For extensions no lease need be signed, no furniture damaged by moving. A pickaxe will build all the new chambers necessary, and the house can be enlarged indefinitely. Fortunately, light and air are not always counted necessary by the people of this land.

Descending from the tramcar near the entrance to

Saumur

Saumur, Angela walked to a villa called "La Jagueneau," which was the retreat of Madame de Montespan after she left the court and had had that famous quarrel with her royal lover, Louis XIV., which was her last. The gossips of the seventeenth century report this wordy storm to have ended in the following fashion: "I have endured your infernal temper, Madame, for thirty years!" Which brought forth from her the furious and intolerably insolent reply: "*Et moi! votre odeur!*"

With her sister secure in the title of Abbess of Fontevraud and an indulgent confessor, *Père de la Tour*, near, who was willing to assure her of pardon for the sins considered peccadilloes at that epoch, La Montespan led as contented an existence in Saumur as her disappointed ambition would allow.

She built the dome rising above the church of Notre Dame d'Ardilliers to conciliate Heaven and to please her religious director.

This church possesses one of those innumerable miraculous statues of the Virgin with which early French territory was apparently thickly sown by heavenly sculptors.

Louis XIV. commemorated the share he took in the religious fanaticism and financial ruin of Saumur, when the citizens, forced in Calvinism by the exactions of the Abbeys of Fontevraud and of St. Florent, were driven from their homes to other lands by his persecuting officers, by placing the following inscription on the frieze below the dome which Madame de Montespan, his mistress, built:

"Louis XIV., by the grace of God King of France and Navarre, drove from his kingdom all heretics and pursued all schismatics by land and by water."

His Revocation of the Edict of Nantes dealt a blow to the trade and energies of Saumur from which it has never recovered to this day.

At the present time, in the houses vacated by those unfortunate Huguenots who took their ability and their riches at this period over the seas, hundreds of workmen are now engaged making millions of chaplets, those beads on which the pious Catholics throughout the world count their prayers. Saumur has practically the monopoly of this industry, and every year barrels full of rosaries are sent off from here to be blessed by the Pope—one of the sceptical manufacturers told Angela, " probably without ever being removed from the barrel."

"What difference would that make so long as they are blessed?" she asked innocently.

If Saumur afforded a residence to the wholly unscrupulous mistress of the King, it likewise had the honour of sheltering within its walls one of those devoted benefactors of mankind who prove to the world how much power for good there is in the simple endeavour of a single earnest individual who gives her life to a cause. Within sight of the Montespan villa, almost under the shadow of the famous dome, and at the very epoch when that costly ornament was being added to crown the church, there lived in one of the old houses still standing Jeanne de la Noue, a poor girl whose tender, compassionate soul was deeply touched by the

Saumur

wretched condition of the indigent poor she saw in her native city. In her own humble abode of only a few rooms she founded an asylum for sick and distressed paupers. Then by entreaties and prayers she finally begged enough money to establish a small hospital in which one hundred beds were placed, carved out like the cave dwellings from the rock. From these meagre beginnings she became the founder of the present great hospital of Saumur, La Providence, whose garden almost touches La Jugeneau, where the fallen favourite of Louis XIV. abode.

The evening sun touched with gold the slender pinnacles crowning the house where Jeanne de la Noue founded her great charity as Angela strolled back along the quay and looked up at the towers of the great castle reared high above that quaint, mouldering house. The colours of the big fortress changed from yellow to pink in the glowing twilight, and the windmills farther along the bank took on all the hues of the varying sky. The washerwomen, who seem never in France to cease their pounding and wringing on the river banks, were still noiselessly chattering at their work. In the square fronting the Hotel de Ville, which was once a king's abode, noisy boys and their dogs raced together at play. Angela, nearing the hotel, leaned her elbows on the wall of the quay, hoping to see the usual long line of placid, unsuccessful fishermen patiently watching their rods by the bank of the river.

What is France without fishermen! But she saw nothing but a full roaring river. Not a rod in sight!

What change had magic worked in the nation which, like Simple Simon, would cheerfully go fishing in a pail? She turned away puzzled, to enter the hotel. Waldman, the dachshund, came bounding out to meet her, wriggling his long body and waving his tail in welcome, as should a proper hotel dog. Guessing him to be a frequenter of the water's edge, she gravely asked him the reason for the lack of fishermen. The only answer he could give was a quick wag. But his mistress heard the question.

"Ah! It is very annoying!" she exclaimed, shrugging her shoulders. "But *que voulez vous*, fishing is not permitted at this season; the game law, you know. And, *voila*, that they are insolent, those fish! I see the impertinent ones leaping gaily every day in the water! *Pas moyen!*" At which Waldman barked loud, like a true sportsman, and got patted on the head by the sympathetic mistress of the Hotel Budan.

Angela then understood the mystery of the fisherman and his frogs she had met at the Ponts de Cé.

After a leisurely dinner she drew her writing table up before the blazing fire, pulled down the bulb of the electric light until it hung at a convenient angle, spread her writing pad out ready for use, hesitated a few moments whether she should use a stylographic pen or a well-sharpened pencil, thought another moment before beginning her long-wished-for book, and then wrote the trite sentence:

"It was spring when I left Paris for a tour—— "

The leaving of Paris drew her mind off in another

Saumur

direction. She hastily left her writing, and, opening her small trunk, took out the tray and dived down to the very bottom to see if her sister had neglected to put in a lace blouse Angela considered became her wonderfully well. She had forgotten its very existence until that day at Fontevraud. "I don't know why I wore that hideous grey gown this afternoon! I think I look like a fright in it. Why did Georgina advise me to wear it out and get rid of it while I was travelling? I am always so silly when I obey. I'll never put the horrid thing on again."

Although the lace bodice was not forthcoming, she found a very pretty light foulard frock; but alas! nothing to take the place of the despised, unbecoming grey suit.

Angela Victoria shook out the skirt of the gown which she removed from her trunk, determined to put it on the next day.

"It is everyone's duty to look as well as possible," she remarked, coming upon a sudden resolve. "Officials and hotelkeepers have much more respect for a woman if she is well dressed." She looked her frock over and discovered that one or two of the hooks needed fastening and a few stitches had broken away in the sleeve, and so, after carefully putting her manuscript aside for the present, she sewed industriously until she became too sleepy to work any longer.

She had a cheerful, confident, expectant feeling about the morrow, as though something very pleasant were going to happen to her. Before she climbed into her high bed she opened the window and saw the moon sailing clear in a sky dotted here and there with little clouds no bigger than lambs in a meadow. A silver sheen was cast by its light on the rippling river and touched the top of the jagged ruins of the "Maison de la Reine de Sicile," standing in squalid streets on the island almost opposite the hotel. Here King Réné and his wife lived when they came to Saumur, among the fishermen and labourers who had formed a little republic on the Ile d'Or. This industrious and extraordinary colony chose their own judges, made their own laws and elected a chief, whom they called king. The first king was a royal archer of the guard in the time of Charles VII.; and an old sailor in the days of Louis XVI. bore the proud title of "Roi de la République de l'Ile d'Or."

The moonlight had been so promising that she awakened at six o'clock, expecting sunshine; but the promises of neither sunset nor moonrise were fulfilled. Instead, her eyes were greeted by a dull procession of dripping, rubber-coated cavalrymen riding over the bridge. It was not mildly raining, the water was coming down in torrents, so she concluded that this was no weather for trudging through the steep, incoherent streets of hilly Saumur. She hated to leave without having found to her satisfaction the house which Balzac fixed upon as the home of Eugénie Grandet, in his powerful but sordid novel; but there was no chance for exploration under these moist circumstances. She bade farewell to her hosts and their amiable doggie and set off for Poitiers by a very early train.

SAUMUR
MAISON DE LA REINE DE SICILE
ROCK HABITATIONS AND A WANDERER'S VAN
A GLIMPSE OF MONTRIEUL-BELLAY

Saumur

Leaving Saumur, she saw the same wet fields and hooded peasants she had seen coming from Angers; the bright genet was the only sunshine visible on ruined walls or among rough stones, but it stood as erect and glowing in the rain as under a clear sky. She polished the window and looked out, fondly hoping to see a glimpse of blue. Strange to say, although Georgina's dismal predictions seemed determined to come true, they were unheeded by her sanguine sister. Angela was a living denial that supreme trust in the effect of mind over matter is as efficient as some philosophers would have us believe; disappointment did not convince her of her error; she went on blindly expectant that the sun would shine to please her, and the most threatening signs of nature were powerless to discourage her.

At Montrieul-Bellay she ruined two handkerchiefs and a chiffon veil no longer new, scrubbing the mist from the window panes that she might see that picturesque town and its fine château while passing in the train. The cars stopped several minutes, but as the glass of the window refused to keep clear for more than one second, she let it down, and braving the pelting shower, leaned out. She saw no castle, she saw no town, but she *did* see a broad, masculine pair of shoulders disappearing into another carriage, following a pair of long legs.

"Cœur de Lion!" she muttered, falling back in her seat. Why did he not choose the compartment she was in! It would have been so much nicer to have a companion. She beguiled the time with trying to imagine who he was, where he had come from and whither he was going. As there was no one to answer her but herself, she settled the question and drew conclusions which were eminently satisfactory to Angela Victoria. Meantime the train, running southward, had left the storm behind, and she found the sun shining in Poitiers.

Chapter IV

POITIERS

THE station at Poitiers was a confused jam of pushing people. Angela, not at all using any caution, but by sheer good luck, managed to get hold of a porter who was making his way through the throng. She nearly lost her ticket in the rush at the *sortie*, but was finally extricated from her dilemma by the man who had her luggage in charge, and helped into the hotel omnibus. When she was comfortably seated there she discovered to her confusion that she had no small change to give him, and was therefore obliged to borrow from the astonished 'bus driver.

By this time her trunk had been stored away on top of the vehicle, and the excitement caused by the arrival of the train having subsided around the station, she looked about, but the manly form her eyes sought was nowhere in sight. Everyone had left the place but a few fat, complacent-looking men, who lounged about talking eagerly and gesticulating violently.

Then Angela Victoria thought to herself: " He was probably going on somewhere else," and sighed deeply, " but I should have liked to see him again; he was very companionable! " With this she resigned herself to her fate, which was to be pulled up a long, steep hill, that,

102   *A Spring Fortnight in France*

although inclined to ascend into the clouds, had changed its mind and ended at the hotel door.

Again she sighed as a somewhat slipshod valet led her through the halls, sliding along in his heelless felt slippers, and showed her into a small room, lacking the homelike charm of her chamber at the Hotel Budan, but clean and passably comfortable.

Angela, who was usually so cheerfully excited and interested in new surroundings, for some unknown reason was not to-day in her habitual state of mind. It seemed to her that the servant's countenance lacked the sweet, smiling serenity of the Jeans she had encountered in the other hostelries. She was unaccountably impressed with the idea that he would neither be as willing nor as competent as Jean of the Budan to fasten that last troublesome hook which modern dressmakers, with fiendish disregard for the temper and nerves of their customers, always put in the most inaccessible spot between a woman's shoulders. The servant's countenance belied him. His attention and willing service drew several well-earned francs from Angela's purse before she left Poitiers.

Angela was idealistic and sentimental, but Angela was also healthy, and her disappointments of the morning were not sufficient to interfere with a wholesome appetite, which craved an immediate *déjeuner*. That meal was announced by the valet a few minutes after she had been installed in her apartment, and she tripped down the broad stairs and entered the dining-room as the first course was being brought on. While enjoying her welcome meal her eyes wandered by the ceiling,

Poitiers

whereon the artist had allowed his remarkable talent to roam between realism and idealism; on a background of beautiful blue sky, sprinkled judiciously with firm, determined white clouds, he had fastened still firmer stucco swallows, coloured with such truth to nature that it is safe to conclude he intended to persuade the public that they were real, airy, light-winged swifts who had been enticed to fly into the dining-room by the realistic blue sky he had painted. His skill not being equal to his purpose, the effect produced was that of huge bluebottle flies hopelessly captured by sticky fly-paper.

Poitiers is a town so securely fastened on the sides of a steep hill that it cannot go sliding down into the small river which protects the base of the city from those enemies wont to assault it in its history as a walled town. After a very stormy and exciting youth the place has sunk into the well-earned sleep of middle age. Hidden securely behind high walls in grim, silent streets, the householders of the twentieth century appear to the casual observer as thoroughly prepared to be roughly aroused at any time from their peaceful slumbers as were the citizens in those days when the English swarmed into the town. The uppermost point of the city is crowned by the palace of the former counts of Poitou. This is now used for the law courts. Angela entered by a long, immensely broad flight of steps and stood in a great hall of splendid proportions. She sat down on the stone bench encircling the wall and thought of the days when Joan of Arc was received here by her sovereign, Charles VII. The hall is ornamented in noble style, but it must always have been

A Spring Fortnight in France

bleak and cold, even when huge logs sent up roaring flames in the three immense yawning fireplaces on the raised dais. Royalty who stood on the platform near these chimney pieces undoubtedly slowly roasted from the heat at their backs, while the courtiers below stood shivering with the cold. Angela Victoria wondered why she always allowed suggestions of personal discomfort to interfere with her romantic visions of striking pageants when she got into one of these cheerless old stone halls?

"I must not let myself do that kind of thing when I write my book," she said to herself. "It may have been summer when Joan of Arc came here." But with the best endeavours in the world she shivered at her own sensations that dark morning and hurried out into the sunshine. The interesting old palace, which adjoins this great hall, is in the process of a much-needed restoration. Some vandals of the last century thought it advisable to put a heavy tiled roof on one of the most beautiful and highly decorated towers, and in order to make this covering fit decapitated the heads of the statues of the counts of Poitou, with which the top was adorned. These noblemen are now getting their heads back. They are to be new ones, but quite in the old style.

Like children around a parent, the old houses cluster close to the palace in the narrow, tortuous streets leading to the Church of Nôtre Dame la Grande, where the white-capped market women spread their tempting array of fruit and vegetables in the open square fronting the richest Romanesque façade in existence, so

Poitiers 105

laden with statues representing the biblical history of man as to be a puzzling study for the passing tourists. The Virgin Mary, one of the chief figures in this decoration, is represented wearing the pointed shoes of that period, made fashionable by one of the many Counts of Anjou, Fulk the Quarreller, that he might hide a defect in his feet.

This church was consecrated by a bevy of saints; the author of the *Te Deum*, St. Hilaire, was the officiating bishop, and St. Martin, St. Juste, and St. Nicholas came to assist him.

St. Hilaire has a church of his own in Poiters, which is justly proud of this father, of whom, says the old chronicle: "People came from the ends of the earth that they might hear him preach."

Poitiers was by far the most puzzling of the cities Angela Victoria had yet visited. Her dexterity in going astray fairly outdid itself in this town. "If all roads lead to Rome, then all streets in Poitiers surely lead to the cathedral," she said, after having come back to it three times, although she took her start toward a different point of the compass. Each time she stumbled upon it she could not resist entering to dream away a few minutes in the noble interior. The effect of a great temple is accentuated by the absence of naves. It must have been a superbly dignified and fitting background for the many pageants which took place during the Angevin rule. Under its echoing vault Joan of Arc unrolled the oriflamme in the presence of her doubting king and the sneering courtiers.

The erection of this great Gothic cathedral was

begun by Henry II. and Eleanor of Aquitaine, his wife, who was hereditary Countess of Poitou. The main portions were finished before that English monarch died in 1189, but the consecration did not take place until nearly two centuries later. The towers then were in their present unfinished condition, except one, to which a part was added in the fifteenth century. They are rude, stately monuments, and the grey dulness of their bearings is lightened by an aspiring tuft of the golden plant of Anjou, which sprouts gaily from the foothold it has gained for itself so high above the earth.

Big and barbaric as the times in which they grew old together, the cathedral and the city of Poitiers are replete with a feeling of antiquity. There are some modern boulevards, but they are unobtrusive, and it warmed Angela Victoria's heart to be in a part of France which still remains so suggestive of the epoch and the heroes of her dreams.

Two old crones selling candles outside, where they squatted on the grass-grown steps, and a solitary beggar woman, sitting by the door within the vast cathedral, were the sole representatives of those throngs whose footsteps had once trodden the low-lying *parvis*. The deserted alley of solemn-looking clipped trees on the Place beside the cathedral added to the archaic charm.

It is but a few steps from the transept door, over the mossy stones of a lane cut through the buildings huddled close to the church, to the baptistery of St. Jean. One of the old candle vendors pointed the way out to Angela Victoria, who never would have found it without that help. Once a pagan tomb, this

Poitiers

queer building is acknowledged to be the oldest existing church in France. The entrance now is sunken low below the pavement of the present city. The guardian, whose venerable age is in keeping with his vocation, was standing at the door anxiously looking up the steps into the street in search of a stray tourist. They were rare birds in this weather and at this season; therefore, when Angela hesitated a moment at the grille, he came hobbling up the stairs as quickly as his years would allow and invited her eagerly to descend.

The old man, enchanted at having captured a visitor, insisted on showing Angela every scrap of the nearly defaced frescoes and every broken stone which has been placed by the archæologists in this ancient fane. Georgina would have thought it a wonderfully interesting sight and have taken down careful notes of all the bits and the old tombs of the Galo-Roman period. She would have pronounced the old man a proper guide, for he had long stories connected with all and each of the stony relics. But Angela took note only of the heavy columns and the wonderful proportions of the old building itself, which seemed to her must many a time have echoed with the clatter of mailed feet and made an admirable background for the high, pointed headdresses and long, clinging robes of the Middle Ages. She stopped the old man's loquacity with a franc piece, and departed, leaving him with the sad expression of a lonely heart upon his withered visage, after he had carefully told her where to find the Church of St. Radegonde, which she next desired to see.

"*N'oubliez pas, Madame*," he called out, "to observe

the imprint of the foot of God you will see in that church."

Angela Victoria might be careless in her appreciation of ancient Christian art, the guide had evidently discovered in her that weakness; but never, never could she be guilty of neglecting a sight which would appeal to her imagination as would this one! The history of St. Radegonde was one of the romances with which she was familiar. This saint was a young German princess whom Clotaire I., the debauched son of Clovis, took prisoner as a child and educated to be one of his many wives. Filled with horror at her fate, Radegonde managed to escape from the royal dwelling and to obtain the protection of St. Germain of Paris; by his influence Clotaire was restrained from pursuing the unfortunate maiden and allowed her to become a nun. It was during one of her frequent ecstasies that the Saviour appeared to her, and to prove the reality of the vision left the imprint of a large foot on a rock which is now the floor of La Chapelle Pas de Dieu. This oratory is a mere grotto in the wall of the church, wherein, protected by a fine iron grille, are life-sized painted statues, without artistic beauty, commemorating the scene of this miracle.

Angela looked with reverent interest at a deep, rather formless, hole in the rock, covered with a sort of cage; she had frequently heard of the heavy hand of God, never before of his foot. On the protecting ends of the arches and on the capitals of the columns surrounding this chapel, a wealth of grotesque figures look down. Angela's easily distracted mind soon wandered humor-

Poitiers

ously away from the ecstasies of St. Radegonde and the foot of God, to the whimsical grinning dogs and frolicking monkeys so amusingly conceived by the old stone masons who erected this church. An abbey was founded by this saint which had one very serio-comic episode in its history. There were two nuns of royal blood who, for reasons best known to themselves, revolted against the abbess, and after having with their followers fought some desperate fights in the streets of Poitiers, ran off to the King of Burgundy. He, anxious for disturbance, not only encouraged them to return, but lent them an army of vagabonds who entrenched themselves in the Church of St. Hilaire. It was only after numerous sanguinary fights in the streets that these troublesome women were forced to submit to religious authority.

After coming back to the cathedral for the fourth time in one short afternoon, Angela somewhat tardily decided never to start out again without a guidebook. The old candle sellers, on whom she had bestowed a penny each time she came upon them, as a sort of penance for her stupidity, again got their dole, and in return directed her to a tramway which would take her vague person safely back to the haven of the hotel.

She gazed out of the window of the car interested by the streets awakened at this hour to life by the labourers on their way to their homes, when her eyes chanced to perceive a well-remembered form standing still, and staring after a small boy who was struggling along with a loaf of bread longer than his whole body and which he carried clasped to his breast like a soldier presenting arms on parade.

"I don't see why I didn't walk home. It would have been so much more interesting!"

She seriously considered stopping the car, but Poitiers conductors refuse to stop their cars when climbing up mountainous streets.

Angela had never done so much consistent sightseeing alone. Georgina would hardly have dignified such drifting about in churches by the title of sightseeing, but Angela considered that she had spent a most improving and absorbing afternoon. Had she not quite forgotten her cake? Mental exertion usually had a good effect upon her appetite. Well, she was all the more hungry for dinner, and many things contributed to heighten this enjoyment. First, there was very good food, and then she was entertained through the whole meal by the guests at another table.

Directly beneath the petrified swallows was spread a long table at which sat some men who delighted and enlivened Angela Victoria's solitary meal by their sprightly conversation. They talked about the wine crop and the weather in various parts of France. They all seemed to come from different localities. They eagerly discussed the present exciting political situation, the troubles between Church and State, and interlarded this serious subject with many amusing anecdotes of their *pays* and merry comments on the experiences they had endured with railroad officials. By the general looks of the assembly and from the boxes she had seen in the hall, Angela concluded that these men were plainly commercial travellers, interspersed, perhaps, by a few notaries. But there was no whisper of trade

IN POITIERS
AS IN THE MIDDLE AGES
ON THE WAY TO THE CATHEDRAL
A FORTIFIED DOORWAY
A PATIENT POITEVIN

Poitiers 111

or money in the entire conversation. They were enjoying a good dinner as only Frenchmen can, and although strangers, beguiling one another by that entertaining talk which gives their nation the right to its conversational reputation.

That evening, sitting before a diminutive wood fire, Angela wrote an enthusiastic letter to Georgina about the charms of travel at a season when tourists stay at home. She forgot to mention the rain, Cœur de Lion, or her own mistakes, but she mildly reproached her sister for sending her off without even one dainty pair of shoes and with forgetting to pack into her trunk a newly purchased and especially becoming gown.

"What could she do with patent leathers and a light blue cloth suit in railway trains and provincial hotels! How like Angela Victoria!" was Georgina's comment when she read this letter.

As she wrote there floated up from the street of the town the sound of men's voices singing in unison; now dying away and now growing stronger as it approached and retreated through the winding ways.

> Fais le beau, Ah,
> Fais le beau, Ah,
> Fais le beau,
> Ah, Ah.
>
> Fais le beau, Ah,
> Fais le beau, Ah,
> Fais le beau,
> Ah, Ah.
>
> Ah, Ah, Ah, Ah.

At least this is how the words sounded to her ears as they floated up through the closed window. The tune was quaint and very French in character. She afterward discovered that it was an old Poitevin rustic song. Something in its quick gaiety excited her fancy and her imagination to picture a line of gay, dancing young men reviving the traditions of ancient Poitou by roaming through the narrow streets, laughing and singing as they went, in honour of the May, with their arms balanced on one another's shoulders like some of the pictures she had seen painted by great French artists. They really sang very well. Was she not in the country of poetry and song! Did not the ancient Counts of Poitou hold court in the palace near by to honour the visit of troubadours? These princes wrote poetry themselves, much of which has survived. Even Eleanor of Aquitaine dabbled in song, and certainly her son Richard played merrily with the Muses when he was not cracking people's heads.

Alas for the romance of the swelling and falling lay which Angela heard going on until late in the night! She asked the valet about it when he appeared with her coffee the next morning. Over his saturnine face flitted the shadow of a smile.

"It was the hired singers for the elections. They were chanting the name of the candidate."

"It was a very charming song," she remarked, unwilling to give up her fancy.

"He won't be elected," declared the man, contemptuously. "He's not a *Liberal*." Then he changed the subject abruptly, and though she had asked nothing about the weather, at once volunteered the remark:

"*C'est bien couvert*—the sky is cloudy, but that does

Poitiers 113

not always mean rain." He opened the window to look out. The wind came in damp and cold. Angela shuddered. With a cloak over her thick dressing gown, and a rug tucked around her knees, she drank her coffee as hot as possible, and marvelled at the birds in the garden opposite, who had the courage to give her such a delicious morning concert, and wondered how the flowers she saw over the wall could send out so much fragrance in such cold air.

When later she went out into the market place surrounding Nôtre Dame la Grande the peasant women were sitting in their market stalls as oblivious of the chill in the air as were the posies they sold. Ruddy-cheeked women in snowy caps and blue aprons, with their picturesque flat baskets piled high with the fresh green salads of all kinds and hues they had for sale, added a variety to the uniform tint by carefully selected bunches of bright crimson radishes laid in among the heads of lettuce, and the peasant women selling bags of dull potatoes tried to make their wares more enticing by brilliant yellow flowers laid on top of the little brown heaps. Pretty country girls stood behind trays of dainty cakes, which bore no kindred to the tooth-destroying sweets sold in market places throughout England. There were booths with every conceivable convenience for housekeeping and personal adornment for men and women, from shoes and hats to pots and pans. The pious were not forgotten; on the railing about the church were hung rosaries and votive candles for those who wished to count their beads or make a vow.

Every merchant was advocating with loud cries the

superiority of his wares, but above all the din and clatter rose the stentorian voice of a ribbon seller calling:

"*Un sou le metre! N'oubliez pas l'occasion!*" "*Un sou le metre!! Mesdames! Mesdemoiselles!* One ha'penny a yard." This peddler had thrown a motley mountain of many-hued ribbons recklessly and ruthlessly on the dusty pavement. They were growing rapidly less at his price of "*Un sou le metre.*"

Angela wondered where the bargains could lay in buying ribbons heaped up on the stones in such confusion that they had to be untangled before they could be measured. The pedlar continued to stir them up like soup, with his yardstick, interrupting his cry of "*Voila l'occasion!*" to do a rushing business among the peasant girls who, with their uncovered heads, carefully and elaborately dressed by skilled coiffeurs, wandered about arm in arm enjoying themselves with merry chatter.

A young French woman, no matter what may be her station in life, rarely neglects to have her hair fashionably arranged, and there are barbers who do it for the girls of the people in the most approved manner, and charge very trifling sums.

A covered market near the *Place de Nôtre Dame,* where all these hawkers are gathered, can be reached through silent streets, or by treading a busy little thoroughfare which connects it with the open marketplace. Here the housekeepers swarm, buying fish, eggs, cheese, poultry, and meats of all kinds, made attractive as raw food possibly can be by tastefully ar-

Poitiers

ranged fresh green leaves and bunches of lilacs laid among the wares to compel attention and attract custom.

Angela had been on her way to find the church of St. Hilaire, when she came upon the marketplace. This is one of the most interesting old churches in France. The guidebook says that it was built in the tenth and eleventh centuries, and within its walls Richard Cœur de Lion was crowned Count of Poitou. Angela reached by devious ways the quiet nook where, midst spreading trees, this ancient sanctuary reposes, still dreaming of the Middle Ages. But the streets were so full of people anxious and courteously willing to direct her that she had no trouble in finding her destination, and managed to get there this time without doubling the cathedral. She went by the Rue Carnot, where there are many delicious antiquity shops which enticed her into plunging into expensive delights. She condoned her extravagant purchases by the excuse that she was buying presents for Georgina, and by the fact that the shopkeepers gave her much entertaining information which she might possibly use in her book. Not one word she gathered from this source was worth a penny, and she squandered many francs on mock antiques.

Both within and without, St. Hilaire is a church likely to awaken the enthusiasm of tourists disposed like Angela to romantic souvenirs. She had gone into Nôtre Dame la Grande by one door and came out by another as quickly as possible, sorry that she had entered at all, but here she could have wiled away with delight many more hours than she had to spare. The choir and the chapels in the transept are raised above the nave by a long flight of broad steps, and against the rough old stone walls and dull grey tint of the pillars the splendour of the gorgeous robes and mantles, the glitter of the armour and plumes, and the brightness of the banners brought by the nobles to witness Richard's crowning, all arose at her bidding to glorify the old fane.

The exterior of this church, although it has been somewhat restored, has an air of ancient splendour and quaint, rugged beauty which entrances anyone who, like Angela, lived during her travels in the age of chivalry and romance. St. Hilaire formerly stood not far from the heavy defensive walls of the city; so near, in fact, that the coronation procession must have been witnessed from towers which are now not far from the railroad track. A bit of these old-time fortifications has been still preserved and surrounds the charming little Parc de Blossac, which is the promenade of the Poitevins.

Angela, who had small faith in her own ability to find the remains of these bastions, in spite of the map which she was carrying about, hailed a despondent-looking cabman whom she saw driving slowly past. The *cocher* regained his vivacity at once, when he found he had captured a fare, and Angela was soon deep in conversation with the loquacious man, who openly rejoiced at having a tourist to drive about, and plenty of time on his hands to conduct her wherever she should choose to go. " Shall I not take Madame to Nôtre Dames des Dunes? She can see the whole city from the terrace in front of the statue there."

Poitiers

Madame was satisfied to put herself in his care; so he drove her along beside the river, which forms islands covered with foliage as its waters unite and part capriciously. They went over the Pont Neuf and up the steep road to the terrace where stands erected an enormous gilt image of the Virgin Mary, overlooking and protecting the city on the opposite hill.

The man descended from his box and, helping Angela out of the low fiacre, left his horse to enjoy a nap while he, with an enthusiasm as marked as if he never before had seen Poitiers, but had only heard about it, first spread out both arms as though to lay the city at her feet, and then crossing them proudly on his breast, threw back his head and declaimed: "*C'est beau ça, Madame! C'est beau!*"

The dramatic manner ennobled the platitude, and Angela, quite as excited by the sight as the driver, replied: "Indeed it is! Very beautiful!"

"And so old, Madame! So old!"

"I have not seen any city that impressed me more."

"Ah, Madame! That is right! You have *raison*. There is no city with more old churches. Madame has seen them all? *C'est quel que chose à voir.*"

A warm ray of golden sunlight shot out from behind one of the heavy clouds on the dusty old town whose very name re-echoes the din of battle. The green, sleepy river below them, stealing away around the islands formed by its own uncertain, lazy, wandering character, began to sparkle as it flowed; the time-worn grey churches showed splashes of dim purple, red and green on the antique tiled roofs; the low clipped lime trees looked greener in the sunlight, while the irregular towers and gables piled one above another on the hillside showed a mass of bright light and heavy shadows. Poitiers from this point looked like a forgotten relic of the mediæval ages. The coachman still stood beside Angela, looking with interest and delight at every expression of pleasure which flitted across her expressive countenance. From time to time he would mutter his refrain: *"Hein! C'est beau, ça! Et vieux!"* She re-entered the carriage; the horse woke up from his gentle sleep, and the man drove slowly down the hill over the Pont Joubert, which has replaced one of the old drawbridges of the town. Angela's mind wandered back a few centuries to the days of the Black Prince, when the renowned battle was fought in 1355, and the French, who had been put to flight by less than half their number of English, found the gate in the wall to which this bridge led closed upon them by the panic-stricken garrison. They perished by thousands like sheep at the hands of their savage English pursuers. A more agreeable picture for the Anglo-Saxon to contemplate is that of the victor in this great fight, the son of Edward III., refusing humbly to sit at the table with the King of France, whom he had captured, but serving that monarch at supper with his own princely hands. Over this bridge Henry II. may have come riding in haste to capture his rich bride, the heiress of Aquitaine, who was being harassed by other suitors. Undoubtedly the gates of the old city frequently opened here to admit the bands of troubadours riding gaily

A BIT OF POITIERS

Poitiers

attired to the courts of the poetic Counts of Poitou. How often the draw must have been let down for pilgrims with their staves coming from the long journey to the Holy Land to lay their tributes at the feet of St. Hilaire and St. Radegonde, on the altars in the shrines of these saints. Perhaps Richard Cœur de Lion clattered in armour down the very hill they had just descended and rode in his usual bold way to demand admittance at the gateway from which this bridge fell over the river.

They turned along toward the other end of the town to find the church of the former great Abbey of Montierneuf, which the coachman pretended to be very much astonished she had not yet seen. The way there led along the boulevard, simple pleasant ways, shaded with trees.

The coachman called her attention to them. "These are the boulevards, Madame. *Pas grande chose*, but very pretty. Not the boulevard of Tours——" He had travelled, too. "But you shall see them, Madame. They lead us to Montierneuf," and with a beaming, sunny smile: "and they suit Poitiers."

The old church which they had come to see was discovered to have settled down with one side in a barnyard. It formerly belonged to a convent which was founded in the eleventh century, and is an interesting mass of pinnacles, queer roofs, small, flying buttresses, and domed chapels. The entrance, which is through a long court planted with lime trees, is more dignified than the view which Angela got in the first place from the barnyard side, and the old tomb of the eleventh century,

A Spring Fortnight in France

of the Duke of Aquitaine, who was its founder, repaid her for coming to see it.

Angela did not go back to the hotel. She ate her luncheon at a restaurant which the *cocher* recommended to her attention, and where no petrified swallows threatened to fall down upon her head. After the meal was over, the man, who had gone off presumably to eat his own *déjeuner*, returned with an expression that implied he was in her private service, and took her where he exhibited with pride the modern Prefecture built in the style of Louis XIII., and the Hôtel de Ville, equally modern and of which he was equally proud, although as a concession to her feelings he remarked with a shrug:

"*Pas vieux! Mais belle tout de même!*"

In the streets about the Hôtel de Ville he pointed out some interesting remains of buildings left over from the seventeenth century, and he drove her patiently in and out through narrow streets and ancient byways lined with houses which might have been standing there when Joan of Arc came to Poitiers to the court of her landless king.

"A lady has been asking for you," said the hostess, looking out from her little box-like office, as Angela entered the hotel. "She will return."

Who could know she was in Poitiers? The lady had left no name. Who did know she was in Poitiers? Angela was consumed with curiosity. She waited nearly an hour in the dingy little drawing-room, tried to amuse herself by reading all the antiquated fashion papers and "Guides to Continental Hotels," with which the

Poitiers

table was littered, and grew very impatient before the keenly awaited mysterious visitor made her appearance. She came at last, with her hands extended in greeting, and Angela welcomed an old schoolmate with surprise.

"Oh! Susanne! How did you know I was here!" she asked amazed.

"Georgina told me. We met her coming from the Gare St. Lazare. You had just gone. Albert and I were out that morning for an early spin. I have been to all three hotels here to ask for you."

"Are there three hotels here?" inquired Angela naïvely.

"Dearest Angela Victoria! You certainly are a wonderful traveller!" laughed her friend, Madame de Sayes. "Will you never change! If you know nothing of the hotels in Poitiers, how did you get to this one?"

Angela thought a moment. "The name on the omnibus attracted me. Now I think of it, I believe there was no other 'bus at the station. Oh, I think I chose it before that, out of the guidebook. Now tell me, what are you doing in Poitiers?"

"I came with my husband. He has some law business to settle here. Besides, we are on our way to mamma's château. I have a niece at school near St. Hilaire. Where are you going from here?"

"I am thinking of going to-morrow to Argenton."

"Then why can't you come with us, at least as far as Le Blanc? We have the car with us."

"I had forgotten that your mother had a country house in this part of the world."

"She never moves from it now-a-days. Paris has no charms for her any longer. She is a faithful Poitevin. Were it not that to-morrow was her birthday, we would take you all the way to Argenton. How is your book getting on? You see we know all your plans. Georgina was so full of your folly, as she called it, she spread the whole of your interesting itinerary out before us."

"Georgina thinks I can't take care of myself, which is a little silly at my advanced age."

"You don't look as if you were having the miserable time she was contemplating: but honestly, aren't you a bit lonely?"

"Not at all," emphatically declared Angela—then she laughed; "but I shall be very glad to go with you."

"We will not come too early, because we are stopping at the house of an aunt who never likes to hurry; besides, Albert and I expect a gentleman, who is to come from some unknown quarter where he has been visiting, and go with us to take dinner to-night with mamma. We'll be here, I think, by eleven."

Angela glowed with delight. "I'll be ready at any hour."

Susanne did not tell Angela that on the Sunday morning she left Paris they met Georgina wandering disconsolately over the Place de la Concorde, and had taken her for a spin out into the country in their automobile. She was very amusing on the subject of the tour to be taken by Angela, whom Georgina fondly loved, in spite of her apparent disapproval of Angela Victoria's general habits. "She wants to write

Poitiers

a book, and I can imagine just the sort of book she will write. She will see everything with magic spectacles and will expect the everyday, fussy, commonplace, stupid people like myself to agree with her."

Georgina was commonplace and everyday, but she was neither fussy nor stupid, as she declared. Most people found her quite as amusing, although entirely unlike, her younger sister, Angela Victoria.

Incredible as it may appear, Angela had never taken a tour in a car before but once in her life, because Georgina only enjoyed motoring for short distances. Her keen expectation of the morrow's pleasure was therefore not surprising. She crept out of bed early, and found the weather propitious, but she could not go to sleep again for sheer, delightful anticipation. When the valet brought her coffee, she gave him her orders, and had her luggage sent off to the station, registered for Argenton by the obliging omnibus driver, and long before it was time to start the *bulletins* were brought back and safely tucked away in her purse. She left her chamber soon after ten o'clock and betook herself to the dimness of the drawing-room, but its melancholy dustiness had no power to depress her that morning. She seated herself at the writing table, turned on the electric light to dissipate the gloom, and occupied herself by writing dozens of postal cards. She did everything but make notes for her book. She was in too restless a mood for that.

Finally her impatient ear caught the whiz and whirr of an approaching machine. She tried to prevent herself from skipping excitedly down the entrance steps in a manner totally unbecoming to her age and dignity, but with all possible effort at restraint she could not help hastening just a trifle. Her feet had nearly reached the bottom step, when she suddenly stopped and drew her breath. Beside Susanne on the back seat of the car sat Cœur de Lion. Angela was allowed no time for speculation. As the automobile stopped, Susanne stretched out her hand toward Angela, saying: " Good-morning, chèrie; you are not one to keep us waiting;" and turning toward the gentleman who had jumped out and was coming round the back of the car, she introduced: " This is my dear friend, Miss Angela Victoria Cheney, Mr. Richard Hardy."

" We have met before," said that gentleman, smiling. " Miss Cheney was good enough to help me understand the guide at Fontevraud."

" Understand! What a fraud you are! Are you going to pretend that you do not understand the language you tried so hard to learn?"

His smile grew broader. " I'm not pretending anything. The man there had such a queer accent. that for the life of me I couldn't make out what he was saying."

Susanne shook her head incredulously, and her husband, who had disappeared the instant the car stopped, to examine some uncertain part of his machinery, now came forward to greet his guest warmly and say: " So you two are old friends! I'm glad of that, for I want Miss Angela for myself on this ride, and I might have thought it my polite duty to resign her to an entirely new acquaintance."

Poitiers

He helped her on to the front seat, waited until Mr. Hardy and Susanne had comfortably settled themselves, and then took his own place at the wheel. The whizzing which had been going on violently and the view she got from the front seat, struck secret terror into Angela's ignorant heart.

"Are we going straight down this horrid mountain?" she asked timidly. The street which, on her arrival in the omnibus, seemed aiming for the clouds, now looked from her place in the car as if it were pitching down into the very bowels of the earth.

Albert laughed in delighted joy at the prospect of driving such a thoroughly unsophisticated passenger. He gave a turn to the wheel and they glided quietly round the corner into a side street, which the car so obstructed by its bulk that had any unfortunate little donkey been strolling along that way nothing but refuge in one of the deep gateways could have saved it from being crushed against a house. They rode slowly through the almost deserted market-place, picking their way through the narrow thoroughfare without accident.

"I thought all roads in Poitiers led to the cathedral. Every street I took brought me there, no matter what street it was," said Angela in surprise; "and here we seem nearly out of town without coming near it."

Albert laughed merrily. He knew Angela, and he knew his Poitiers. They had slipped down on to the boulevard, past St. Radegonde, and were over the Pont Neuf, and when they did see the cathedral again they looked at it across the valley from the top of the plateau where they had reached the green country full of fragrance and of the breath of spring.

"The field of the great battle was over there," said Susanne solemnly, touching Angela on the shoulder, who looked around surprised to meet a pair of dancing eyes. "You see, my dear, I have not forgotten your hobby. I am sure you came down here to get into intimate relations with these squabbling old ancients you have adored ever since I knew you. How well I remember at school seeing you pore over that expurgated History of France the good nuns gave us to study. No one else found any interest or excitement in it but you."

Angela laughed heartily. "Oh, yes, there was another. You forget Claire de Vaudrieul, who used both ingenuity and energy in convincing us that all the French kings from Clovis to Louis XVI. looked exactly alike, by cutting out carefully with her knife the true portrait of the former and fitting it into all the other illustrations in the book, to prove that except for the hairdressing there was no difference whatever in the resemblance between all these kings. Her passion for enlightenment got nothing but a severe penance."

"Say, rather, she got punished for her mischief," laughed Albert.

"I never learned anything at all at school," said Susanne.

"Except how to be charming," said her gallant husband.

Poitiers

"That's an accomplishment they taught you all," whispered Richard.

The low words muttered in Susanne's ear escaped Angela, who turned and supplemented Albert's compliment by adding: "And how to make yourself beloved."

"I think, chèrie, you, too, learned a little of that art."

The blood surged gently into Angela's smiling face, and, as she turned quickly back facing the road, a little expressive pantomime took place on the back seat, which pleased and amused Susanne so much that she made a remark sufficiently equivocal not to disturb the equanimity of those in front if it chanced to reach their ears.

"It is as I told you, is it not?" To which Richard Hardy replied warmly: "Far ahead of anything you said."

At this point Angela again turned toward them and joined her praise: "Nothing could be more perfect," which seemed to cause Susanne great merriment.

The rains of the previous days had freed the roads from dust, and the car began to roll smoothly and swiftly along a beautiful highway on the ridge above the banks of the river.

As the car sped on, Angela began to experience the delicious excitement of rapid motion. She lost interest in both ancients and moderns. For a time she uttered queer little squeals whenever she saw a dog, a child, or a peasant who seemed likely to get in the way, but, as the trees, cottages, and fields went slipping by, quicker and quicker, the fever for flying took possession of her. A broad, straight road, smooth as a floor, fulfilled the driver's idea of the ways of Paradise. Albert was as radiant as Angela, who became jubilant as she watched the distant objects come rushing up to meet them. He put on full speed whenever he could as they slid down the hill into the little town of St. Julien d'Ars.

"*Mon ami*, I beg you to drive slower," said Susanne. "There is an ancient church and a château here we might see, if you would permit us."

Albert held the car back a little, but the demoralisation of automobiling had taken full possession of Angela. In the novel charm of that first, short, fast run she had lost all desire to do anything but fly.

Where was the mooning sister Georgina so deplored?

"Oh, please don't stop," she begged.

"Angela! Angela!" muttered mischievous Susanne. "And your princes? This is a town of the Middle Ages!"

What did Angela Victoria care to see! All she wanted was the broad road again. The twelfth century was very far behind and hopelessly slow. The delicious recklessness induced by speeding in a motor car can drown all other sensations. The sentimental, tender, vague Angela Victoria had become a regular wild woman by this time, perfectly willing to run down peasants or scatter sheep. It is possible that she might have regretted killing a dog or frightening horses, that she could have been sobered if a child was pinned

Poitiers

under the wheels, but she certainly resented any interference which churches, or châteaux, or ancient towns might have with their flight. This was her first swift automobile ride, and it had aroused some new and astonishing emotions which Angela's face was too mobile to conceal. Albert de Sayes was enchanted, her companions on the back seat immensely amused. From time to time she would turn a glowing countenance, which looked very girlish, flushed with excitement. Richard Hardy did everything to indulge her weakness by urging the driver, who was only too ready to speed, to renewed exertions.

"Here's a clear, smooth stretch, Albert, give us a run."

Trees, fields, bushes, and the wind went scurrying by, while the car seemed to stand still. Georgina would have been shocked if she could have seen her sister. For the first time in her life birds, colour, landscape, all the beautiful things of nature, lost their importance.

A little donkey standing in a field with its head over the hedge brayed at them.

"Jealousy!" exclaimed Susanne.

"Reproach!" said Richard Hardy.

"Oh, no! He is greeting us," laughed Angela. "You know they always recognise their kind, and to-day I belong to his family, and, what's more, I don't care. I revel in my degradation. I would rather go fast than see anything in the world."

"Such is the fruit of evil companionship," said Susanne, pointing her finger at her husband.

"Or a taste of the poetic pleasure of the birds," said Albert, with theatrically sentimental airs and graces.

"*Mon ami!*" exclaimed Susanne. "Do you compare your insane speeding with anything so enchanting and graceful as a flying bird?"

"I do, and so does Miss Angela. *N'est pas, Mademoiselle?* Some day I shall take you out without Susanne, and show you what sailing through the air really means."

"*Que le bon Dieu vous garde!*" laughed his wife.

They were in sight of Chauvigny, with its five ruined castles, and, as they came over the bridge, the sunshine flooded this ancient hill town and its great church with sudden beauty. The River Vienne, flowing down here from Chinon, waters a lovely valley dotted thick with castles, fortresses, and mediæval towns. The highway runs around the base of the hill and the steep street leads up to the eleventh-century church. Susanne tried to insist upon stopping, but Albert maintained there was little to see, except a curious fresco, "and that is of the fifteenth century. Much too modern for our party!"

Angela, in her new motor rage, encouraged him, but Susanne's influence carried the day sufficiently to make him take a detour through the hilly old town by the broad curving street before resuming the highway to Le Blanc. From the first elevation they looked back. The five great strongholds, now jagged ruins, but still imposing, stood out sharp against the sky. They saw the Tour de Flins and the Château de Gouzon,

POITIERS—AN ANCIENT DWELLING

THE DOOR UPON THE STREET THE DOOR WITHIN THE COURTYARD

Poitiers

of which but little remain, the Château de Montleon and that of d'Harcourt, now converted into a small historic museum, and the baronial castle of Chauvigny, which belonged to the bishops when they were lords of the town. These five feudal castles made Chauvigny, in the olden times, a place of great importance, yet Angela in her modern fury for motoring, which had grown up like a mushroom in a few hours, took more interest in rushing along through a wild, unkempt country where the road alone was good, to considering a stop in this interesting old town.

The character of the territory they entered after leaving Chauvigny suggested many well-remembered corners of her native land by its rocks and rough aspect. The state of the road alone betokened that they were in France, where " A Touring Club " takes a deep and practical concern in the highways. This road probably existed centuries ago, for it leads from Chauvigny to St. Savin, where there were monks settled as early as the reign of Charlemagne in the rich valley watered by the River Gartempe. During the reign of the great emperor, and under his patronage, a splendid abbey was built up there, which existed until destroyed in the troublous times of the Revolution.

"At St. Savin you *must* stop, Albert," said Susanne. " I refuse to pass it, and so does Mr. Hardy. I am going to break Angela of her passion for racing by forcing her to enthuse over the delicious old church. There it is now, on the other side of the bridge."

They were rolling over the old gothic bridge, and in front of them shot up high into the blue sky the

A Spring Fortnight in France

graceful spire of the church whose foundations were laid in 811. Angela's enthusiasm for speeding had not cooled, still she was glad to rest, for her breath had been growing shorter and shorter as they raced onward in the cutting air. They stopped before the impressive church, where an old sexton came out to meet them. He would not allow them to enter until they had admired the spire.

"*La plus haute fleche qu'on connait en France*, except—" he added gently, sotto voce, "one at Bordeaux."

Bordeaux is so far away that they all gazed up at the spire of St. Savin with wonder, convinced that it was the most extraordinary thing in the world.

Within the church the restoration has been carried on a trifle too vigorously for real artistic beauty, although such an authority concerning antiquity as Viollet le Duc is responsible for the work. The frescoes on the pillars cannot consort properly with the ancient paintings on the walls until the softening influence of time has dulled some of the crudeness of the modern painting. The older frescoes were executed in the eleventh century, and are unique in France. The landscape is absurd and perspective ignored. The figures are stiff, long, and thin, as all Byzantine artists loved them, but the draperies are adjusted with an antique and charming grace. The subject is from the apocalypse, while the crypt is devoted to the legends of St. Savin and St. Cyprien. Surrounding the choir, a circle of pillars with splendidly carved capitals is still standing

Poitiers

where they were placed when the church was built, and in some of the chapels which radiate from the ambulatory there are several stone altars, bearing curious and interesting inscriptions, which were set up when the sanctuary was consecrated in 811.

"Would you have missed this for the sake of beating the record?" asked Susanne, putting her arm around her friend.

Angela looked a trifle shamefaced, her excitement had subsided, and she secretly resolved never to try to combine sightseeing and motoring again, for she knew in the innermost depths of her soul that the slightest hint from Albert would have made her pass that church had not Susanne forced her to stop.

Much of the ancient abbey has been destroyed; in the present quarters of the gendarmes a portion of it still survives. The most antique portion of these buildings, the Abbot's Palace, has been beautifully restored, and is now the property and private dwelling of a distinguished civil engineer.

Albert looked around at the town of St. Savin and its surroundings with marked approval.

"Why have you never brought me here before, Susanne? The good monks knew when and how to choose their habitations; they left the steep hills and the rugged rocks and the fighting to the lords they expected to use as protectors, and took the fat land and the feasting with a little prayer thrown in for themselves. I should like to have been an abbot. I would have made everyone work while I amused myself!"

"*Mais*, Albert! Shame upon you!" cried Susanne.

Susanne was a pious Catholic, and her husband's irreverent remarks shocked her immensely. But Richard upheld him.

"I agree with you. I should like to have been abbot, but not to have passed through the ranks of begging monk or preaching friar."

"Albert would have enjoyed preaching," laughed Susanne.

"Not if the congregation were as inattentive to my wisdom as my wife," he answered, as the car started off.

Between St. Savin and Le Blanc flows the River Anglin, a charming little stream, in whose waters are reflected the towers of many picturesque dwellings of the nobility, and ruined feudal remains.

Susanne insisted upon going slower, that she might see the country, and Angela made no objection. She had been satisfied by their last furious flight. Albert obeyed his wife, and then praised himself as a model husband. It was past noon when they entered Le Blanc, passing into the village under a lofty railway viaduct of whose graceful proportions the townspeople are justly proud. It is the only thing of interest in the town except a modest vine-draped old château and its adjoining church.

"We have not killed a peasant or even a pig," said Albert, pretending to be disappointed, as his car stopped at the inn door, "but we formed Miss Angela's taste for speeding."

"Say demoralised her virtue as a tourist, rather," Susanne exclaimed.

Poitiers

"You Frenchmen," said Hardy, " recognise no limit to speed, except that forced upon you by the inequalities of the ground, and you are all as indifferent to the beauties of the landscape—as——"

"An American on a smooth road! Wait till you ride with him at the wheel, Miss Angela!"

Angela shook her head, and again she blushed just a little.

The funny old inn, where they were served with an admirable meal by an agile waiter, was of that indescribable age which arouses speculation as to whether it was not built in the time of the Crusaders, and renovated at intervals in later centuries. The most modern efforts had been expended on the restaurant. Albert and Richard made bets as to when the hangings had been put at the sunny windows, and the dingy tapestry hung on the walls. The tables and chairs and the splendour of a chandelier with Welsbach burners were concessions to the taste of the twentieth century.

Angela was forced to part from her friends and the fascinations of motoring at Le Blanc. No persuasions could induce her to alter her plans. She was determined not to turn aside from her present purpose. The train she expected to take for Argenton did not start for half an hour, and before she went she meant to ask Susanne a few questions about Mr. Hardy, if she got the chance. They seemed to know him so well, and she wondered she had never met him at their house; he had crossed her path by such persistent accidents on this trip that, she told herself, it was quite natural her curiosity should be excited.

Madame de Sayes played into her hands by expressing a desire to wander about the village. Albert had taken Richard off to look over the machine. When the two ladies were walking off toward the bridge near which the château and the church rise above the river from a bank of velvety green, Angela asked without preliminaries:

"Who is this Mr. Hardy, Susanne? Where did you come across him?"

"He's charming, isn't he?" evasively replied Susanne.

Angela made no answer to this, nor did her face express any response. Susanne looked roguish and hesitated a moment. Her companion was so calm that she stopped teasing and answered her questions.

"It was in New York that Albert knew him years before we were married. My husband went over there to study international law, or some such stupid thing, poor dear! which I never could understand. Richard Hardy became one of his best friends. They have met since many times, and he always spends some days with us when he takes what he calls a flier across the ocean." She laughed a little rippling laugh. "So you translated for him at Fontevraud! Wasn't it droll that you should meet him with us?" She was going to add that she had been telling Richard a great deal about Angela before they met at the hotel door, but she changed her mind and kept her counsel. "His French is a trifle halting, but not so bad as my English, so we love to talk together, each in a foreign language."

"Your English is the dearest, prettiest tongue on earth, and you know just how fascinating you are whenever you look up and say, 'Is it naught?' Susanne, you are a fraud! No man can withstand you."

"Oh, yes!" smiled Susanne, "Richard can withstand me. Albert says so." And she chuckled merrily. "To-day he did not even listen to me. He spent his time watching you, and said it did his old heart good to see anyone so full of pleasure in life. His *old* heart, indeed!" And Susanne's laugh rippled again.

"Nonsense!" was all Angela uttered. She promptly dropped the subject, although under ordinary circumstances she would have confided to Susanne how she had called him Cœur de Lion for lack of a better name and laughed well about it; but, somehow, she had grown afraid that Susanne might be mischievous and repeat it.

When it was time to leave they took her up to the station at the summit of the village street, Albert driving the car at a snail's pace, and assuring Angela at every moment that she was breaking his heart by taking away his moral support and leaving him at the mercy of a cruel wife and a friend who allowed him no pleasure.

"Don't let him tease you, Angela. You know we shall miss you horribly. I wish you would not go!" said Susanne, with genuine regret in her voice.

Mr. Hardy said nothing, but got out, took Angela's handbag, and went into the station with it, while she stopped to bid her friends good-bye. He tried likewise to take the two-franc umbrella, but she clung to it and refused to commit it to his care. She suddenly hated that cheap, ugly, useful article, and felt very glad that she had insisted against Georgina's will in bringing a very beautiful new bag her sister objected seriously to allowing her to take.

As she followed Mr. Hardy into the station she turned round to throw a kiss to Susanne, and saw that lady lean forward and smilingly whisper something to her husband. Angela was sure it was some nonsense about her, for Albert looked mischievous and shook his finger at Angela's farewell.

The guard stopped Mr. Hardy at the entrance to the platform. He could not go on without a ticket, and was about to buy one when Angela nervously begged him not to do so. "Please go back," she exclaimed; "Susanne hates to be kept waiting."

She was so evidently in earnest that he gave her the bag, and held out his hand:

"This is *au revoir*, I hope!"

"Thank you," was all she said, as she shook hands with him.

He walked slowly away, and when he reached the outer door he turned to raise his hat again, but she had disappeared.

Angela Victoria crossed the line to another platform, where the train for Argenton stood waiting, and clambered up the high steps of a second-class carriage, which had every appearance of being the oldest car in existence. It was the only one on the train, so she had no choice. Travel between Le Blanc and Argenton was plainly not rushing. With that

Poitiers

fine system of economy practised by railroad companies all over the world a little branch road like this was the final haven of all antiquated coaches before they eventually fell to pieces.

The compartment in which Angela seated herself had rafters like a canal boat and a roof so low that, although she was not very tall, the plumes of her hat brushed the top every time she stood up. Faded blue cushions were laid on the hard wooden benches, the diminutive windows were overcast with the dust of ages, and the floor, of some mysterious composition, had retained the impression made by generations of excited feet.

Angela took entire possession of this antiquated vehicle and then waited for the train to move. Having a whole line to itself at Le Blanc, it goes when the officials get ready; it was high time for it to be starting, but these worthies, perhaps detained at their coffee, were in no hurry. A soldier who, with his wife and little son, after excitedly examining all the compartments of the coach had finally selected the carriage next hers, beguiled the time for Angela by affording her some mild amusement.

The man of war installed his wife and child comfortably in their places, and then began solemnly marching up and down the platform, earnestly discussing politics with the conductor, the only official in attendance. At regular intervals a baby voice calling "Pa—Pa—," in a sing-song fashion arrested his flow of wisdom.

The soldier would then stop short, and, instead of

being annoyed by the interruption, would exclaim in tones of indescribable pride and tenderness:

"*Mon fils!*" with a rising inflection, and then continue his conversation with the guard and his strut up and down the platform.

"For all the world like a cuckoo clock," thought Angela to herself.

No train in France starts without proper ceremony. The etiquette is as severe as at the Spanish court.

First: a dinner bell rings violently.

Second: a shrill whistle blows.

Third: a loud horn sounds

Fourth: the locomotive utters a squeal like a distressed animal, and the cars move leisurely off.

At the sound of the whistle another "Pa—Pa—," this time in distressed tones, came from the baby lips; the soldier leaped into the carriage, his friend shut the door, and the train was off, winding away on the high bank above the river.

Angela settled back with a sigh. She felt unaccountably melancholy. "It is better never to have been in an automobile than to be obliged to leave one for an antiquated second-class carriage on which all the wheels are flat."

She began to feel a trifle uncertain about the wisdom of continuing her tour alone. She even considered for a moment taking a quick train from Argenton and joining Georgina at San Remo. Suddenly the idea of "the book" popped into her mind. She would never dare face Georgina after the determined stand she had taken with only one line of that celebrated work

ON THE WAY TO ARGENTON

completed. With her happy faculty for finding consolation in the inevitable, she dismissed the motor and loneliness with one shake of the head and devoted herself to the view along that charming river, the Creuse, whose waters, green with the reflection of the steep banks and trees bending over to drink, were visible from her carriage windows.

She now began to perceive that this short journey from Le Blanc to Argenton was one of the loveliest she had ever taken.

She looked down into a shady hollow at Ruffec-le-Château where it nestled in the valley. A league or two beyond came Ciron, where a curious Lanterne-des-Morts, erected beneath a spreading oak, was plainly visible from her perch in the high coach. Along the course of the river the towers of the imposing Château de Ronfort, with its triple enclosure, reawakened dreams of feudal times; beyond, the tourelles of the Château de la Barre mirrored themselves in the smooth waters of the river, and the double towers of the Château de Corse raised themselves among the shining groves of green trees along the bank. The train crossed and recrossed the little river, and at least four or five more châteaux, both restored and falling into decay, interested her before they finally drew into the station of Argenton. The Creuse and the Anglin, rippling along quietly by the road she had followed to-day, excited her imagination to enchanting pictures of the social life in ancient Poitou.

Chapter V

ARGENTON

*A*RGENTON was *en fête*. Although rain had evidently fallen there and the streets were wet and muddy, young girls in white shoes, dainty white dresses, and long tulle veils crowned with wreaths of white roses, were picking their way about from house to house in company with their mothers, likewise in Sunday gowns, receiving congratulations on their First Communion. Boys in shining new black suits, with gold-fringed white ribbon tied around their right arms to show that they were likewise communicants, modestly brought up the rear in each one of these little processions.

In the balconies of the curious houses overhanging the Creuse, in the galleries closed in with glass along the river, tables with wine and sweetmeats were spread, and the young communicants flitted in and out, making a very pretty picture. Angela controlled her desire to linger in the street and make herself a part of the festivity, and went directly to the hotel, where a smiling, elderly valet gave her the choice of the best rooms. She selected one on the side of the water overlooking the pretty little hotel garden, growing in the shadow of the long bridge, and from which she had a view of the quaint houses piled one above another on the opposite side of the river. The valet left her after she had

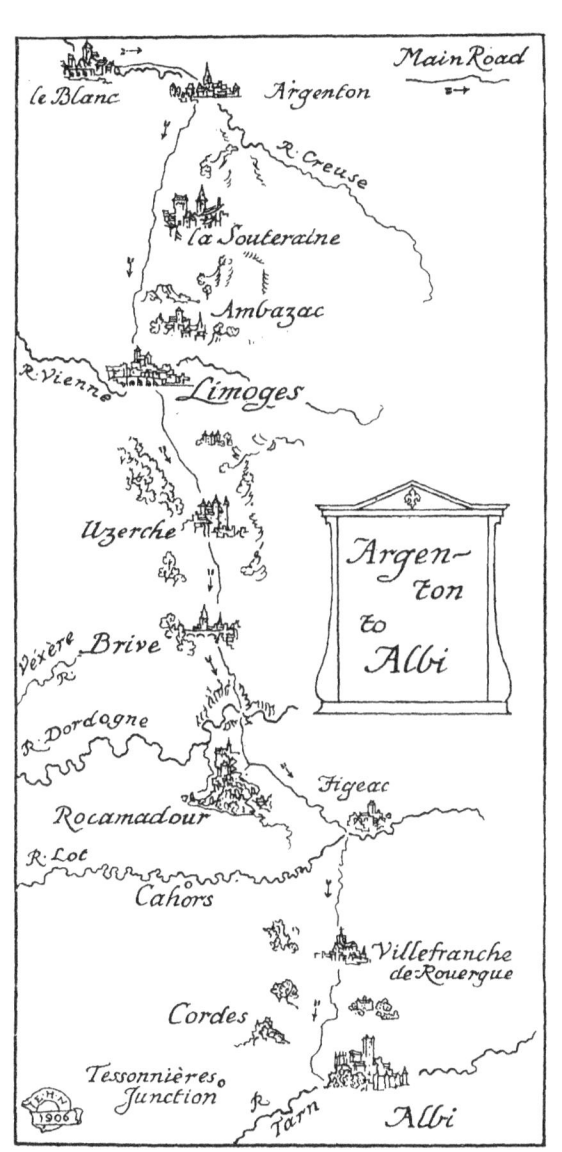

decided which room she preferred, and when he came back with her trunk he handed her two letters.

"These have been awaiting madame all the week. They are for her *n'est pas?*"

Yes, they were; although mademoiselle stood written on the address instead of the desired madame she had adopted.

One was from Georgina and one from a young girl cousin. She turned the envelope over. How nice of Margot to write her. Nevertheless, she prepared to read Georgina's letter first. Angela Victoria sat down by the broad window overlooking the garden and opened her sister's epistle. It was very long. It began with several pages of good advice, and had been written on the very day which she left Paris. She "hoped that Angela would not be lonesome," and then after cautioning her for at least a page on the subject of many things about which she was certainly in need of caution, but never would acquire it even with Georgina's help, it ended thus: "Margot has just been here to wish me good-bye, and to declare that the thing she most desires to do in this world is to join you and come to Italy. I hate to think of your being quite alone. Why do you not let her meet you at Argenton? It is on the direct line from Paris to Limoges, and so few hours in the train that she could easily travel there alone. She says she can be ready to leave in two hours' time whenever you send her a telegram. I advise you to let her come. She speaks the language, does not wear showy hats, and knows how to behave.

"I can't imagine why she wants to leave Paris at this season. Perhaps she's trying to escape some admirer. But whatever the real reason may be, she pretends it is preference for your society and the desire to travel."

This little touch was very characteristic of Georgina.

Margot's letter was short, and written after Georgina was well on her way to Italy.

"DEAR COUSIN ANGELA:

"I am sitting with my trunk all packed and ready to stuff the last things into my bag, for I know you will send for me the *moment* this reaches you. I must come! I am so tired of running around in an Anglo-American-French circle. I want to strike out on some new, strange, unexplored path. I don't want to do all the things over again I did last year when I was abroad. Mamma loves society and cannot understand how I feel, but now that Constance is out she has an ever-willing companion, so she says I may go to you if I choose and take Robinson with me. He's a good dog and I am sure no hotelkeeper in France objects to dogs, so do say I can come and bring him. Do—do—dear Cousin Angela; I shall be very miserable if you don't, and if you will have me shall be more than ever your loving

"MARGOT."

This very much underlined and girlish effusion quite touched Angela's heart. She hesitated a moment on account of Robinson—a small Boston terrier from

Argenton 145

whom Margot was rarely separated, and whose personality and intelligence made him a credit to the dog world. Angela was very fond of him, but she feared for a minute he might be a bother; then her desire for society, which had so unexpectedly developed in the last twenty-four hours, triumphed over all obstacles. That evening Margot received in Paris a message by telegraph:

"Come, both of you; wire hour of train."

As a result of this message, the next day when the noonday express from Paris stopped at Argenton, a tall young woman, with a little bull-faced doggie under her arm, both looking smiling and happy, stepped from the train and clasped Angela in a loving embrace.

"We can walk to the hotel, can't we, Cousin Angela? We've had a delightful journey, and we are so glad to be out of Paris, but it was very hard for one of us to keep still! So good of you to let me bring Robinson! He doesn't get on with mamma's Flou-Flou, and no one at home loves him as I do. I simply could not have come without him."

Robinson, by graceful pirouettes, singular wriggling antics, by racings backward and forward, and all those forms of delighted expressions known to dogs, was endeavouring to declare his excessive appreciation and thankfulness for the invitation he had received to enjoy the freedom of provincial pleasure. He led the way to the hotel, and was there received with exuberant welcome by a frolicsome pointer, who played the rôle of canine host. To tell the truth, Robinson's insinuating manner, tact, and proper policy, of which he had enough to make the fortune of a whole diplomatic corps, won the hearts of the mistress and all the servants of each establishment he visited.

After Margot had been comfortably installed in a chamber adjoining that of Angela, and had eaten a luncheon to which she did ample justice, for she was hungry after her long morning in the train, the trio sauntered out and took their path through the narrow streets of the town until they reached the lower bridge. Here they lounged on the parapet, fascinated by the many hues of the gables and wooden galleries and picturesque jumble of houses thrown against the green hillside and clustering thick above the broad river, in which all the colours of the rainbow fight for mastery, but are made soft and harmonious by the artistic touch of time. Behind the houses overhanging the water, where it goes fighting its way over the stones, the graceful spire of the parish church rises on the lower side, while on the upper, the Rive Droite, quaint and interesting, an old chapel and bits of the ancient towers of castellated times, nestle under the protection of a great gilt statue of the Virgin erected where once the castle keep frowned down upon the narrow dell. A mighty castle it was crowning the top of this hill—a castle with eleven towers which defended the pass and all the châteaux and feudal halls which cluster so thick on the banks of the Creuse. It was destroyed in the time of Richelieu, and given over to the natives as a quarry. Nearly all the houses of the present day and one of the bridges, it is said, have been built from this splendid old fortress.

ARGENTON

THE RIGHT AND LEFT BANK OF THE RIVER CREUSE

Argenton

"How did you discover Argenton, Cousin Angela?" asked Margot. "It is supremely lovely."

Angela had not discovered Argenton. Long ago poets wrote of its ancient mill, which to this day holds the middle of the stream, throwing out water with its busy wheel like a mischievous boy kicking about spray with all the strength of his small feet as he wades in a pool; painters innumerable have tried in vain to reproduce the charm of the overhanging houses, with their deep sweeping roofs, and wonderfully beautiful etchings exist of the old bridge and the ancient houses huddled close at either end of it.

While Margot and Angela leaned over, looking down into the water, Robinson explored every inch of the territory far and near; he sniffed at the children who passed and received with as cool condescension as became his birth any attempt at friendly advances. He could not see what conceivable object would possibly detain his mistress and delay his walk. He jumped lightly on top of the parapet and tried to follow their eyes with his own. The sight he saw was so unworthy of his notice that he promptly jumped down and invited them in loud tones to be moving on. The sound of a drum just then mingling with his entreaties, excitied the ladies' curiosity. Climbing up the zigzag street, they came to an open space before the chapel they had been admiring from a distance, and found the drummer, who was likewise the town-crier. He was mumbling a piece of news quite unintelligible to his listeners, for the reason that besides being the oldest inhabitant the poor old person had lost all of his teeth.

148 *A Spring Fortnight in France*

Nobody but Angela and Margot, and a few open-mouthed children, were at all interested in his announcements, which seemed to concern the elections, as nearly as they could make out. The townswomen lounged in their doorways, gossiping, and the old man, after uttering his muttered news, pounded his drum again with all his might, and, calling out to them, " Bonjour, Madame Leon—bonjour, Madame Constant," he hobbled off, noisily beating with all his might upon the instrument strung around his neck. A circle of dogs had gathered, which Robinson first joined, then routed, when he was promptly suppressed by his mistress and forced to trot abjectly by her side up the steep way which led to the top of the hill.

" How I wish we had four legs! " said Angela, as she watched the agile little beast spring lightly up a flight of steep steps mounting to the statue and the chapel beneath it. The little doggie stopped occasionally to look back pityingly at their toilsome advance. Suddenly he began to bark and leaped four steps at a time in his hurry to reach the plateau above.

" What can he be barking at so furiously? " said Angela excitedly. " He doesn't chase sheep, does he? "

She was not quite sure yet that it had been wise to invite a dog to join her travelling party.

" If such a thing were possible in this strange town," said his mistress, " I should think there was someone up there whom my little doggie knows and likes. That sounds like joy. I understand all his tones. Who can it be? "

Argenton

Margot began to follow in the wake of the little animal with flying steps, but Angela Victoria still toiled up laboriously. A man was coming to meet them at the top, around whom Robinson was bounding and circling. Margot hurried still more, holding out both her hands.

"Oh, Mr. Hardy, how glad I am to see you! Where did you come from! Did you know I was here? Have you met my Cousin Angela?"

"Not so fast, not so fast, Margot. I can't answer everything at once. I can only tell you one thing at a time. I have met your cousin; we spent yesterday morning together."

Margot looked around amazed and delighted. Angela seemed slightly vexed. She thought to herself, "Why does he always say he has seen me before?"

Margot went right on with her questions. "Are you stopping at our hotel?" she asked.

"I am not stopping at any hotel yet. I left my luggage at the station and came up here to look around before deciding what I should do."

"You can't find any higher place to look around in Argenton for a hotel than this one," laughed Margot, sweeping her extended arm over the broad view beneath them.

"I couldn't find one more enticing."

The high hills, following the course of the winding river, appeared low from the elevation; rows of poplar trees, bordering the course of the stream, stood up like stiff green plumes bowing and bending slightly with the breeze. There were angry clouds near the horizon, but the sun shone serenely above them and touched the edges of the dark masses with a ripe, golden-red light.

"Did you ever see such a sky, Cousin Angela! Above us there are the softest clouds floating in the brightest blue, and down over there behind the town there is a gathering of regular storm fiends."

Along the river bank the women were pounding wet linen, and the sound of their voices as they laughed and talked together floated up to the high hilltop; a white road wound away over the emerald hills until it disappeared like a bit of whipcord in the distance. Peasants in their black cotton blouses were ploughing every strip of land available for planting. Their wives were digging the small gardens, and with figures outlined sharply against the vivid sky sowers with extended arms trod the furrows, engaged in the most graceful of all bucolic labours. The birds hushed their songs for a moment, their melody drowned by an invisible military band somewhere down in the narrow streets of the town. Not a living being could they see moving about except two men on one patient donkey crossing over the upper bridge, and a small dog who, while keeping guard just beneath, on the steps of a cottage, was engaged in a staring match with Robinson, who stood stiff-legged and frozen like a small growling machine at the top of the steep flight up which he had just sprung with such eagerness.

"Come and have tea with us, Mr. Hardy—can we get tea, Cousin Angela? Oh, I don't mean tea, of course we can't get any tea in a village! Well, then, come and have a cake—we can always find cakes in France."

"I'll come and treat you to a cake; I won't promise to eat one myself."

They left the heights for the river streets below, and in one of the narrow lanes found a bakery in which very good cakes were approved and eaten. Women came to their house doors to look at the strangers, to bow pleasantly, and to laugh at Robinson, who introduced himself to new dog friends at every corner.

The houses, so picturesque on the riverside, show uninviting façades on the unpaved inner street. The little party stepped high over the mud-puddles, and came out at last on the lower bridge in front of their hotel.

"How much more interesting everything looks, seen in the right company," said Richard Hardy to Margot. "I did not fully appreciate the artistic beauty of this place until I met you ladies."

"We like it ever so much better since you came, don't we, Cousin Angela?"

"Considering that you only discovered me fifteen minutes ago, I don't believe your cousin can answer that question satisfactorily."

Angela laughed. "And considering that Margot herself only arrived in Argenton about two hours ago, I do not think her opinion is worth a great deal."

Mr. Hardy turned to Angela and asked about the history of the town. "Do you know," he said, "whether the Richard in whose company we first met ever spent any of his warlike genius on this place?"

Angela was about to reply, when Margot laughingly said, "No, I think he never came here; I don't think anyone came here but Richelieu, who pulled down the castle, and the Revolutionists, who hunted all the nobles living in the vicinity, and set up a reign of terror here." She said this in such a sing-song way, with such a mischievous look upon her face, that both Hardy and Angela gazed at her in surprise.

"Where did you learn so much?" exclaimed Richard Hardy.

Still smiling, chuckling, in fact, Margot replied, "I studied it on the train coming down here. Cousin Georgina said I couldn't come unless I tried to teach Cousin Angela something. But that's all I've learned so far. I mean to study every evening and instruct her by day."

Angela, laughing heartily, went off into the hotel, and left the two others to watch a tandem of two little donkeys being skilfully driven along by a peasant boy. Margot was so enchanted by country sights and sounds, and Robinson so wild with the delight of freedom and the company of the hotel setter, that Mr. Hardy felt he was quite safe in leaving them to enjoy themselves, while he went off to the station to make arangements about his luggage.

It was nearly dinner time when Margot at length decided to go in and join her cousin.

"Why didn't you stay out on the bridge with us? It was lots of fun."

Argenton 153

"I wanted to see the landlady. You see we must leave here to-morrow."

"Leave here to-morrow!" cried Margot. "Oh, Cousin Angela! and Dick Hardy has just come; I thought we could stay and motor about awhile. I want to see all the valley of the Creuse, Gargilesse, and some of those places Georges Sand writes about. I've been reading some of her books on purpose. Mr. Hardy says he can hire a motor car and that the roads are splendid about here."

Angela was noncommittal. She asked, instead of replying, "Where did you know Mr. Hardy?" Again she was questioning concerning a man whom everybody seemed to know but her.

"Oh, mamma has known Dick Hardy for ages! They are terribly good friends!"

Angela became very dignified. "I don't think it sounds very well for you to call a man of his age by his first name, even when you are talking behind his back."

Margot's face became a study in merriment. "I like men of his age, as you call it! And, Cousin Angela, everyone calls him Dick. I believe even Robinson does in his bark talk—why, what has happened to you? You're getting just like Cousin Georgina!"

It was Angela's turn to smile then. She tried in vain to repress her amusement and to look stern.

"Of course I never call him anything to his face but Mr. Hardy; I often want to, and some day my tongue may slip. He gave me Robinson, that's why the little doggie loves him so. Papa adores him, and

I'm glad he's here. I must ask him how he happened to come. He's worth all the silly youngsters I left behind in Paris. Now come, truly; don't you think he's *great*. You must like him; *everybody* does!" said Margot, using a favourite and very American argument.

Angela's smooth brow wrinkled into as severe a frown as her amiable countenance could manage. "I haven't thought much about him. He was with the De Sayes yesterday when they took me with them in their car, but I first met him at Fontevraud, where he pretended not to be able to speak French. I hate deceit. That prejudiced me against him."

This excuse sounded lame to Margot for not liking a man altogether attractive. She laughed so heartily that Robinson came bounding up to see what was the matter. "Poor dear; did you expect him to tell you the history of his life—just so—*comme ça*—and as to the French—well, you should hear him speak it and you would not wonder that he felt somewhat modest! Imagine the most English accent you ever heard, and it will be only half as English as his is. He manages to get on some way, and has gone this minute for his luggage. He's coming here to stay. I asked him to."

"Why, Margot! You should not have done that. We are two unmarried women alone here!"

"Oh, Cousin Georgina, go away! I want my Angela Victoria! She is not fussy; she lets me do what I want," sang Margot, catching the unresisting lady round the waist and half lifting her off the floor.

"If you are so wild, Margot, and so slangy, I will send you back to Paris."

"No, you won't! Not now! I tell you I'm quiet enough there and I will be good here. How can I help being a little silly when I am with you in this lovely place and such a nice man has come. You like nice men yourself; you know you do. Mamma says you would never have escaped matrimony if it wasn't for Georgina. Robinson will chaperone us all."

Angela Victoria had not the character to resist the spirits of a girl with a temperament so like her own. Robinson, on hearing his name mentioned, wagged his stump of a tail to the best of his ability and expressed his willingness to do his best as a guardian by springing on Angela's knee and flinging his little blunt head against her shoulder; after which demonstration he quickly jumped down again, and making his way to the door, glued his nose to the crack. He was ready to go again.

"Must we really go to-morrow, Cousin Angela? Did you mean it? Can't we make one little trip up the valley?" Margot put her arm around Angela's neck and became insinuatingly affectionate.

"I must do so much for my book before I get to Italy, and Georgina expects us very soon." Angela was wavering perceptibly.

"Bother Georgina!" Margot merely said, when her cousin arrested that irreverent ejaculation by exclaiming: "Ring for Jean; we must find out about the trains and see what we can do."

Jean No. IV., his fatherly smile broader than ever,

answered the bell promptly and gave them at once that air of interested attention by which a good French servant invariably invites confidence.

Margot laid her desires before him.

He swore his favourite oath.

"*Sacre nom d'un chien*," at which Robinson quivered; "you have great time to see everything before the train for Brive shall depart at nearly three o'clock to-morrow. There is only one tram going to Le Châtre and, *sacre nom d'un chien*, the train stops at every gate! If Madame would only take an auto!" He had a friend who charged only twenty-five centimes the kilometre and *essence* extra. "*Un rien!*" It is but forty-seven kilometres to Le Châtre, but that is not the most interesting point in the valley, even if Georges Sand did live there. She wrote her books in a village they should see. The road is "*un peu accident*," but very good. By starting early the ladies could make a fine excursion through this *veritable* little Switzerland we have here and get back in time for a good luncheon before starting. Should he fetch his friend, the motorist?

Margot glanced imploringly at her cousin, who needed no such inducement to yield to her own desires.

"Please, Cousin Angela, please!"

Angela was only too willing to be persuaded. The friend was fetched in an incredibly short time, and he came provided with a map and the certain assurance that "his auto (accent on the o) never broke down."

When he left, the plans were arranged for the next morning.

Argenton

"You may ask Mr. Hardy to join us," said Angela, not wishing to be too hard hearted; "he knows so much about motor cars it might be nice to have him along."

"I don't see why you didn't let him engage the automobile, Cousin Angela. He asked me if he might not do it, and now I am afraid he will be hurt."

"I am not quite certain," said Angela, with dignity, "about the propriety of asking him at all, but if he comes we must not be under obligations to him. Now, let us go down to dinner."

Margot had vanquished her cousin; Mr. Hardy had joined the party. They all sat at the same small table for dinner, and Robinson lay stretched contentedly under it at their feet.

"When I hear the rich rolling accent of Midi and watch the hotel guests carefully wiping off their plates and polishing their goblets with their napkins," said Margot, "I realise that I am really travelling in France."

A rosy-cheeked young waiter served everyone in the dining-room, attending with such skill and alacrity to his duties that Richard declared had his clothes not been several sizes too large for him he would surpass in every respect the best waiter in Paris.

After dinner they went out into the soft evening air to see the young moon, hanging like a crescent of mother-of-pearl in the lovely twilight sky of topaz and amethyst. The storm clouds Margot had called fiends were no longer visible. They had taken themselves off to some other part of the country. The reflection of the sky made the waters of the Creuse like opal. The ladies and Mr. Hardy lingered on the bridge until the river darkened to the colour of dull metal, the moon disappeared and the lights in the houses looked like stars reflected in the flood.

Jean's friend the chauffeur was waiting for them when they came in, and although Mr. Hardy at first protested strenuously against being the guests of ladies, Angela's very serious and sober air when he objected had the desired effect of making him accept the position as gracefully as possible.

The man was ordered to be at the hotel by half-past seven that they might get as long a morning as possible in the valley.

The sun rose on one of those soft spring mornings when lovers' hearts grow tender, young poets plunge more enigmatically into verse, and tourists draw heavily on their fund of enthusiasm. Down in the garden below the hotel windows the blossoming fruit trees looked like masses of frosted silver. The jonquils in the round beds had all got up early and were holding their heads together gossiping about the end of the wet weather. The iris, planted thick near the river, hung over to admire its beauty in the clear water, and the cook-boys, the *marmitons*, in snowy aprons and white caps, flitted back and forth at their duties, drawing water or carrying provisions to some cool storehouse under the stone arches of the bridge, where overhead were passing numerous placid little donkeys carrying panniers piled high with fresh lettuce, carrots, radishes and the tender green cabbage they were bearing to the market.

The peasant boys driving the little beasts leaned over the parapet to shout at the little cooks below in the garden, giving their slow-moving asses an excuse for blocking the way and the driver of the next behind them a chance to use his lungs.

The haze of the atmosphere hung like a veil around the great golden statue of the protecting Virgin, making the huge figure look like a heavenly apparition; the walls, gables, pinnacles, towers and roofs of the confused little town on the hillside had more colours and shades to show than were ever gathered together on one painter's palette; and the most telling touch of it all was furnished by a mass of peach blossoms which pushed itself into view between the old galleries and made a splash of pink above the grey foundations of the houses overhanging the river. The clear waters of the Creuse went flowing on tranquilly, unruffled by the changing colour that it mirrored, reflecting sky, houses and gardens.

"*Quel jour! Quel jour!*" Jean IV. exclaimed when he brought the coffee. He had an air of proprietorship, as if he had made the weather to order. "Madame should stay a week."

Margot, taking the words out of Angela's mouth, promptly replied that they expected to come back soon for an unlimited visit. She had been out early with Robinson for a run—lazy Robinson, who looked disgusted at being routed out of his bed so long before the coffee came. She had met Richard Hardy sitting smoking on the end of the bridge, and he had romped with her and the little dog.

"Oh, Cousin Angela!" she cried, as she came in with her face all aglow with freshness and joy. "I am having the time of my life! Such a day! Such darling little donkeys! And such good company as you and Dick Hardy!"

When they were ready and went down to start on their expedition it was not yet eight o'clock. The car stood ready, and Richard was walking round and round it in company with its proud owner and having its beauties and perfections carefully pointed out to him.

"Not pretty, but all right," he said to the ladies in English.

The auto in question was indeed a very humble member of the family to which the car belonged wherein Angela had distingushed herself as a speed maniac a few days before. It was not new, showy, or very large, but it was roomy and comfortable.

Jean, who felt more or less responsibility about the trip and was determined to make the expedition a success, came out bringing a good-sized basket, from which the neck of a small bottle protruded and wherein, among snowy napkins, invisible dainties were evidently concealed.

"*Ces dames* may want a picnic breakfast in some one of our *ravines ravissants*, and it is impossible that the peasants should give them proper food," he said to his friend the chauffeur, confiding the basket to his care with as much solicitude as if it had been a baby. He then stood with his hands tucked under the bib of his long blue apron and superintended their departure with many nods and wishes for a "*bonne journée.*"

Argenton

Margot chose her place beside the driver. " I have primed my memory with all the poetical and descriptive phrases I could gather about the valley of the Creuse in either George Sand or the Guides Joanne, and I simply must fire them off to astonish the *mecanicien* when he begins with his ' *Voilas*,' his ' Ohs ! ' and his ' Ahs ! ' and I must keep ahead of his enthusiasm to make my ride perfect."

" Just throw a few of your original superlatives at him and he will never be able to rise above them," said Richard, as he took his place beside Angela Victoria.

This lady, glancing into his face, thought she had never seen eyes so expressive of ardent admiration and affection as when they dwelt upon Margot's vivacious countenance.

Robinson divided his attention between the front and the back seat. Sitting bolt upright beside his mistress, he kept up a rumbling, growling soliloquy, directed with perfect impartiality at the donkeys, cats and dogs they met as they rolled through the streets of the town. When the last houses had been passed he scrambled over the back of the seat to find a comfortable and less crowded spot between Angela and Richard, there to curl himself into an incredibly small circle of dog and resume his interrupted morning nap. Scenery had no charms for Robinson. He had not read Georges Sand.

They ascended a long, sloping road, until at the top the driver stopped his car and they looked back upon a semicircle in which green fields and grey cliffs mingled in the amphitheatre falling down to the river. Far beyond were the blue outlines of the hills. The

A Spring Fortnight in France

valley of the Creuse, called by a French author the Highlands of Berry, deserves all the praise lavished upon its charming and diversified scenery by admirers. Among fertile fields, rugged crags and romantic ravines the valley road winds up and down hill, following sometimes the wanderings of the river and then, turning inland, affording glimpses of brawling brooks and mildly trickling streams, which gush from the folds of the cliffs and meander sedately in the shade of the glens.

Ancient grey villages, with ruined châteaux and churches dating from the Crusaders, cling to the hillsides, turning their backs upon the precipice. There are rolling, highly cultivated uplands and enchanting wild hollows.

"All our good bourgeois and the young poets from our cities come here to see the precipices and then naïvely believe that the Alps and the Pyrenees have nothing to teach them."—*Georges Sand*.

Among the groves of trees, their tender leaves a juicy green, were numbers of wild pear trees in full blossom, and here and there the delicately tinted branch of a wild plum or peach tree made the landscape a lovely thing to look upon. Labourers in their blouses were working in the field, old women passed them on their way from one village to another; and Margot quite forgot the lesson she had learned in the expressive ejaculations called forth by the genuine pleasure she experienced. It was only as they approached the quaint little hamlet of Gargilesse, where that novelist " lived, loved and wrote," as the wise chauffeur expressed it, that she began to spring upon him some of the quotations with which she had stored her memory. His tongue was loosened completely, and he found as many wonderful adjectives with which to express himself as if he had never seen any of these romantic views before. He did not rush his car; he halted at the best points, he knew every turn and twist of the road, and was as proud of the beauty of the country as if every inch of it was his own property.

"Behold how like velvet the fields are! *Ce sont des veritables montagnes de verdure.* And the rocks, are they not forbidding? They were good safe places on which to put those castles." He pointed out several ruined towers in the far distance. "*Ah, Madame!* Those were rude warriors who lived here! They fought much! *C'etait des gens, ces vieux guerriers!*"

"I wonder if our friend Richard," Mr. Hardy said quietly to Angela, "did not storm about these parts on his way down to fight his brothers and the nobles in the south."

"I am sure he led his knights through here many times," enthusiastically answered Angela Victoria, and then they plunged into speculations concerning the Middle Ages, while the driver on the front seat, between prolonged exclamations of delight, entertained Margot with the local sayings and customs of the neighbourhood. The comical humour which he expressed in his face when he told her that the Poitou peasant believes that if he washes on the twenty-fifth of March, "*le jour de Nôtre Dame,*" someone in his family would die before the year was out, and therefore, to be on the safe side, he never washes at all, pleased her more than all the literature she had acquired. Gargilesse and Le Pin are both villages of which Georges Sand writes so enchantingly in her " Promenades autour d'un Village." They took their luncheon in a cool dell beside a brook in the shade of a ruined castle. The snowy napkins, spread out on the turf amidst a growing bouquet of charming wild flowers, a decoration of which few tables can boast, revealed at their undoing little rolls of bread, crisp and dainty, some chicken, which appealed to the sharpened appetite, fresh cheese and butter, and a bottle of very good wine. After they had quite finished to the very last crumb the appetising refreshments prepared for them by Jean they came home by another road, still within sight of the capricious torrent of the Creuse, and reached the hotel after what had been a morning of infinite delight. The sentiment of the entire party echoed the words of Georges Sand: " *C'est une Arcadie, dans toute la force du mot . . . Une journée d'Arcadie au cœur de la France, c'est tout ce que l'on peut demander au temps ou nous vivons.*"— *Promenades autour d'un Village.*

Jean came out to receive them with an air that implied he had been the person who invited them to enjoy all this pleasure. He stood by beaming with interest and delight as Angela paid the man and expressed her warmest gratitude at the same time. Richard secretly added a generous fee as soon as she had turned her back, and expressed his sense of obligation to the man in mangled French, thereby earning Jean's friendship for life.

Nothing had been said about Mr. Hardy's departure.

Argenton 165

If Margot knew his plans she kept them to herself. She followed her cousin upstairs after the chauffeur and his car had reluctantly rolled away and found her gathering up the last odds and ends. Angela did not mention Richard or appear to think anything about him, but when the omnibus drove up to the door to take them to the station he joined them quite as naturally as if he were personally conducting the party. He calmly asked Angela about her tickets when they reached the station, bought one for Margot and himself, as if it were quite his business to do so, and had the luggage registered for Brive. As he handed Angela the bulletins he said, with a smile:

"You see I know quite enough French to be useful, although I should not like to speak it where you linguists could hear me; and I must confess I can't catch it when one of those rapid-firing native tongues shoots off the sentences at random. I only know travellers' French."

Chapter VI

BRIVE

BETWEEN Argenton and Brive lies a country of great natural beauty and romantic historical interest. Here begins Central France, a district full of variety and charm. It is the land of mediæval battlings, this centre of France, fought over by Anjou, England, and Poitou; the keynote to the quarrels of the turbulent Counts of Toulouse and Dukes of Aquitaine. It is sprinkled thickly with the remains of the most impregnable strongholds which stood through many sieges to fall in times of peace; castles whose walls have echoed with the songs of troubadours, for the minstrel was ever welcome in these halls, and from which trains of noble ladies issued through the splendid ruined gateways to visit the rich abbeys endowed by kings, which flourished in the fertile hollows watered by the numerous flowing rivers of this territory.

The party had no sooner taken their places in the compartment than through Margot and Robinson they gained a friend in the person of an old gentleman, who up to that time had been occupying the carriage quite alone. He would have frowned severely on any other intrusion; but a bright, healthy young woman with a bright, healthy young dog was not to be resisted by an elderly Frenchman of social instincts who had not

Brive

opened his mouth except to yawn since he quitted Paris that morning. The old gentleman's tongue, once loosened from its long rest, became even more active when Richard won his approbation by offering him an American cigarette, and Angela Victoria confirmed his liking by saying she enjoyed smoke.

"Which is not astonishing," he said, politely, "since Monsieur smokes." Angela blushed violently, a trick which always confused her very much, because she considered it juvenile, but which immensely amused the mischievous Margot.

The old gentleman spoke a little English. He was not at all shy about using it. He grew merrier than any one of them when he made a mistake, and was the first to lead in the laughter.

La Souterraine, one of the highly interesting stations along their journey, was reached almost before they realised that they had started on their way. It is the curious old mediæval town, and the name comes from the deep crypt under the big church. Nearly everything of interest in the place, the fine old gateway to the citadel, the strange church with its twisted spire, and the great convent, now used as a hospital of some sort, can be seen from the railway.

The old gentleman, who before this time had confided to them ingenuously that he was a citizen of Brive, a native of La Corrèze, and a director of the railroad on which they were travelling, appreciated the interest they displayed in his *pays* with a delight equal to that showed by Jean and the chauffeur of Argenton the night before. He was quite ready to give them all the information in his power. La Souterraine was, according to his judgment, an ancient town well worth seeing if " one made the voyage in an automobile."

This introduced the subject of roads. Richard Hardy asked about them with deep interest.

" I have made the trip," said the citizen of Brive, combining French and English with skill and fluency. " The highway is *comme ci comme ça*, very hilly in places, but not dangerous, and most interesting."

He then, like all motorists, began to praise his car. " It is not big, it is not grand. I drive a *Richard* and it serves my purpose excellently. It has taken me from Limoges to Brive in an hour, although the road between those towns is *très accidenté;* in other words, mountainous."

The line now began to run through tunnels and to skirt precipitous heights crowned by both ruined and restored châteaux. It then entered a wild valley, through which rushes the stormy little torrent called the Gartempe. High hills, covered thick with deep, dark-serried groves of splendid chestnut trees, which produce the major portion of all the *marrons* eaten in the world, rise above this stream, which has likewise been utilised for electrical works. The tunnels now came thick and fast, but the scenery between each was so diversified and lovely that Margot said it made her think of letting down a curtain to surprise the audience. The old gentleman entertained them by an amusing narration of the inauguration of the road. He said that when the line had been finished the

A RUINED CHÂTEAU OF CENTRAL FRANCE

Brive 169

news was spread over the country, and from far and near the peasants came and camped out in parties on the hills to see the first trains go by. Many had never seen a railroad before in their lives, although this was not so many years ago, seeing that he was a director at that time. They came thirty, forty, even fifty, kilometres, bringing with them all the members of their family, grandfathers, grandmothers and babies. The women's caps and the men's costumes were something worth seeing as they all stood up shouting, waiting for the cars to pass. What they expected to see no one was ever quite able to find out, but when the train really came along they all fell on their knees, holding up their hands as though awaiting something. When the cars had passed they looked at one another in amazement.

"*C'est tout?* Is that all?" and then, as though something ludicrous had happened, they all fell to laughing uproariously and spread through the villages to enjoy themselves.

Under the car windows at this point they looked down at the stones over which flowed a limpid, pearly brook.

"*Il n'y a pas mal de truite, mais je tiens pas beaucoup à la peche*," which, literally translated, is, "There are not there badly of trout, but I do not hold much to fishing." This confession from the mouth of a Frenchman was as extraordinary as the language in which it was couched. He declared himself a devoted follower of "*la chasse*" and pointed out many of the châteaux he had visited in pursuit of that sport. Before they reached Limoges they passed Ambezac. Beyond the wild gorge which runs back into the country near this town are some meagre remains of the former great Abbey of Grandmont. The monks of this mediæval monastery were in high favour with Geoffrey Plantagenet and his wife, the ex-Empress Matilda, as well as many of the other powerful nobles of the Middle Ages. The abbey was enormously rich in treasures of gold and silver lavished upon it by these princes. At its dissolution in 1772 they were divided among the neighbouring churches and monasteries.

That miserable young king, Henry Court-Mantel, eldest brother of Richard Cœur de Lion, who went about ravaging and stealing everything he could, and who was even a greater curse to these provinces than were his younger brothers, took with his own sacrilegious hands a magnificent golden pyx from the high altar in the Abbey de Grandmont, having in vain tried to find the other treasures which the wily monks had hidden safely at the news of his approach.

Richard Hardy, seeing that Margot and her elderly admirer were deep in a French conversation that flew so wildly from ancient castles to the dishes eaten by the *gourmets* of Limoges, and from trout brooks to the comparative merits of hunting dogs and Boston terriers, that he, with his slow comprehension of the language, found impossible to follow, seated himself beside Angela Victoria and plunged into speculative reminiscences concerning the doings of their pet hero.

Limousin was one of Cœur de Lion's chief battlegrounds. The bloody feuds, rebellion and intrigue from which he was never free kept him busy with battle-axe, fire and sword in this hilly district. Every ruined tower, every crenelated wall, suggested his memory; yet the talk between Angela and Richard drifted away from deeds of prowess to the softer side of Cœur de Lion's career. It was the singer of *sirventes*, the player of the lute, the lover of the ladies, of whom Mr. Hardy spoke. " He was as tender as he was rough," said Angela, leaning dreamily back against the cushion. Her lids were dropped half over her eyes and she talked as if to herself. The sentimental mood was upon her very strongly in this country, where the memoirs of a romantic age are recalled among scenes of entrancing natural beauty.

" I won't answer for the tenderness," he laughed; " but his love was quick to grow and flame. How constant it was is another question."

" He had too big a heart," she said, smiling; " he loved too many, but all very strong men have big hearts."

" But do all strong men love too many? "

" I don't know," she said, musingly. " Queen Berengaria knew more about it than I do."

" Yet he tumbled all in a heap at her feet when they first met and stopped at nothing until he got her." Mr. Hardy turned suddenly and asked abruptly: " Don't you believe that love at first sight can last? "

" I have never thought anything about it," she said, slowly. " I don't think I believe in sudden affection."

" But have you never thought that what you now

A Spring Fortnight in France

name sudden affection may possibly not be sudden at all, only latent?"

"Then your faith is the faith of reincarnation."

"I am as uncertain on that score as you are about love at first sight. Don't shake your head and laugh. From the tone of your voice I know what your faith is."

Angela woke up and said with energy: "I believe there are people in the world who imagine themselves to be suddenly overwhelmed with such unforeseen passion for a stranger, but I have never yet been brought to believe that such an emotion was love as I understand it."

"What *do you* understand by love?"

He asked the question earnestly, lowering his voice slightly as he glanced toward the chattering Margot and the amused, absorbed old gentleman.

Angela Victoria caught the glance and hesitated. Like a flash, the determination entered her spirit to break up the travelling party so far as Mr. Hardy was concerned. Margot's mother and father might, as the girl had expressed it, " adore Richard Hardy," but she, Angela Victoria Cheney, did not propose to be the means of encouraging a match between a pair so unequal in point of age.

Richard Hardy was still looking at her face with a quizzical expression in his eye, waiting for an answer and little suspecting where and how her thoughts were wandering, when again the train ran into the darkness and the old gentleman turned to him and explained:

"We are now beneath Limoges."

Brive 173

"Under Limoges in a tunnel! Don't we see the city at all?" cried Margot, disappointed.

"If I had foreseen this little journey, *chère Mademoiselle*," said the gallant old gentleman, " as director I should have voted that the railroad pass all the principal monuments of the city."

Beyond Limoges, despite the many tunnels, the journey grows constantly more interesting. The conversation had become general, and the old gentleman proved himself as interested in mediæval history as anyone in the carriage.

"You should stay long in this country and explore it fully. We are very proud of it *"nous autres."*"

"Was it not near Limoges that Richard Cœur de Lion came to his death?"

"Ah, yes, Madame. It was at Chalus-Chabrol that the poisoned arrow 'met him.' A most interesting place. It is to the west of us here, on a branch road between Limoges and Angoulême. A most inspiring village for artists! There are two castles not so badly ruined and a lot of irregular old houses piled up among trees below them on the hill. The flowers and the vines have buried all remembrances of siege and assault, and a tumbling brook turns the wheel of an old water mill within sight of the very spot where that *vieu lion rageaux* Richard got his final wound. It is a little out of the way. But why do you not stop at Uzerche? Few foreigners visit it. It is a queer old town; I am sure you would enjoy it. You cannot see it from the railroad, but if you choose you can stop there now and reach Brive by a later train in time for dinner. The ancient houses are very well worth seeing. We say in this *pays*, 'Who has a house in Uzerche has a castle in Limousin.' It is full of twelfth-century streets."

"Come on, Cousin Angela; let us see Uzerche! What a blessing we have a man with us! We can do anything with a man along, can't we, Mr. Hardy? Oh, thank you so much, Monsieur! Of course we must stop. I am travelling expressly to see queer towns, and so is Robinson!"

The old gentleman laughed merrily at the young girl's light humour.

"*Eh bien!* It gives me great pain to lose you, but I can't retract my advice. I will earn your gratitude. Besides," he said, slyly, "I am to get out there, too. Are you to go to the Hôtel de Bordeaux, in Brive, Monsieur?" he said in English to Mr. Hardy. "I know the proprietor well and can promise that you will be comfortable."

The train began to slow up as Richard Hardy carelessly answered "Yes" to the foregoing question. He had either not understood or paid any attention to the preceding words of the old gentleman, and was therefore much surprised when Margot began to tuck Robinson under her arm and to hand him the bags.

"This is not Brive, is it?"

"No, but there is something to see here. We are going to get out and stop over a train." Whereat he quietly went about taking down the wraps, as if he were their courier.

Angela decided that her reign as a leader was over

Brive 175

for to-day. She allowed herself to be gently lifted out of the uncomfortable high railway carriage by Mr. Hardy; they parted from the old gentleman, who got into a vehicle waiting for him, with many expressions of gratitude and regret on both sides, and took the omnibus for the town.

Uzerche is half a mile or more from the station. They took a short cut through a tunnel about one hundred yards long which led directly up into the hilly streets of the unique town. The place, as the old gentleman said, was well worth seeing. It stands on a promontory, with the river doubling around the point; the old walls and ancient gates encircle streets full of interesting houses topped with numerous pignons, like candle extinguishers. At the point of the conical hill whereon the town has grown stands a fine church. Uzerche has two châteaux; one is now used for a girls' school, but the story of the place is but that of a day in the life of Henry Court-Mantel, young King of England, who, though crowned while his father, Henry II., lived, was destined never to reign or to have any real power. He kept all of Aquitaine in a constant state of turmoil during his short life by his bickerings with his brothers and his senseless rebellion against his father's will. The people of Limoges detested this young king; when he tried to re-enter their city the inhabitants met him with volleys of stones, shouting: "We will not have this man to reign over us! He shall no longer have our money and treasure!" and they drove him forth.

It was then he fell ill, and, weary and ailing with

the effects of his own passions, came to linger in Uzerche while waiting for the Duke of Burgundy and the Count of Toulouse to join him. He then took his turbulent person south to Rocamadour, where, ill though he was, he pillaged and wasted the town and the sanctuary and returned northward to Martel, near Brive; there to die.

"I shouldn't mind stopping a week in Uzerche at all, Cousin Angela. The hotel looked very clean," said Margot.

"Hear the child!" exclaimed her cousin. "She thinks we have months instead of days before we are to join Georgina!"

"It's a pity you have not," said Richard. "This part of France is not only full of beauty, but it takes such a powerful hold upon my imagination that"— he looked laughingly at Angela Victoria—"it quite turns the tide in favour of reincarnation. I should like to believe I had once lived here in the rough ages myself."

Margot laughed aloud. "I don't believe you would have liked it a bit. But then, if you must choose some old creature as your former self, why not select the mighty Richard? He had the same name."

"Thank you very much. Perhaps I will, and choose Robinson as the pet lion I brought with me when I returned from the far-off East. To be sure, he fawns and jumps and pretends he is only a dog, but he has the spirit of a wild beast at times, particularly when there is a bone about."

"I didn't know Richard had a lion," said Margot, "and, anyway, he shan't insult my darling lamb of a Robinson by calling him a wild beast."

"There are a great many things you don't know. You don't know you were shut up in a castle and bored to death until I walked up close, as brash and brave as you please, and knocked it down like that one." He pointed to a ruin near Allasac.

From the carriage window Angela looked up at the machicolations in the floor of the projecting gallery, where the great holes were left for the besieged to pour down missiles upon the foe.

"Were you not afraid of the boiling oil?"

"I was afraid of nothing, not even of the women. Not even of Margot, and she was always a pretty dangerous person."

The young lady in question tossed her head without deigning to answer; instead she began piling her ci-devant knight's lap full of travelling bags.

"I will take care of the lion, poor despised lion, and when we get out of this surging mob he will take care of himself," she said, and clambered down with Robinson into the dense crowd swarming the platform of the station at Brive.

Richard Hardy took all the bags he could hold in one hand and unceremoniously linked Angela's arm with the other. "I can't afford to lose your opinion that a man is a useful travelling companion," he said.

Angela did not see fit to answer, but that had been Margot's expressed opinion, not hers. The young girl and Robinson were waiting at the sortie.

"The personal conductor is needed here to give up the tickets."

"What trouble these French methods do make. Must I drop all my traps and fish out the tickets?"

"Tell me where they are," laughed Margot, "and I will fish them out." But he had already found them, and, merrily joking with one another, they found the hotel 'bus, in which one passenger was already seated. The driver had gone for the voluminous and heavy luggage belonging to this man, whom, to judge by the size of his trunk, was a commercial traveller; so Margot and the lion, alias Robinson, trotted up and down while waiting and made warm friends with a donkey attached to a little car.

The man who was the additional passenger was very much of a dandy after the French fashion. He glanced at the blooming Margot, turned up his weak moustache into what he considered an irresistible curl, and then, perfectly satisfied with that last touch to his personal charms, opened a pen-knife and proceeded to pare his nails, glancing up occasionally from that occupation to cast sheep's eyes at the highly amused young lady.

"Cousin Angela! Wasn't it amusing to think the landlord took you for Mr. Hardy's wife?"

"I didn't find it amusing at all. I was thankful it happened when he had gone into the *bureau*. It serves me right. I should not allow a man to trail around with us, even to please you!"

"Why, Cousin Angela, you are cross! I thought

you were never cross." Angela Victoria, usually so amiable, was this time distinctly out of humour. She went soberly on, changing her gown for dinner, and looked so serious that Margot thought it wiser to pursue the delicate subject no further. So instead of teasing she said:

"Isn't this a delightfully funny old hotel? Such a perfect combination of the old and the new. Outside staircases, narrow, curious halls, yet with such comfortable-looking modern beds, not to mention electricity and really generous wash-stands. I wish it was warm enough to eat in the garden," she sighed. "You haven't seen the garden. It is very nice; the scent of the flowers is simply delicious, the birds are trilling away like a whole chorus of opera singers—no, I don't mean opera singers; I mean something better than that. Never mind what I do mean. I can't think of a simile myself. Anyway, they are very obliging with their music, and the twilight is so bright, and nobody to be benefited by it except Robinson. Mr. Hardy says it is too damp and cold for us to sit out under the trees."

"Of course, if Mr. Hardy says so, we cannot go," said Angela, with dignity.

So only the four-legged member of the party enjoyed the fresh fragrance of the spring flowers. He stood outside the window, as near to his mistress' table as possible. The hotel dog—there is always a hotel dog in France—was this time an amiable old setter who was trying to be hospitable and was at least ten times Robinson's size. He had accompanied the new arrival to the garden and lay stretched on the ground behind him, endeavouring to be as polite as possible; but Robinson rudely turned his back and discouraged all advances. He had eyes only for the humans.

"What do you say to a stroll by moonlight?" said Mr. Hardy. "Margot is still angry because I would not let her take cold by eating in the garden."

Angela Victoria said politely and as amiably as possible under the circumstances: "Are you responsible for Margot's health?"

"I think I am in a measure," answered Richard Hardy, coolly.

There was no more to be said.

"Oh, do let us go, Cousin Angela! I am always begging to go somewhere. We might have our coffee at some little café in the town. Couldn't we, Mr. Hardy?"

"I think it is quite possible to find one," he said, with a smile, "and we shan't have much time to see this place to-morrow morning if we start out early, as your cousin proposes to do."

Angela made some feeble objection to the plan, but it was impossible for her either to be harsh with Margot or to deprive herself of the pleasure of a stroll before bedtime.

Brive never looks more picturesque than by moonlight. It is a town quite safe to recommend as a centre for excursions. The region about is delightful and its own fascinations will not absorb much time or attention. There are wide boulevards shaded with elms and with beech trees; comfortable houses in pleasant

Brive 181

gardens; a universal air of prosperity; a broad canal bordered with plantations of lilacs and magnolias, and in some of the more interesting crooked old streets a few enticing antiquity shops. As the little party, with Robinson and his friend, the hotel setter, in close attendance, strolled about, it all looked very serene and the air was heavy with the fragrance of the gardens flooded with the light of the growing moon.

"Oh, I wish I could have some ice-cream soda!"

"Oh, Margot!" exclaimed Angela, in horror.

Mr. Hardy grinned. "That's right, Margot. Wave the American flag! And hold fast to your thirst. I will give you all the ice-cream soda we can find in Marseilles!"

"I am afraid you will have to wait longer than that." Angela's tone sounded very quiet and chilly. "I doubt if we stop in Marseilles."

"Cousin Angela, we just *have* to go to Marseilles. You are tired now; we'll talk about that later." Margot made such a funny face and put on such ridiculous airs that Angela could not help laughing. "Go upstairs and I will help Mr. Hardy loosen his French tongue and struggle with the landlord's English. Unless I do we shall never discover how or when we can get away from here. They will tie us up in some hard knot, and if I must be left high and dry I prefer a more entertaining city than Brive. Don't you?"

Angela Victoria had found the little town very pleasant that evening. She said so.

"Oh, yes," Margot went on, "it was mildly pleasant, but how can one like a dull, little commonplace provincial city after the deliciously entrancing Argenton?"

"My dear Margot! how can you judge of the dulness or interest of this town after stumbling around a few streets in the dark?"

Margot was not afraid to judge anything, but she laughed and skipped across the court into the cosy office of the hotel to help untangle the difficulties into which Richard and the landlord would be sure to plunge when they talked about morning trains and the best way to pursue the journey to Rocamadour.

Angela was still busy unpacking and repacking her small trunk when Margot came upstairs. She was trying to make place for some old brass she had found in a queer shop that was still open when they went out that evening. She never longed for Georgina so much at any time as when she tried to pack into her trunk articles which she had foolishly bought and were too big for the place she had to give them. Georgina frowned severely upon the reckless expenditure of money; still, if in spite of her remonstrances her sister was extravagant, she displayed a veritable talent little short of genius for tucking away such purchases where they would be safe from damage without wrinkling every garment in their vicinity. Angela had no such skill, and consequently her arms were usually laden down with packages she knew not what to do with. Georgina absolutely refused to travel with one extra bundle. Angela Victoria always accumulated a dozen or more in the course of a short journey.

The entire contents of her trunk were spread on

Brive

the bed when Margot entered. "Why, Cousin Angela, what are you trying to do?"

Angela sat down with despair on her countenance. "Tell me first," she said, "when we are to start?"

"We must take the train at eight if we want to see anything of Rocamadour, and go on the same day. The landlord says we are to have '*une promenade ravissante*' on the railroad. I wish we could motor there. I would be willing to ride in any kind of a car. I would even go in a *scroot*, if necessary."

"What in the world is a scroot, Margot?"

"It is only my name for one of those nasty little, smelly, noisy, ancient automobiles that go shaking past our country place at home. I stole the word from papa. It is what he calls a ragged little cur, just plain dog. My scroot is just plain ragged motor, without fancy trimmings."

"I think, my dear, I prefer the landlord's suggestion of a comfortable train. I have changed my ideas about the delights of motoring."

"Oh, have you! When did you do that? You will have to reform, dear Cousin Angela, for my sake, because Mr. Hardy says he means to bring us all here some day in the best car he can find, and to visit every town in this neighbourhood. He and the landlord are talking gibberish about it this very minute. I left them because my tongue got tired trying to translate while they both went on talking together all the time. How could I make them understand one another? I wish Richard Hardy wouldn't leave us to-morrow."

Angela did not answer immediately; she went to the bed and began to fold the clothes lying there.

"Is he going to leave to-morrow?" she said, coolly.

"Well, I don't know! He only said he would cut off somewhere else if you didn't want him to keep on with us any longer. But you do want him to go with us to-morrow. I told him so."

"Margot, how can you say such things? I said I did not think it was right to let him tag along with us. I don't think it is proper."

"Proper! I didn't know you were so awfully proper, you dear old cousin!"

Angela suddenly rebelled against an expression that Margot had long used unreproved and which in the young girl's mind did not signify the weight of years. Robinson, aged three, was "a dear old dog" to her. She went on: "I don't see why you feel that way. Mamma thinks it is delightful that he is with us! I have just got a postal card from her. It came while we were gone. I wrote her the minute we met him."

"I do not think your mother uses her best judgment. Of course, for your sake, I tolerate him."

"Tolerate him! And he is so nice! And he has loved me so many years! And mamma idolises him!" all of which Angela had heard before in other words. "Well, if you tolerate him now, you will adore him before our journey's end, so he shan't go away."

"I wish you would not use such exaggerated phrases, Margot. We cannot, of course, prevent him coming our way. The road is free to everyone who pays."

Brive 185

"I am glad it is. Of course we can't prevent his coming, and I don't want to."

Angela was annoyed to a point which prevented her sleeping very well that night; nevertheless, such was her temperament that she arose smiling, serene, and apparently very amiable the next morning. Margot threw her arms around her cousin's neck and kissed her so enthusiastically that Robinson was impelled likewise to join in the demonstration.

The packing had not been entirely successful. She had managed to find a place for the brass among her frocks, but several small boxes and a portfolio had found no resting place in her trunk. Margot looked at them as they lay on the table.

"Don't you want me to take care of those things, Cousin Angela? They are not valuable, are they?"

"Oh, no," said Angela, absentmindedly; "they are nothing but some papers."

"Well, give them here. I will get rid of them," said Margot, as she gathered up everything lying loose.

Angela went down to breakfast. Coffee was served in the garden. The bright morning sunlight had removed the objection of chill and dampness, and although the loquacious waiter lamented at length on the abominable weather and the late spring, the birds and the flowers did everything in their power to compensate them for these disadvantages.

Brive looked peaceful, and even picturesque, as they jolted along in the 'bus on its way to the *gare*. Market women were coming into town with the smallest donkeys they had yet seen, harnessed into little waggons, full of appetising vegetables and potted plants. The milkmen, with little carts full of shining brass cans, were going their rounds, stopping at the gates of comfortable, roomy houses.

"I wish I could have one of those bright jars as a souvenir from Brive," said Margot.

"And how would it do to take a good-looking milkman along to carry it for you?" asked Richard.

"No, thank you. I'll leave him, blue cap and all, for someone who likes him better," laughed Margot. "Just give me his battered brass can."

The station at that early hour was nearly deserted. A pretty, fresh-looking woman with grey hair, who was the proprietress of the news-stand, greeted them with such amiability that Richard bought of her not only sufficient local literature to furnish reading matter for several weeks, but also a bundle of postal cards and three indelible pencils to forward *impressions de voyage* to absent friends.

Angela Victoria wrote a line to Georgina, before the train started, on a card ornamented by a view of the canal:

"Am getting on delightfully. Find Margot a great help. Brive is a beautiful city."

Margot scribbled all over a picture of women washing in the river and sent the following off to her mother:

"Brive is a stupid little hole, but the hotel is good. We are just starting for a better place. Cousin Angela is a sweet thing, but she doesn't like

Brive 187

Richard Hardy. Isn't it strange? Robinson sends a snap to Flou-Flou. M."

Richard wrote a greeting to Monsieur and Madame de Sayes.

The steeples of Brive had hardly disappeared below the horizon before the two heavy towers and the great donjon of the ruined castle of Turenne stood out from a background of deep blue sky. This castle fell before the levelling hand of revolutionary bands. No more important stronghold in olden times existed in the province, and its vicomtes were princes in the land.

"This must have been a gay neighbourhood for you and me when we were living in the Middle Ages," said Margot to Richard. "The whole territory is peppered with castles. That boredom you spoke of yesterday could not have been caused by lack of society."

"But you fail to realise, my dear young lady, that there was some difference between travelling at railroad speed and picking one's way over bad roads on slow-going horses. I don't believe that dinner parties and junketings were altogether the rage in this neighbourhood when we last visited it."

"I love riding so much that I am sure I must have acquired the taste when I lived around here."

With the guide book Richard had just bought in one hand and making magnificent gestures with the other, she pointed out the numberless ruins dotting the landscape and showing their pitiful jagged skeletons on every elevation.

"Here, facing Turenne, is the Château de Linoire. On the left you see the castle of Cavagnac, dating from the thirteenth century. That restored affair on the right is the Château de Croze; it did not exist in my time. The people are regular parvenus, nobles of the sixteenth century."

"Oh, we never could have known them!" exclaimed Richard, with contempt; "could we, Miss Angela? For, of course, you were one of the chatelaines of this neighbourhood as well."

Their nonsense was interrupted by their arrival at the station of Martel, and there the conversation turned solely toward that interesting but exceedingly wicked young prince, Henry Court-Mantel. It was here the young king died. His old father, Henry II., held the sceptre and the revenues, and held them very tight; but when his unworthy son, the youthful monarch, although burning up with fever, his strength failing, still went ravaging about Aquitaine, pillaging churches and stealing from the people, the old king tried by force to stay his progress. Young Henry came to Martel from Rocamadour, where he had emptied the sacred treasury of all the thank offerings bestowed upon the sanctuary by generations of grateful princes. He was stricken down at this little town in a house which is pointed out near the present Hôtel de Ville. No sooner did he feel the hand of death upon him than he plunged into the futile business of a deathbed repentance, after the most approved manner of the twelfth century. He sent messages of affection to his father, praying the old king to come to him. But that wily potentate did not trust his fascinating son. He had played too many miserable tricks on his father. The sovereign, therefore, sent off a bishop whom he felt he could spare with forgiveness and a precious ring to bestow upon the dying prince. For once, young Henry was not shamming. He confessed his sins aloud in the presence of his retainers, ordered his attendants to clothe him in a hair shirt, and, holding in his hand the ring he had received from his father, he was by his own orders dragged out of bed by a rope fastened around his neck and left to die on a bed of ashes.

" I don't think I am as crazy about the Middle Ages as I was before you read that bit of history. But look out! Do! Here is something to make us glad we are living right now."

The strong little locomotive dragging its light train was puffing and pulling laboriously up the path cut for it along the side of the rugged hills, from the fertile plains of La Corrèze to the sterile plateau of Les Causes. The road makes a circuit on the flank of the craggy mountains, ascending perpetually, while below lies the immense circus of rich, productive land through which flows a tranquil river bordered by the neverfailing poplar and dotted with pretty villages and thriving farms.

The châteaux of Floriac and of Mirandol hang on savage cliffs above the Dordogne. Across the plain is the rough, natural fortress, where behind the primeval rocks the Gauls made their last stand against the invading Romans. All the way up the precipitous route flowers grow in abundance, and great bunches of royal-looking iris and a profusion of bright broom cling to the hillside among the rough grey crags. On reaching the summit of the pass where stands the isolated station of Montvalent, the trains in following the ascent look like giant black earth worms slowly crawling up a granite wall.

Handsome peasants with lively dark eyes shining from under their rakish big flat blue caps were lounging about the desolate *gare*. The train left them idly gazing, and the engine, with a high, piping whistle, went diving into a region among savage fields, on which were lying, strewn thick as leaves in autumn, stones and pebbles of every size.

Margot, thinking they were a strange sort of flower, exclaimed with pleasure. The sheep, in large flocks, looking fat and healthy, were apparently eating the grass which grew in these extraordinary fields with greedy delight. This strange high moorland, "*Les Causes de Gramat*," extends for leagues on these uplands.

"Isn't it wonderful!" cried both Angela and Margot again and again, until even Robinson was moved to raise himself on his hind paws and look out of the tiny side window, but seeing only stupid nibbling sheep he lay down again with a growl and a sigh at the strange fancies of his adored mistress.

From the remarkable soil of these moors spring forests of sickly looking oak trees, but in the meagre shade they afford lies hidden the wealth of the district—the highly prized truffle.

Chapter VII

ROCAMADOUR

"*ROC-AMADOUR!*" called out the conductor at a dreary station on a barren plain. They looked about the lonely fields.

"The supply of stones is still with us," said Richard, "but where is our wonderful shrine?"

"Follow those people; they must be pilgrims, and we shall find it," said Margot. "They all seem to be getting into the omnibuses."

A line of shabby vehicles labelled "Hôtel St. Marie," "Le Lion d'Or," "Au Grand Soleil," "des Templiers" and "Nôtre Dame" were drawn up at the desolate *gare*, and as five of them had a proportion of at least three passengers each, Angela and her friends took the remaining vacant waggonette. Robinson, after having carefully examined both driver and horses and expressed his satisfaction in his own way, was called by his owner to spread his small person over as much space as possible and keep out a mother and child who were following.

"I should have died," said Margot, when the horses started, "if that woman and her terrible child had come with us."

"Why, Margot! How cruel! The poor child was horribly afflicted with those frightful sores. One side of the unfortunate baby's face was so pretty, and her skin and cheeks so soft and clear! It was pitiable! It excited all my sympathy."

"I'm awfully sorry for her, but I couldn't bear to look at her!" insisted Margot.

"Perhaps the mother hopes to have her child cured by a miracle," said Angela.

"The Age of Miracles has passed, and the Age of Cleanliness is here. That woman doesn't seem to know it. She is very well dressed, but did you see her hands?" said Margot.

"Oh, let's dismiss that subject and look at the landscape. Where do you suppose Rock-amadour, as the guard pronounced it, has hidden itself?"

"Why, this country is nothing but a garden of stones! How the farmers have toiled to grow these crops! They seem to promise well."

"And the stone fences look just like New England. Are you or are you not on your native heath, Cousin Angela?"

After two miles of uninteresting road they finally stopped at an antiquated little collection of houses, where some of the rickety omnibuses were discharging their passengers.

"Is *this* Rocamadour?" asked Margot, in disgusted tones, of the driver.

"*Eh non! Mademoiselle!*" answered the man, echoing the contempt in her voice. "Those men and women who got out are going to walk over the hill to save a sou or two. *Nous autres*, we will ride."

Nous autres referred to himself and Robinson, who

ROCAMADOUR
FROM THE CAHORS ROAD

Rocamadour

had pulled his four legs over the barrier between the coachman and his friends and was encouraging the slow-going nags from time to time in his own harsh, peculiar way, a proceeding denounced by his owner as " loud, rude barks."

L'Hospitalet, where the first halt had been made, in ancient times was a shelter for poor pilgrims visiting the sanctuary and where hospitality was free.

The shaky little waggonette went on to the top of a plateau, from which the road falls suddenly down the side of a long hill into a narrow winding valley. Rocamadour, a mass of towers, battlements, turrets and spires thrown against the side of a precipice, here bursts suddenly, theatrically upon the view, clinging like a nest on the crags above this deep, winding gulf of green.

The surprise, the wonder and the impressiveness of this spectacle is greatly enhanced by the dull, commonplace approach to the brow of the hill, where abruptly the earth opens, as it were, and reveals the unexpected panorama of a wild, unique gorge, with a little town hanging among the boulders on the rocky side of the valley.

Legends obscure the foundation of this place of pilgrimage. Tradition has it that Zaccheus the Publican, he who mounted the sycamore tree to watch Christ pass, retired to this wilderness after the Crucifixion, and, becoming an Anchorite, passed his life in one of these many caves burrowing the mountainside, where now the sanctuaries are erected. It was a perfect morning on which to see Rocamadour for the first time.

Clouds as soft as down were floating in a sky shading down from a soft turquoise blue to delicate amber as it neared the horizon. The tiny River Alzou trickles between marshy banks, like emerald velvet; the rude rocks of the hills are streaked with strong black lines, as if they had been daubed by mischievous, playful giants. Small trees and meagre turf find little to nourish their roots in the soil of the precipitous uplands, but their soft colouring fitted the landscape, and bold wild flowers dared to dress in orange, pink and purple to brighten the dull crags.

The road to Cahors winds through the narrow ravine like a curling yellow serpent, until it is lost to sight among the hills. The 'bus jolted down the zigzagging approach to the village and entered it under a gate of the former fortifications. The inhabitants came out of their crumbling houses into the one narrow, muddy street to see the visitors roll past, the children pointing with amusement at Robinson's sober bull face, and the grown-ups smiling at his friends. The omnibus came to a halt at the foot of an immense flight of steps leading to a pile of noble buildings, which appeared to be clinging to the sides of a sheer precipice.

Angela's eyes glowed; her imagination could roam here in Middle-Age splendour without an effort.

"I will now ascend the heights with my lion," said Richard, seriously. "We will cautiously enter the *bourg*." The lion was already half way up to the stone platform above, and Richard had to resort to the undignified expedient of taking two steps at a time to catch up with him. With his long legs he soon reached

Rocamadour

the top, but Angela and Margot stopped every few minutes to look down into the solitary street of the village beneath them, where a long line of houses with an ancient fortified gateway at either end curved around the base of the rock.

The outer row of dwellings still hangs over what was once the city wall, rising abruptly from the little curving River Alzou. The long flight of stone steps leads to a terrace cut in the rock, where a shop, the Hôtel St. Marie and a few houses are plastered against the precipice. The place looks like an old fortress turned to sacred uses, but as long ago as when Charlemagne ruled France it was a sanctuary and a place of pilgrimage. Through a narrow fortified passage on that terrace more steps lead to another natural rock shelf higher up. Here the sanctuaries are built in the virgin rock. The inner court of a beautiful mediæval château must have looked very much like that bit of Rocamadour, and it did not need much imagination on Angela's part to transform the gentle nun, who, within a picturesque shop, sells rosaries and " *objects pieux*," into a noble lady in the costume of early France.

The holy lady and a boy lolling on the steps wearing a broad Basque cap shading his handsome face were the only persons about when the party entered this court. All the other booths, like martins' nests clinging to the walls, were closed tight. The first of May was clearly not the season for pilgrims. Richard and his lion made friends with the modest young shopkeeping nun in the most substantial way. Richard purchased

A Spring Fortnight in France

samples from the pretty nun of all the wares she offered him. Robinson got a tiny copy of Durandal, the sword of Roland, to ornament his collar.

"Here are candles to burn that our wishes and prayers may be granted," said Richard, handing over a bunch of tapers. "I will keep one for myself. A single wish granted can make me happy."

"Only one?" asked Margot, mischievously, giving back the smile he sent her. "I'll take a dozen, and Cousin Angela wants at least five to wish back to life each one of her old heroes."

"If any one of those gentlemen should appear as he really was," remarked Richard, "I think she would take flight to something more modern."

But Angela tossed her head. Dead heroes would do for her! She took her candles and went up a few more steps to another platform, where in a shallow cave is the tomb of St. Amadour protected by a grille. Near it is the great iron-bound chest which held the rich offerings made by royal pilgrims in the Middle Ages. Thrust into a cleft in the rock is a copy of the mighty sword of the Paladin Roland, Durandal. Henry Court-Mantel stole the original and left his own worthless blade in its place.

Opposite the iron-bound chest on this platform they entered La Chapelle Miraculeuse through a graceful Gothic portal adorned with exquisitely sculptured cabbage-leaf decorations. Behind the fifteenth-century façade is a chapel dug out of the living rock, where the strange little black Virgin, rudely hewn from the trunk of a tree by St. Amadour, is enthroned. It was before this image that Henry II. went to make his vow of reconciliation with Becket.

Into the rough cavern half filled with jutting rock Angela reverently carried her candle and her prayer. The rugged walls are black with incense and the smoke of torches and tapers. Hundreds of little marble tablets, thank-offerings to the Virgin, inscribed with grateful words in gilt letters, line the walls of this chapel in many places, completely concealing the grey rock. Among them is one which was placed in the sanctuary by Monsieur and Madame de la Mothe-Fénelon to commemorate the recovery of their infant son, the future Archbishop Cambrai, who was cured through the intercession of this virgin.

Margot gazed at this little tablet with profound interest.

" Saved that I might be bored by Telemaque! " she muttered.

Richard Hardy smiled a wicked smile.

" I don't think I enjoyed Telemaque very much either," gently said Angela, " but he was a great man —I mean Fénelon."

" My only acquaintance with his greatness is through that mild young gentleman who talked such perfect French," said Margot solemnly.

The miraculous image, clad in tinselled robes and elevated on a jewelled altar, recalls the past centuries. The tawdriness of the hangings and brilliancy of the gilt is softened by the hand of dingy antiquity.

On the jutting rock at the back of the chapel hang some rusty, heavy manacles, offered to Our Lady of

Rocamadour by prisoners who had been released through her intercession, or escaped by her aid. Richard and Margot scoffed at the weighty fetters.

"If a man managed to get such irons off, I don't believe he could run far with such a load in his pocket without being speedily caught."

But Angela had supreme faith.

Robinson, like a sensible dog, had kept out of the chapel, and spent his valuable time exchanging views with one of his own kind, a worthy protector of this holy citadel.

A flight of steps descended from this platform to the inner court, where the picturesque nun still smiled at them from her romantic little shop. Here they entered the large church of St. Sauveur. The supposed portraits of St. Louis, Robert d'Artois, Charles of Anjou, Alphonse de Poitiers, Alphonse de Bologne, who came here in 1245, their crude colours softened charitably by the dim religious light, are frescoed on the walls. Louis XI., the superstitious monster who neglected no miraculous image, is also portayed here, with the date 1463, the time when he visited the shrine.

"He probably crawled up all those hundreds of stone steps on his knees," said Richard, "and hanged a dozen enemies before and after to flavour his devotions."

Some of the old portraits are falling rapidly into decay. Charles of Valois, marked 1524, has entirely lost his face. The dates painted below each of these pictures probably denote the time when these princes visited Rocamadour—Jean de Valois, 1344; John, King of Bohemia, 1324; Marie of Luxembourg, Queen of

Charles de Bel, in 1324, and Alphonse of Boulogne in 1242.

Angela sighed deeply and regretfully at having been born so late that she could not be present at any one of these great processions.

"I wish I could have witnessed such a royal pilgrimage!" she said.

No great princes come here now, either to pillage or to pray, but the summer religious gatherings still have much of the twelfth-century character. Accompanied by their curés carrying floating banners, with much chanting and loud praying as they walk, the peasants, some on foot, some in the trains, and nearly all natives of the near-by provinces, come to Rocamadour to implore help of the miraculous statue. Before the pilgrims arrive each season they are preceded by a vanguard of beggars and pedlars who encamp on the great stone stairway leading from the village street to the sanctuaries, and who keep up a hideous din with their entreaties and lamentations.

The pious pilgrims kneel at every step of the long flight, some crawling all the way up to the top, praying and singing as they go. The noise is inconceivable! When they arrive at the church of St. Sauveur the first care of these peasants is to confess their sins, and the priests, who fill the long row of confessionals stretched under the portraits of the former august pilgrims, are kept busy listening to a string of misdeeds having none of the exciting quality which those of Louis XI. had to offer. Even St. Louis, if history speaks truly, had a few interesting crimes to confess.

There is no secrecy about these peasant confessions. The boxes wherein the priests sit are open on all sides, and the pious pilgrims are in such a hurry to obtain pardon that they not only crowd on one another's heels, but hasten to shout their sins to the priest before he has had time to deal out the proper penance and absolve the predecessors.

"What a famous opportunity it must be for them to discover their neighbour's faults. But I suppose each one of them is too busy with himself to listen!" This was Margot's idea of the rite. Angela Victoria again was pensive.

When a "successful retreat," as it is called, is in progress, the church and the chapels adjoining are filled at night with pilgrims, some sleeping on the hard floor, others praying and chanting aloud to an accompaniment of snores.

It is the idealised camp meeting! A certain and a large mass of humanity crave this sort of religious excitement. The doctrines may be different, but the naïve emotional simplicity is the same, whether the way lies to Mecca, to a grove in New England, or to Rocamadour.

When Angela Victoria and her friends left the church with its royal frescoes, the boy with the Basque cap again met them, this time accompanied by a pretty young woman, whose simple black dress hung about her in graceful folds, and whose hands were busy with knitting needles.

"Monsieur and Mesdames wish a guide!" she said confidently.

ROCAMADOUR

VIEW OF THE VALLEY FROM A ROCK GALLERY

THE PILGRIMS' STEPS

THE COURT OF THE SANCTUARIES

THE CRUMBLING GATEWAY OF THE TOWN

Monsieur gave one glance at the modest, charming face and felt that without a guide he could go no farther.

"Why don't you conduct us?" Margot asked the boy.

He smiled. "*Ma foi!* I have not yet eaten. This is my sister; she has the keys of the Château gate. She likes climbing," and he went back, laughing, to his place on the steps.

The girl led them through another of the imposing fortified gateways, and out onto a broad zigzag path which meandered up the mountainside amidst blossoming shrubbery, waving masses of iris, and a wealth of flowering laburnum and cytisus. The Bishop of Cahors has constructed this lovely and graceful path to the Grotto of the Agony, near the top of the hill. It is called "The Way of the Cross." There are *Stations* at each bend of the path where beautifully carved statuettes, coloured and placed in stone niches, represent the sufferings of Christ on his way to Calvary. The Grotto of the Agony is a large, natural cave, containing a group of figures in stone, life-size, and recalling the scene in the Garden of Gethsemane. Half way up this steep hill, a little to one side of the path, is a terrace overlooking the valley. On it has been placed a great wooden cross, once carried in procession through Jerusalem, and then brought here by barefooted French pilgrims.

As the party stood under its shadow their girl guide was so overcome by enthusiasm that she put her knitting in her pocket, and, with many exclamations, said: "Ah, you should see how magnificent we are on the September evening when the *grande retraite* ends. Then all the pilgrims wind up this road carrying lighted flambeaux and singing as loud as possible."

Angela involuntarily clapped her hands over her ears at the suggestion.

"Ah! *Mais, Madame! It is superbe! magnifique!*" said the girl, who noticed the unconscious movement. "The voices are splendid in the open air. And the sight is wonderful! Here under the cross are pulleys and wire, which they stretch way across the valley and hang with coloured lights."

"Pilgrimages have become modern," sighed Angela, "with modern decorations."

"I prefer to be here on this lovely morning," exclaimed Richard. "We have, instead of pilgrims with rough peasant voices, the song-birds cracking their little throats in praise of Nature, and the sun, and the clouds, following each other to vary the light in the valley. Flowers blooming everywhere to brighten this stern pile of rock and sanctuary, and Robinson frisking wildly with the godgiven joy of animal spirits."

"Just my sentiments!" exclaimed Margot.

The girl had been listening to the English speech with puzzled face. She did not understand a word that had been spoken, but she nodded encouragingly, thinking it might be something concerning the pilgrimage.

"*Oui, oui, il y en a souvent des Anglais,*" politely wishing him to know that the gatherings were not exclusively French.

The Château, no longer the stronghold it once was, when it defended the surrounding country and protected the treasures of the church from the ruthless ruffians and invading Angevins, is now the habitation of missionary fathers. It has been restored and is kept in a state of fine preservation. The view from the ramparts is inexpressibly grand. Far below the whole the deep cañon, rolling off toward Cahors, is seen, while almost even with the castle wall stretches the plateau and the wild, monotonous region of stones and moorland which forms Les Causes, the arid plain through which they had driven on their way to Rocamadour.

The girl pointed to a grove of sparse oak trees beyond the castle wall on the top of the hill. "The Fathers get many hundred francs from the truffles they dig there in the winter."

Angela looked with interest, but Margot cried out:

"The mention of truffles sharpens my appetite. Do let us go to breakfast. I think I can enjoy it more than sightseeing just now."

Richard laughed and so did Angela. They cast a last look at the wide stretch of the valley, and then cautiously climbed down two hundred and sixteen steps, a short way the guide took to lead them to the Restaurant St. Marie. There, on a sort of balcony hanging in midair, far above the roofs of the lower village street, amidst hanging vines and great tubs with flourishing oleanders about their table, they were served with an inviting *déjeuner*.

The pleasant-voiced waitress not only gave them

truffles to eat, but told them about the Father's clever pig who had dug up the delicious tubers.

"That pig adores truffles," she said. "*Mais, voila!* one that is well trained! She roots them up, but she does not touch them. If her ear is pulled, or even tapped, she gives up the truffle and takes a bit of corn instead."

"And we dare to speak with contempt of pigs! Are you listening, Robinson?" asked Margot, offering the little dog a truffle, which he promptly and resentfully spat out.

It seems that in Rocamadour, according to their waitress, the seasons of pilgrimage bring material as well as spiritual joys. Many of the maidens from afar find homes here, as well as absolution, while the men from over the Dordogne carry back wives which the Virgin is good enough to find for them in Rocamadour.

"I hope the Virgin will be as good to us—don't you, Cousin Angela?"

Angela was happy; she said lightly, "If she is, I will bring Georgina."

Margot held up her hands in supplication and made a wry face.

"Don't you think she might do something for me?" said Richard.

"I'll speak to her about it," said Margot.

The waitress knew not one word of English except "yes," which, with smiles and many interested nods, she uttered at stated and most inappropriate intervals. When she was bored by listening to the foreign tongue, she re-entered the conversation by giving them what was probably a standard piece of information.

"We have no king here," she said, "but we have a tyrant," she groaned comically, in pretended rage. "He holds the key to the town pump and we can get no water unless he chooses. When he is ready in the morning, he thumps on a big drum for us to come, but long after we are all waiting he continues to pound his instrument, instead of serving us. He's a musician, that one! He thinks he can play the drum," and she chuckled at the thought as gaily as if the circumstance was something new.

Margot went off with the waitress to feed Robinson and see the kitchen, but Richard and Angela sat contentedly among the oleanders and vines, which draped the rest of the terrace, and gazed down at the sluggish little river between the lovely green banks.

"I am going to brush up my French at the rate of a lesson a day when I get home," he remarked. "I never before realised how much enjoyment is gained by getting all the fine points and the fresh exclamations with which the French tell a story they must have repeated a hundred times. To tell you the truth, this is the first time I have ever really travelled in France with enjoyment, thanks to you."

"Georgina, my sister, would be surprised to hear you say that. She always contends that I do not know how to travel."

He was about to answer when Margot came flashing back. "The *patron* says we ought to go to Padirac!"

Richard grinned. "Somehow or other that doesn't sound very polite. What is Padirac?"

"*Mais*—but—it is *quelque chose de* wonderful! *Immense! Splendide!* and several other adjectives besides.

In plain English it is a big cave. It would seem that these hills are full of subterranean wonders!"

"Thank you," laughed Richard, "but I prefer the top of the earth."

"So do I," said Angela quietly. "I hate dark, mysterious caves and smoking torches."

"There aren't any torches, now! You have electric lights! On the underground rivers there are motor boats, and we all go down in an elevator."

"Worse and worse!" exclaimed Angela, horrified.

Richard made a grimace.

"Very well, if I can't persuade you to go under the earth, I must content myself with descending the two or three hundred steps that go down to the street. The omnibus is waiting for us! Come on Robinson!" and she was off.

Angela Victoria and Richard went down more leisurely, casting lingering glances at the lights and shadows on the hills and the golden patches of sunshine on the yellow winding road to Cahors.

Down in the village street women and children were carrying home loaves of bread as big round as a barrel top.

"Baking day!" announced Margot.

One beggar alone was visible in the town. She asked nothing of this party. She went from door to door, followed by her child, and the humblest of little donkeys, walking straight into the houses to ask for a bit of the stale loaf.

"*Une ânesse, et sa petite.*" Nowhere was her petition denied.

Rocamadour

The rickety little waggonette, which the driver dignified by the title of omnibus, received them, and they rumbled away through the crumbling fortified gate, stopping once while the driver offered to give a lift to some school children who had come down into the valley to gather learning, which they found rather too heavy to carry successfully uphill. They clambered up beside the driver and turned round to ask permission to pat Robinson, who submitted condescendingly to a caress from each one of the fat little hands.

"How I hate to rush off so soon. This is the most enchanting, deliciously funny, fascinating, perchy place I ever saw!" exclaimed the superlative-loving Margot. "I shall never see anything again like this in my life. Could anyone ever make you believe there was such a place, Cousin Angela, slammed right up against the side of a mountain? I don't see how they ever stuck it on! I wonder it hasn't fallen off." Seen from the road they were then mounting, Rocamadour fully justified Margot's exclamations, but as Richard declared: "It has been sticking there ever since before the time of Charlemagne, so I do not think it will fall off before we come back again."

The vivacious driver, not to be left totally out of the conversation, began to describe with more exactness than delicacy the ills of some of the afflicted pilgrims who were brought to Rocamadour, that miracles might be performed in their favour.

The school children listened with that awe and intense interest the young take in the horrible, but Margot stopped him short by asking him to describe some miracle he had seen performed. He scratched his head with the butt end of the whip, flicked a bold fly off the horse's flank, and said: "*Mais ca—Je ne sais——*" and quietly relapsed into reflection.

The children munched great pieces of bread, offering every few minutes a crumb or so to Robinson, who accepted all they gave him with eager politeness, then quietly dropped the bits on the floor as soon as they devoted themselves to the next bite. Dry bread was hardly worth the trouble of swallowing.

The lean horses pulled the vehicle slowly up the long hill, and, as the noon sun shone brightly on the scene, they could look back down the whole of the long street, and on the luxurious sweeping vines mingling with bright flowers that grew along the steep city wall next the river; on the yellow tints of the castellated sanctuaries, clinging like swallows' nests beneath the grey overhanging rocks; on the dark trees, growing beside the castle, whose crowning glory was the slender towers so perilously balanced on the edge of the precipice. Black rooks were circling around the valley, and the whole scene was a marvel to their eyes. With every step of the straining animals the tints in the landscape changed until suddenly at the beginning of the plateau they turned inland, and the whole scene vanished as if by magic.

They were early at the station, and Margot spied a man in an automobile coat, whose machine was waiting outside.

"It's nothing but a scroot," she whispered in An-

ROCAMADOUR

A TERRACE 'TWIXT HEAVEN AND EARTH

THE BEGGARS OF ROCAMADOUR

THE VALUABLE TRUFFLE HUNTERS

gela's ear, " but I wish we were going off in it just the same! "

"We wouldn't get to Albi for a week," replied Angela.

" I wouldn't care if we didn't get there for a month," said that incorrigible dawdler, Margot.

At this moment Richard called her to help him ask the man some questions.

Yes, he had come from Brive. *Pas mal de collines,* but a good road.

" Always a good road," whispered Margot. " Do you notice that? "

He expected to go through Rocamadour by the highway they had seen in the valley, and so on to Cahors.

The poor woman, with her unfortunate and repulsive child, was also waiting for the train back to Brive. Angela, moved with sympathy and the great love the mother evidently felt for the afflicted little object, entered into conversation with her.

The child looked big and healthy, except for the wretched sores. She kept fretting a little, constantly muttering, " Ma-ma—ma-ma—ma-ma," to which the mother would answer tenderly, "*Mon rat!*" a pet name which made Angela shudder.

The woman said she had been to the shrine to pray, to give alms, to procure some holy oil, which she thought an all-sufficient cure. She did not hesitate to rub the afflicted spots with her far from clean fingers to ease the itching which made the child complain. Angela was in agony. She could not help saying: "Oh, don't do that! Get some fresh warm water, some clean old linen, an antiseptic, and a doctor!"

"*Mon dieu!*" A *doctor*, all right, *mais de l'eau!*" and the train came to end all discussion on that subject.

Chapter VIII

ALBI

"*M*R. HARDY is not going with us to Albi; he says he is going directly on to Toulouse." Angela did not reply. The gentleman in question had gone down the corridor of the car into the smoking compartment.

"He says he thinks you do not want him," went on Margot.

"That is hardly a fair thing to imply."

"He didn't exactly say those words, but I am sure that is why he has decided to leave us." Angela Victoria looked out at the sky. "Won't you ask him to stay, Cousin Angela?"

"No, my dear, I will not." She spoke with decision. "You have had him a long time, and you should be satisfied."

"A long time! Why, how can you call three or four days a long time! I really think you might ask him to stay with us until we get to Carcassonne. It is so much more convenient to have a man, and Richard Hardy seems to know so many nice things about all the towns that we don't really need a guide book."

Angela Victoria was still silent. So, after Margot had pouted a little, she gave Robinson an extra squeeze or so, which he bore with equanimity, but turned his head away feebly in protest. After this conversation Richard's first remark, when he returned to the compartment smelling of smoke, was neither totally unexpected, nor did it cause Angela the faintest surprise.

"This," he said, as he put his cherished briarwood into its case, "will be my sole consolation to-morrow." Angela did not respond, and Margot made up a pouting face. "I ought to go on from Tessonières to Toulouse." He spoke as if he were feeling his way. "I have some business there. It is at Tessonières, I believe, that you change for Albi. You are going to Albi now, are you not?

He looked furtively at Angela, who thought to herself, "What a fraud he is!"

"Yes," she replied, so pleasantly that Margot pinched Robinson's ear. Then, feeling that something more was demanded, she stammered: "It has been very nice to have you with us so long."

Margot looked out of the window, and said abruptly: "The rain of stone fell over all these fields, too, didn't it? I wonder where it stopped."

So the subject of parting was ended for the moment.

Although they had left the station at Rocamadour some miles behind, they were still on *Les Causes de Gramat*. Sheep were grazing on all sides in the fields. At one small station a farmer was putting two of them into his cart; they lay curled up in a great melon-shaped basket, strapped firmly down, but looking quite comfortable, nevertheless.

The dark-skinned, black-haired peasants, with their blue flat caps jauntily set over one ear and the wide

Albi

trousers bound at the waist by gay handkerchiefs, chatted merrily in patois, the rich rolling tongue of the South. The trainmen shouted incomprehensible remarks to the loungers at each station, and the *maitresse de la poste* gossiped in that rich dialect to the railway postoffice clerk as she delivered into his care the small mail bag and the iron box with registered letters always brought down to every French express train.

The rugged industry of the hard-working French peasant has wrenched from the rocky soil luxurious green fields, which grew broader and broader until at length they spread out below this stony region into a land of smiling valleys, of flowering hedges and rolling, fertile fields, the hills richly cultivated to the very top. Along the road villages clustered around a ruined tower or an imposing church, and weather-beaten châteaux, now turned from their former uses to prosperous farm houses, had in the dooryards the enormous dove-cotes of olden times, around which fluttered great flocks of cooing doves. Piles of fodder denoted the richness of the land; the corn was growing tall enough to nod in the breeze, and great white oxen were busy in the fields. Gorges, deep and dark, guarded by the ruins of a castle or ancient fortifications, succeeded these broad, sunny stretches. In this mountainous country, where the struggles of the Middle Ages made battle a constant necessity, no height proved too inaccessible, no rock too steep on which to erect a feudal stronghold.

Margot flew in excitement from one side of the carriage to the other; going now out into the corridor to look far down below the track at a lovely valley, and then back to the other side to crane her neck at a turreted château set high above the green fields. Her sorrow at Richard Hardy's departure was entirely forgotten in the pleasure of the varied scenery. Her eyes were so constantly busy with the surprises of the landscape that her tongue found it difficult to utter expletives capable of describing her enthusiasm, as garden land succeeded savage deep defile, and ruined castles followed upon peaceful, rustic villages crouching beside babbling brooks. Robinson, accustomed more or less to his mistress' excitable temperament, squeezed himself up close to Angela Victoria and rested his head on her knee, rolling his eyes in sentimental fashion while she stroked his ears.

"How a dog loves to be loved," said Richard, meditating. "And the lucky beggars usually get it, too!"

"This is Figeac, is it not?" said Angela, evasively.

Like many of the towns of Aquitaine, Figeac owed its beginnings to a monastery as far back as the days of Pepin, that prince who gave the popes their temporal power in exchange for the throne of France. Figeac has been through many vicissitudes since that time, but it remains a queer old town where the Château de Balenes, which once belonged to Edward III. of England, and sold by him before his death, still exists, now turned into a schoolhouse, beautifully adorned with carved roses and shamrocks.

The ancient monastery church has this quaint inscription in the choir:

"*Dieu m'a ornée* 1540—*Dieu m'a reparé* 1761."

Champollion, the greatest of Orientalists, was born in this town, and on the curious narrow streets there are still remains of many lovely bits of beautiful Gothic architecture.

Capdenac is the next station to Figeac, and at no great distance from the latter. Here the train made a wait of some twenty minutes, and they got out of the carriage to look across the broad flowing River Lot at the town which crowns a precipice high above the bank of the stream. The conductor, smiling at Angela and at the franc she slipped into his hand, said to them: " Go to the end of the platform and look up and down the river. I won't permit the train to go without you, and you can see nothing from here." Robinson and Richard galloped to the buffet to buy cakes and incidentally to stretch their legs, while Angela and Margot looked up at the proud old fortress and the the beautiful river winding off into a splendid valley below the town.

" If I were going to write a book about this trip, it would be a short one," said Margot. " I would put in the middle of every page, ' It is great; come and see it.' "

" Which would not be entirely satisfactory to those unfortunates who do their travelling beside the winter hearth."

The steep rocks rising straight up above the red roofs of the houses, and the old castle walls sheer above them, were yellow with broom flowers and draped heavily with hanging vines, in which purple, pink, and yellow mingled with the green. Sully, the noted minister of Henry of Navarre, owned this castle, in which his ancestors had once lived and fought.

"What lots of colour there is here," was Margot's next remark. "Look at the walls and roofs of this old town, Cousin Angela; how gay they are! Not a bit like the sad violet tints of the north. The people splash on pink, green, red and yellow to suit themselves."

"Each region has its charm," said her cousin, earnestly, "and the colours of each suit the region. I can't imagine Angers or Le Mans wanting to look gay."

Margot very nearly imperilled her head leaning out of the window for a parting glance at Capdenac and the River Lot.

Another little stream, the Diege, now kept them company on the way to Villefranche, where the train enters the beautiful valley of the Aveyron. The region through which the line from Villefranche to Tessonières finds its way has few rivals in France; it is a district where nature has taken pleasure in displaying all her many moods and where human interests abound. Grey, surly gorges, almost closed to man by natural walls formed of overhanging rocks, without possible roads, are succeeded by groves of bronzed chestnut trees, and the valley spreading out on the banks of the sinuous Aveyron. From the rolling, smiling plain rise abrupt elevations, on which were planted castles by the defenders of this passage to the southern countries for the protection of themselves and their vassals. Nearly all of these feudal strongholds have fallen at the hands of ruthless destroyers, leaving in the present age only

Albi 217

jagged walls and falling towers to make the natural picturesqueness of the landscape more human and interesting.

Villefranche, a populous city with a truly splendid church and an old Carthusian abbey, lies sunken in a hollow. The Black Prince fought desperately outside its walls, beginning with the capture of this city a conquest which ended in the final expulsion of the British from Aquitaine. In later centuries the Huguenots and the Catholics stirred up bitter religious strife in this ancient citadel, and the Protestant chiefs were hanged from the windows of the Hôtel de Ville for the murder of the Catholic governor. After leaving Villefranche the train pulls slowly up a steep grade into a dreary mining district, where coal and iron abound, and the banks on either side of the track are dull and grey with the refuse from the mines; then again by a quick change the road turns a sudden bend and enters a valley of exquisite beauty, where upon a rock of perilous height is the great Château of Najac, one of the most romantic spots anywhere on the journey. The castle, looking down over the land from this high point, awakens many souvenirs of romance and chivalry. It was built in 1110 and for centuries guarded the smiling country and the winding defiles from any approaching force. It was almost impregnable, and the ruins to-day are among the most picturesque in existence. A little village nestles at the foot of the precipitous castle rock and an old bridge spans the flowing river. The castle itself, after centuries of glorious memories, was sold for twelve francs during the Revolution, and after serving as a quarry for the entire neighbourhood the present proprietor bought it for fifteen hundred.

Margot and Angela gazed longingly up at the singular old town and its crowning towers.

"How I hate to let these heavenly old bits get away from me!" cried Margot.

"Heavenly in more ways than one," laughed Richard.

"Don't joke; I am coming back here on my wedding tour!" said Margot.

"Then I'm coming with you," he answered.

"Perhaps."

Angela did not join in the fun, but she felt with Margot that it was becoming more and more difficult to go past these enchanting remains of ancient France, beckoning and enticing them to stop by the way and dive deep into the memories hidden in their massive walls.

She was becoming discouraged herself at the difficulty of describing adequately what she saw. She therefore mentally changed her projected literary work from a book of travel to a romance of the Middle Ages. It would not be any more difficult to write and a great deal more entertaining. She was sending her hero with a train of knights up the heights and over the drawbridge into reconstructed Najac when the train shook on noisily over the bridge and into a tunnel. When they came out she found Richard sitting quietly before her, calling her attention to the last and most beautiful picture of the vanishing ruin framed between a cleft in the rocky precipice beside the track.

"Another spot we should linger in," he was saying,

IN CENTRAL FRANCE
A STRETCH OF FERTILE COUNTRY
ON HIS WAY TO TOWN
OLD CHÂTEAU

Albi

"with its old gates and vine-grown towers. It rained castles in this part of the world. But is there not something very sad to you in the relics of wild, reckless, turbulent spirits long laid low? The empty shells left by all the throngs of knights and retainers as their only souvenir?"

"Ah!" eagerly answered Angela, "history has not forgotten them."

"What does history tell us about Najac, and the trains that came and went over that drawbridge through generations?"

"Whether history speaks of them or not, the monument remains, and I cannot look upon it without thoroughly loving those human old knights full of a simplicity we call barbarism. I shouldn't in the least mind their ignorance or brutality if I could only tumble back among them once more. I am sure they were chivalrous at heart."

Richard laughed incredulously. "We are more sophisticated, but cleaner and more comfortable."

"How do we know that we are? We only think so. Future generations may look back at us and denounce us as being quite as savage! I don't believe our emotions are half as strong or as natural as they were in the Middle Ages."

"Perhaps not as violent, but I will not agree that they are not quite as strong. No old knight setting off for the Crusades could feel more desolate at parting than I shall be to leave this little party in an hour or so."

"I don't think it is quite an hour to Tessonières,"

Angela answered, unconcernedly. Then again being overcome by her politeness, and feeling these were not very courteous words, uttered the banality of which she had been guilty the last time he spoke of leaving: "It has been a great pleasure to have you with us." In spite of her attempt at extra cordiality, it seemed to her her voice sounded very frigid.

"Here we go in among the black rocks again," was the way in which he accepted her attempt at politeness, and the subject closed.

On flew the train past La Guepie and its frowning donjon; then again, as though to counteract a dark impression, the spreading valley appeared stretching away beside a shady stream, through tilled lands and thick-walled farm houses, which had sprung from the spoils of the nobles' castles. Every acre was cultivated, and the men were ploughing in the warm fields with sturdy oxen, while the women, laden down with great heaps of fagots, trudged along the well-made road.

The plenteous rains had filled every stream to the very banks and polished up the young foliage and freshened the fields. The lilac, iris and fruit blossoms of the early spring were left behind in the north; here the brighter flowers of approaching summer grew along the wayside and trimmed the hedges with garlands. Again, beyond Lexos, a dull hamlet, the valley closed in and sharp black rocks rose on one side of the deep ravine, through which a brawling river tears and frolics. At the desolate station of Vindrac-Alaynac the landscape widens again; there were more velvet fields and wide-leaved trees, while over the plain in the far distance

Albi

appeared the ancient city of Cordes, resting on the top of a cone-shaped hill and looking like a bit of Italy escaped into France, bringing with it the radiance of an Italian sun, with which the hill town shone pink and yellow in the flash of the late afternoon light.

Margot did not attempt to conceal her regret at Richard Hardy's departure, and he was evidently very unwilling to leave her. It was not in the nature of things that Angela's tender heart should not likewise feel depressed at what she considered her duty in sending him off.

All the world loves a lover, and a sentimental old maid feels more intensely than the rest of humanity when her innermost soul is warmed by the spectacle of mutual affection. Angela Victoria decided that it now existed under her very eyes, and had not her conscience reproached her as a negligent chaperone and the vision of Georgina's inquisitorial questioning and possible wrath thrown a deep shadow over the future, she would even now have changed her mind and asked Richard to come with them to Albi.

She sat absentmindedly petting Robinson and turning the question over in her mind. Margot and Richard stood outside in the corridor, talking in low tones and apparently forgetful of all but one another.

The road here passes through an undulating wood-clothed country which hides La Cayla, once the home of Maurice and Eugénie de Guerin, whose journal, a French classic, Angela had received once as a prize at school. She had meant to look out from this place on the cemetery near Andillac, where his devoted sister came so often after he lay buried there, and then went home to continue her journal " still to him, to my dear Maurice, to my Maurice in Heaven." But in her excitement she forgot all about it.

Richard left Margot and came back into the carriage to call her attention to three châteaux which they were about to approach. " I hope this has been as much of a red-letter day to you as it has been to me," he said. She wilfully misunderstood him. Margot was the only one to whom he should use such pretty phrases. She answered by another platitude: " The landscape has been very changeable." He smiled quietly, but took the cue at once.

" Yes, quite as variable and as delightful as the nation which has grown up in it."

Just then the train drew up at Tessonières, a supremely dull, uninteresting junction, in a supremely dull, uninteresting plain. Richard helped them out with their rugs and small bags, and went across to install them in the train for Albi, which was standing on another track.

Margot lamented unreservedly that Richard was to leave them.

" Your train will soon be leaving. You must not get left!" said Angela Victoria, nervously, as he walked slowly beside them across the line.

He smiled at her anxiety.

" Don't fear; there's no such evil in store for you, nor such good luck for me. My train halts here for ten minutes."

" I envy you your day to-morrow," he said, turning

Albi 223

to Margot, not venturing to open the subject again with Angela Victoria.

"I have often wondered if the cathedral at Albi looked as smooth in reality as it does in the pictures."

"Oh! I don't see why you're not coming with us," said Margot, despairingly. "We shall miss you horribly, and the lion will pine for you." The lion in question was sitting calmly down on the seat of the carriage, looking with a very disgusted air at the leash Margot had hooked on for fear he would bound after Richard.

"En voiture! en voiture!"

The adieux were made.

"I hope I shall some time meet you in Paris," Angela said, with cordiality.

"I shall hope to see you long before we get to Paris!" exclaimed Margot, leaning way out of the carriage window and forcing the lion to offer a limp paw, almost to the peril of his existence.

"*Au revoir, au revoir!*" waved Margot, and they were gone.

There was no more romantic scenery. From Tessonières to Albi the way lies over a flat plain, with here and there abrupt hills crowned with towers. They imagined each one of these to be the city they were seeking, although finally when the great cathedral really loomed into sight they wondered how it was possible they could have been so stupid as to mistake the smaller churches for this extraordinary edifice.

Angela Victoria had regained her composure, and

Margot's spirits did not seem to suffer at Richard's departure. She began eagerly to discuss hotels.

"Where are we going, Cousin Angela? Hare says that all the hotels in Albi are dirty."

"But the Guide Joanne recommends La Poste. The Guide Joanne can never lie!"

"*Va pour la Poste!*"

The Hôtel de la Poste proved quite as satisfactory as the guide book had said. There was no fault to find, from the green parrot welcoming them in the entrance hall to their own comfortable bedroom and Robinson's dinner. It is a clean, quiet house, and after they had eaten well they slept the sleep of wearied travellers.

The finest view of Albi's extraordinary cathedral is to be had from a bridge a few steps below the hotel on the boulevard. They went there by the advice of their newest and latest Jean to look at it before taking their way through the narrow streets for a nearer inspection.

"It looks to me much more like a fortress than a church," said Angela, and so it does from this point above the river, rising on ragged rocks, overtopping the grim palace of the archbishop and the square donjon, where many a wretched heretic who was imprisoned during the great heresy of the Albigenses suffered torture and death for daring to deny the might of the Pope.

It had been raining again the night, and the way to the cathedral led them through squalid, muddy streets, lined with houses, among which here and there a fine bit of architecture peeped out; but the general impres-

BETWEEN ROCAMADOUR AND ALBI

A PEASANT OF LES CAUSES

THE CITY OF CORDES

Albi

sion they had of Albi was that of a true *ville méridionale*. The boulevards are of the same shabby description common throughout Southern France: the broad promenade of a town easy-going, neglected, and given over to that simple social enjoyment which the citizens find in small cafés. These avenues were once the ancient city moat. The cafés swarm everywhere, particularly on the Place la Perouse, where they stand crowding one another, shoulder to shoulder, while plenty hide themselves away on the humbler streets in the inner town. One wonders in a city of the Midi how all these cafés manage to exist, but they always seem gay and full of patrons.

"Here we are at last, Cousin Angela! *Dans le Midi!* Listen to the accent! All the s's are z's. I love these genial people." Notwithstanding the rain, the boulevards were not muddy; they were dusty, another characteristic of the south; but Angela and Margot trudged bravely through the middle of them, while Robinson pursued his triumphant way among the friendly southern curs.

"The cathedral looks as if it were made out of chewing gum," was the young lady's first exclamation when they came in view of that splendid edifice. The pink brick wall is in reality not unlike the colour of spruce gum, and as smooth as if the whole structure had been sandpapered after it was finished. It clearly suggests the American delectable dainty to which Margot compared it at first sight. But further inspection of this chewing-gum cathedral revealed to her that it was adorned with one of the most superbly carved portals of stone known to the world. It is an unequalled marvel of delicate lacework fashioned by a sculptor's chisel.

It was a strange fancy to mix the severity of this carefully constructed brick edifice with such rich and elaborate stone carving. The choir built inside the vast church, which is without a nave, is a miracle of intricate sculpture, where, in elaborately wrought stone niches, stand statues of the apostles, saints, and sovereigns clad in the costumes of the time when those who cut them from the stone were living. These statues are coloured, and now a thick coat of dust has gathered over them, softening each line and improving the beauty by deepening the shadows. The walls of the main church are covered with strange old paintings, while above the high altar the Last Judgment is depicted with a vividness of imagination calculated to alarm the most hardened of sinners.

A bustling sexton prepared to show the cousins about. They could easily have explored the church without his help, but talking with guides afforded them more than half their amusement when they went sightseeing. In this particular, Margot and Angela Victoria were exactly alike and quite different from the dignified Georgina. The sacristan in question was evidently strongly divided between a desire for the fee they would bestow upon him and his religious duty. He told them that he was about to be the chief functionary at a wedding soon to take place at the high altar. He entreated them to wait for the ceremony, so they bought a package of postal cards for his benefit, and he immediately gave them seats on chairs reserved for the

Albi

guests, not even objecting to the presence of Robinson. These chairs were the low, rush-bottom affairs with which French churches are strewn and which serve equally well as seats or praying stools.

Robinson tried to poke his stub nose out from his place of concealment under Margot's cloak, which he found altogether too warm for his taste in that southern climate. After exhibiting his discomfort by audible pantings, which disturbed and alarmed his mistress, he was cautiously lowered to the stone floor, where, cool and comfortable, he crouched quiet and unnoticed, observing the ceremony.

The wedding was a very simple affair. The bridal party plainly belonged to the bourgeoisie.

"You can always tell their station in society by the men," whispered Margot. The groom, in fact, looked like a shoemaker in a hired dress coat, but the young bride and her mother were as stylishly attired as Parisian aristocrats. She wore a white satin gown beautifully made, with a long tulle veil, and looked like a fashion plate, while her mamma, who perhaps in everyday life occupied the position of a washerwoman, wore a graceful and pretty costume of soft grey.

The new husband was an ordinary and very insignificant personage, but he had a kindly face and looked like a good man. The father was a peasant.

The officiating priest in rich robes, the acolytes in brilliant red soutanes, their white surplices edged with broad, beautiful lace; a soldier brother in his best uniform, with plenty of yellow worsted trimmings, and, first and foremost, the sexton, transformed into a splendid beadle clad in shining array of gold and gorgeous apparel, lent an air of magnificence and festivity to the scene.

"Our weddings won't be half as grand as this," whispered Margot. "Couldn't we manage to be married in France?"

Angela looked into the mischievous young face; but this time she did not smile at her girlish cousin's nonsense. The wedding party had brought a sense of momentary depression to her.

An old lady, who had come into the cathedral to enjoy a quiet snooze while pretending to tell her beads, woke up at the first sound of the priest's voice and left the church in haste. Margot looked after her in surprise; and Angela thought with sympathy that the ancient dame was perhaps overcome by emotion and sad souvenirs. The true cause of her flight was revealed in the tinkling bell and collection bag of their friend the "Suisse." Each one of the cousins dropped a franc into the slender fund.

"I wish the bride could have it. I would like to make her that much of a present," again whispered Margot.

"*Pour l'Englissse!*" hissed the sexton.

"Do you suppose he will take it himself?"

"Of course not!" indignantly answered Angela the unsuspicious.

The little wedding party went out as quietly as they had come in. Margot, Angela and the bold Robinson followed in its wake, thus escaping the eager sacristan until they should come again in the afternoon.

The square at the back of the cathedral is grass-

Albi

grown and neglected. The market women with their gay umbrellas and attractive wares on that warm spring morning had ceded the place to half a dozen small boys playing ball. The showy acolyte who had considered himself of primary importance at the wedding suddenly appeared at the head of the stately flight of steps under the porch, and, like a great crimson ball, whirled himself down and out under the castellated archway into the group of his companions, stopping their game to call attention to the peculiar charms of Robinson.

The four little fellows ceased throwing the ball to follow their bright-robed friend, who, holding up his gaudy skirts over unspeakably shabby trousers, intercepted the two ladies and the small dog.

"*Je vous prie, Madame;* will he bite? We have never seen his like. What kind is he?"

"A boul-doug," she told them.

"*Un Anglais!*" proudly announced the acolyte.

The youngest of the group, a bold little chap of eight, ventured to pat the frisking little beast. Finding that no evil resulted, other small hands were put out cautiously, and Robinson, in spite of feeling horribly bored by the undesired admiration, was condescending enough to lick one of the dusky little human paws.

Their delight knew no bounds.

"He has entered *la cathédrale!*" excitedly announced the youngster in red; "he has assisted at the wedding!"

"*Té! té!*" cried the others in chorus. Then Angela

made the acolyte happy by telling him how well he looked marching up to the altar.

"Do you wear your red gown all day?"

"*Mais non, Madame!* but papa is still there," and, glancing the way he had come, they saw a comfortable group gathered under the canopy of stone lacework from which he had descended upon them. The sexton, with his feet on the rail, was balancing himself as adroitly on the two back legs of his chair as ever did any Maine farmer outside the village store, while two other little boys in red soutanes played marbles at the feet of a man sitting on the balustrade talking to the curé.

"We are really now in a land where the people are at home in the churches."

After converting the ball players into capitalists by distributing two *sous* to each, the crimson boy flashed back to "papa," and the cousins went their way, leaving the tiny lads with their heads together, eagerly and vehemently discussing the question whether Robinson was the ugliest or the prettiest dog they had ever seen.

Fifty years ago this uninteresting place was crowded with ancient houses having carved beams, interesting gables and overhanging stories, all huddled so close to the cathedral wall that the beauty of the splendid south portal was obstructed. These antique structures exist now solely on the picture postal cards. They were undoubtedly as decrepit and unsanitary as they were interesting, but they have been replaced by modernised buildings, farther away from the church, quite as decrepit and unsanitary, besides being ugly into the

IN CENTRAL FRANCE

WHERE THE HILLS CLOSE IN HOUSES CLUSTERED ALONG THE BANK

Albi

bargain. Albi was never noted for its sanitary conditions. Leprosy and frequent terrible pests killed off quite as many of the inhabitants as did the swords of the Crusaders or the tortures of the Inquisition. Albi was always a hotbed of strife and contention, and heresy was rife from the early days of the rebellious Albigenses to the later period, when the Inquisition drove forth the Huguenots. The Albigenses, those early schismatics who revolted against the authority of the church, are not credited with either having invented any new religious doctrine or improving on the old. A crusade was carried on against them mainly for the reason that crusades were a popular way the potentates of the time took to perform penance for their sins; being at once exciting and affording an outlet for turbulent spirits to keep from interfering with the workings of the governments. When the Albigenses sect arose Jerusalem was out of the question for many reasons, one of the most salient being that nobody wanted to go to the East. The Albigenses furnished an excuse and an occasion to wear the Cross. Persecution created obstinacy, and the primary cause was obliterated by party hatred. Raymond of Toulouse defended the heretics of Albi against the superstitious fanaticism of the multitudes and got himself into such serious trouble that he nearly lost all of his domains. The river, now so lovely and peaceful, then ran red with blood, and horrible carnage filled this little town with slaughtered victims.

The cathedral was not built until after this period, but when the Inquisition was crowding the donjons of the archbishop's palace with trembling, tortured victims awaiting their doom, this splendid fortress-church was rising, and its terrors were still raging when the German mason sculptors from Strasburg went unconcernedly about their work and carved out of solid stone the most exquisitely beautiful exuberant "frozen music" ever devised.

The cousins looked back at the cathedral porch before they entered a squalid street.

"A feudal tower on which the chatelaine has draped her rarest lace that she might honour the expected king."

"Or the knight of her choice," finished Angela Victoria, musingly.

They were looking up past the round, smooth brick-crenelated tower to the masses of filmy fretwork, scarcely possible at that distance to associate with solid stone. It seemed as though the fairy-like fabric ought to float in the breeze.

They were nearly in front of an aged church, against which some wretched houses lean, as if for protection. A fine tower, and an old woman who came down the crumbling steps, crossing herself many times, decided Angela to enter. There is one splendid tomb, but nothing else which enticed her to linger. Margot had not followed her. She stood out in the dirty street listening with rapture to the strains of a Beethoven sonata, which, played by a master hand, floated down from the open window of one of the decayed Renaissance houses.

When the adagio was ended the music ceased, and they went on in silence.

Albi

Wandering further through the sprawling streets, past the Hôtel de Ville, they found more interesting bits of architectural memories sandwiched between hideous modern houses.

Margot, who was somewhat in advance of her dreamy cousin, suddenly disappeared in a doorway. Robinson followed with a bound, and Angela hastened after to find herself in a dingy little shop where ugly modern bric-a-brac and genuine antiquities consorted amiably with one another and were crowded confusedly together, all covered with the same mantle of dust.

The old woman who owned this mixture of treasure and rubbish was laboriously removing something from the window as Angela entered.

Robinson, having whispered "Rats!" to himself, had vanished on a hunting expedition under chairs and behind wardrobes in pursuit of the prey he was forever chasing but never captured.

Margot was helping the shopkeeper, and when finally the object of their endeavours was dragged into the space they had managed to prepare to receive it, there stood revealed an enchanting old Spanish desk of undoubted antiquity.

Angela uttered an exclamation of admiration. Margot examined it with ecstatic ejaculations.

"Mamma has been pining and looking everywhere for years for a desk like this; Aunt Julia got one somewhere in Spain. It isn't half as lovely as this. Mamma will be crazy about it. She will do anything I want when she sees this, and forgive me ten times over for running away with you. Look how exquisitely the

234   *A Spring Fortnight in France*

ivory and the silver is inlaid, and the little ebony columns are carved! Isn't it a jewel?"

The old vendor wiped it carefully with a very dingy silk handkerchief, opened the drawers of the cabinet, showed the secret compartment and elaborated on the perfect condition of her treasure. She told them she had bought it from an old house of the last member of a family that had lived there for centuries. The house had been torn down, but judging from some other effects she had acquired at the sale it must have been furnished as incongruously as the antiquity shop.

The woman knew the value of the desk. She frequently disposed of her most lucky finds in Paris. Neither Angela Victoria nor Margot was good at bargaining; her mother must have the desk; she would never forgive her daughter for letting such a prize slip through her hands. It was agreed that for three hundred and fifty francs it should be boxed and delivered in Paris.

"How much money have you in your pocket, Cousin Angela?"

"I have two hundred francs, but I will draw more to-morrow."

"I want only twenty-five of them. That will settle this bill, and you can pay my way until the next allowance comes."

The twenty-five francs were followed by another fifty on her own account, and in exchange she bore away a choice bit of deliciously faded old tapestry and a roll of coloured prints. Had it not been that her cheques were in her trunk and her trunk *en consigne* at the

Albi

station a second hundred would have gone galloping after the first, but she remembered in time and kept enough for current expenses.

Angela Victoria sometimes had her wits about her.

The long afternoon was spent among the wonders of the cathedral carvings, sitting first before the " Jubé," which Hare compares to " a thousand interlacings of a mossy bank, a harmonious mass of labyrinthine stonework," and then strolling slowly around the choir to look with delight at the statues. There is a sense of the sculptors' intimacy with the kings and saints and angels expressed in the costumes in which they have clothed these high personages which amused and delighted Angela Victoria, and the coating of dust to which her cousin objected made them more attractive to her.

Margot had been seized with a mania for taking photographs, and discovered as she was starting out that the camera she had not opened since she left Paris was without films. She therefore made her way to " *le grand bazar* " while Angela wended her way to the cathedral

A small company of canons, which seemed composed of the oldest and youngest priests in the service of the cathedral, had just entered the choir and disturbed Angela in her contemplation of the unusual woodcarving of the stalls when Margot appeared at the south portal.

She had a tale to tell of the amiable hospitality of the southern people. At the grand bazar, after taking infinite pains to find a film proper for her kodak, the shopkeeper gave up the unsuccessful endeavour and sent a small boy with her to a drug shop where he thought she might find what she wanted. The druggist, like the proprietor of the bazar, searched through his stock from top to bottom. When his search proved in vain, with pleasant smiles and as many excuses as if he had committed an unpardonable blunder in not laying in a supply of those particular *pellicules*, he went with her himself to the street corner and pointed out a photographer's establishment.

"It may be, Mademoiselle, he will have what you wish; although he does not sell supplies. He but takes portraits."

Margot, by that time interested in the possibilities of the chase, went to the photographer's. Of course he had not that film *exactment*, but inviting her to repose herself in the loveliest of gardens, he endeavoured with the end of an extra spool and some ingenuity to make the film he had fit her camera. It did not prove very useful, although perhaps her own unskilfulness and the late hour of the day when she attempted her work were both responsible for the failure of the views; but she had enjoyed her afternoon ten times more than if the bazar had at once supplied her needs.

The last walk they took next morning in Albi, like their first, was to the Pont Neuf. They had been there by moonlight the evening before and watched the silver light spread over the overhanging houses on the opposite side of the stream and gain at last the massive ugly tower of the cathedral, transforming it by an enchanted touch into a marvel of stately beauty. Now, in the

ALBI

THE VIEW ON THE BRIDGE

Albi

early daylight they came to stamp upon their memories the picture of the individuality and strength of the strangest cathedral their eyes had ever enjoyed.

"How I wish Richard Hardy had come with us! It was cruel to send him off."

But her cousin evidently was not listening. "Come," she said, "we have barely time to settle the bill before the omnibus leaves."

At the Hôtel de la Poste, besides the genial smiling landlady, there lives in perfect harmony a dog, a cat, and a parrot. Robinson as a guest entered perfectly into the spirit of this company. He convinced Madame Ronchoneau, the cat, of his peaceable intentions by turning away and sitting quietly down when she humped her back and her tail grew large. The landlady in consequence loved him for his considerate conduct. "*En voila un qui n'est pas bête,*" she reiterated, unconscious of the pun. Robinson ended his sojourn in Albi by a famous romp with the two four-footed friends, to the accompaniment of squawks from the parrot. After a final race of "three times round" the little dog vanished from sight by diving after his mistress into the depths of the omnibus, leaving his comrades staring in amazement and *Madame la Proprietaise* shaking with laughter.

"*Allez!*" shouted the porter, banging the door, and they rattled down *les Lices* past the many cafés crowded with imperturbable pleasure-seekers, who will sit out in the dust after *déjeuner* and enjoy life over a cup of coffee until it is time for a siesta, and then come back and lounge away an hour or two over their *apéritif*, and later return after dinner to spend the evening in harmless amusement.

The South is the country of cafés. There are cafés for the rich, cafés for those of slender means, cafés for the poor. The majority of these places of entertainment are out of doors, with tables spread on the sidewalk almost out into the street, for the greater pleasure of a people who find it impossible to enjoy themselves within four walls, and for whom the café, with the simple innocuous refreshment it offers, is a necessary joy in life.

The boulevards of Albi are planted more thickly with cafés than they are with trees.

Chapter IX

CARCASONNE

"*To* Carcasonne by Castres, Castellemaury!" called out the baggage porter to the registrar. "On the other track, Mesdames; I will bring the bags."

"We are in the land of garlic and rich accent, Cousin Angela."

The porter pronounced the name of their destination "Car-ra-ca-sun-a," and the perfume of the odorous vegetable hung thick about him.

From the apple blossoms and light spring foliage of Normandy down through the sunny splashes of the gênet in Anjou, the blossoming hedges and iris of Central France, Angela Victoria and her cousin had now come where the brilliancy of the poppies, the opening roses and the high-waving fields of grain proclaimed the summer.

"Here are more cleft rocks, more enchanting ravines, more well-tilled fields torn from unwilling nature; more villages tucked away in safety beneath a church, and castles, castles, castles!" Still they were in the land of the Crusaders, where wild Brabant mercenaries and jingling knights had passed over the hilltops and through the stony ways in the valley. "I fancy," said Angela, "I can see groups of mediæval warriors and their squires trudging along on their horses through all these mountain paths!"

"Steeds! You must say steeds, Cousin Angela. What I wonder is, whether the Brabant-hired soldier of the olden times was anything like the Belgian of to-day."

"He was undoubtedly a very rude, formidable person," said Angela, which little piece of humour amused them very much, as they had once passed a summer in modern Brabant together.

The road leads through the romantic country where, during the twelfth century, the *jongleur* and the knightly troubadour wandered from castle to castle gaining material for their songs and coming finally to the Court of Love, which was held so long near Castres by Constance, Countess of Toulouse, and Adelaide, Vicomtesse of Albi. On what remains now of the once noted château where these ladies received the poets, singers and minstrels from far and near, the busy wheels of life run, manufacturing commodities for the modern world.

"I wish we could fill a box with old chronicles and travel around this country in a van," said Angela, musingly, "stopping to read, to imagine and to reconstruct among all this wild scenery and these splendid ruins. Wouldn't that be an ideal summer!"

"I'd rather do it in an auto, if I could come with the right person," said the more practical Margot.

Angela sighed. "An automobile seems desecration among these scenes of chivalry and romance."

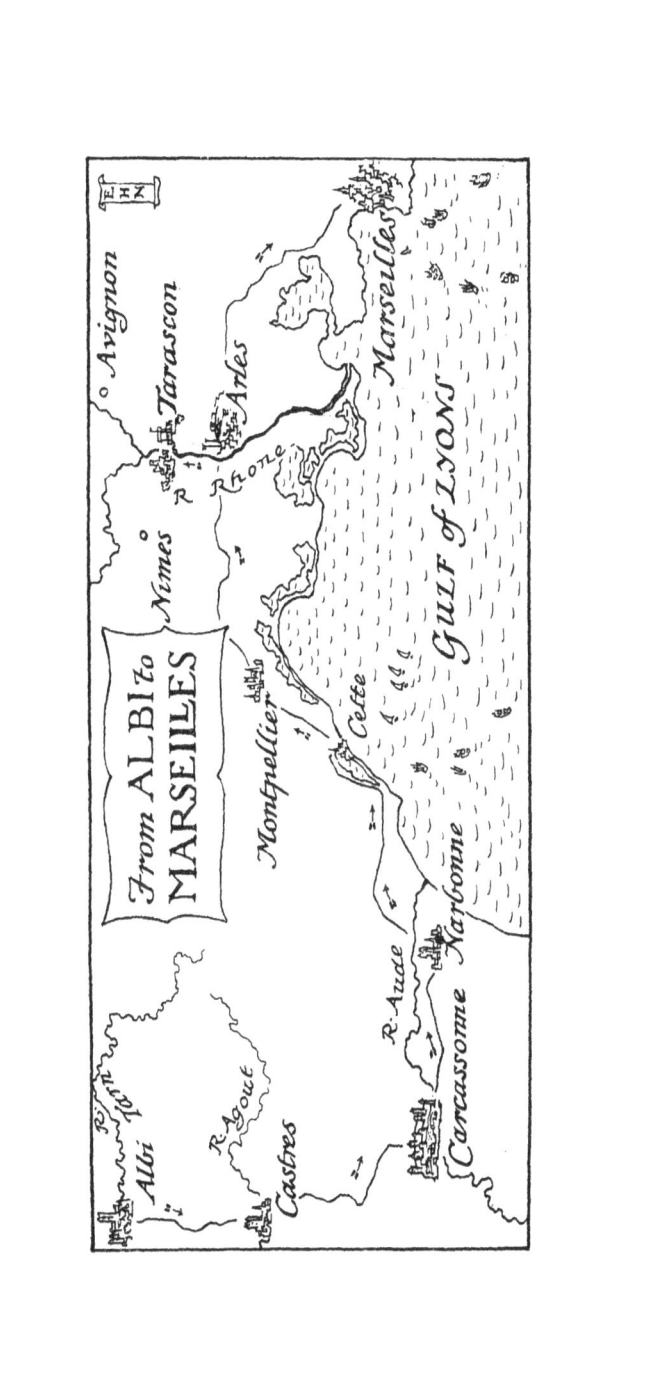

Carcasonne

"Perhaps! But me for the motor car! The miles are marked by châteaux; we could never get around to them all in a van. They must have been the cafés of old Provençe!"

"You sacrilegious girl!" laughed Angela. "How can you trample so on my sacred weaknesses!"

"You are an old darling. I love your sentimentality, but I also love motor cars. So do you."

Before they reached Carcasonne darkness had shut down over the landscape. Angela and Margot stared curiously about as they left the station, for the walls of that old city with which the pictures had made them familiar; but they saw nothing but streets barely wide enough for the passage of a donkey cart, through which the driver who piloted the hotel omnibus announced his approach at every turn by blowing a horn until, with a final fanfare, he swung his vehicle with supreme address into the courtyard of the Hôtel Bernard, and before them lay an attractive entrance, where modern electricity lights up ancient outside galleries overhanging a courtyard garden with a sparkling, trickling fountain.

A suave landlord advanced, bowing, to greet them, smiling at pretty Margot, as all men did, and making a profound reverence to Angela Victoria.

"A landlord!" whispered Margot, as he disappeared into the house to give orders. "Perhaps we shall find a chambermaid here, too." Her conjecture was answered by a trim little maid in the frilled cap of the Midi, who came back in the wake of the host, and, taking their bags, conducted them by devious ways up broad flights of stairs and through salons into a bedroom of palatial size.

It was not until she had left them provided with hot water and the luxuries so keenly appreciated by tired travellers that the cousins' continued surprise found voice. They looked around the roomy apartment at the comfortable beds, the generous washstand. The up-to-date pieces of furniture quite obliterated the shining inlaid floor, the carved frames of old panel walls decorated with huge mirrors, and the evidences of antiquity in the interesting fireplace. Angela sank down on the sofa. " And this is Carcasonne! At the very least I expected to be pulled up a hill; to clatter over a drawbridge, and come in under a raised portcullis and finally to be put down at a quaint little inn clinging to high city walls——" She glanced around in contempt. " Why, I can't see even a tower! "

" I saw some fine cake shops on our way here; Robinson and I are going to try them to-morrow."

" How can you joke? You know I am cruelly disappointed. This is serious. I have been anticipating Carcasonne more than any place on the whole of my travels. Indeed, it has long been a Mecca for me!

> *Mon Dieu, que je mourais content,*
> *Après avoir vu Carcasonne!'*

Eh, Cousin Angela? Don't despair yet; perhaps the ramparts are behind the hotel and we came through the portcullis in the dark. The omnibus driver was making such a hubbub with his horn and everything was

Carcasonne

rattling so that no human being could have told if we had been clattering over bridges all the way here. Do get ready for dinner. I am starving!"

Angela got up slowly. Still looking disconsolate, she said weakly: " I'm sure this is one of those railway advertisement frauds. We shall find in the end that Carcasonne is nothing but a painted panorama. I always did think the pictures were too lovely to be true!"

" Don't despair! Under the shadow of that disappointment we must pull ourselves together with substantial food. Robinson, you wait here, and I promise to bring you a fine dinner. If they tell me that dogs are allowed in the dining-room of this fine hotel you shall lie under the table to-morrow. You are a tired doggie. You need rest."

Robinson rolled his eyes in meek denial, retired slowly to a spot where his mistress inadvertently had dropped her handkerchief, and turning three times slowly around, laid himself down upon it, with his eyes glued to the door out of which she had vanished. " That's the way humans treat us! She thinks I can sleep on an empty stomach!" was the reflection which filled his canine soul.

The little doggie did not pine in solitude very long, for in the midst of excitement caused by a dream fight in which he had just conquered the biggest dog in all France, he regained triumphant consciousness as his mistress' quick footsteps brought him up on his feet.

" Come on, Robinson," and Robinson, with pirouettes and valse steps, executed with incredible swiftness, danced down onto the terrace in the courtyard near the fountain to be regaled with the sumptuous repast. His mistress and her cousin sat beside him at a table sipping coffee and listening to inoffensive music furnished by a mild orchestra in the shape of a music box, which could be stopped at will without taking offence, in the middle of any one of its five selections from "Faust," "Matitche," "The Valse Bleue" and other light, choice gems.

Robinson divided with a mouse-coloured poodle the admiration of all the guests on the terrace. He strutted around like a king, sneezing for sugar with all the sweet simplicity of a creature accustomed to adulation wherever he went.

A large notice hung on the wall giving the prices of cab fares to "La Cité."

"Doesn't that sound just like a panorama." exclaimed Angela Victoria. "I know it's some horrid old fraud! If it is, I won't stay here another day! I had made up my mind to take my manuscript (as yet all blank paper) and sit among those wonderful old walls and towers in the sunshine and write chapters and chapters. How cruel!"

"Don't despair yet, Cousin Angela; we've only just come. Suppose we go out now and take a walk before bedtime; we might possibly find the ramparts by moonlight."

Angela Victoria was rich in possession of guide books, but she had a habit, of which Margot was likewise guilty and which filled Georgina with indignation. She never consulted her guide book at the right time. In consequence of this peculiar method of self-instruc-

CARCASSONNE—THE LOWER TOWN
LES LICES A MAIN STREET
AN UNDECIDED VOTER COURTYARD OF HOTEL BERNARD

tion, neither of them found that evening either walls or towers. In the narrow streets the people were taking the air and visiting their friends who sat before the shop doors enjoying the mild spring evening. Crowds were promenading the broad boulevard beneath the splendid waving beech trees, whose trunks glistened like silver in the flood of white moonlight.

"Walls or no walls," cried Margot, enthusiastically, "I'm just crazy about Carcasonne!"

"Perhaps the cité is up there," said Angela, glancing up at a kind of a bastion which jutted out upon the boulevard. There was no entrance nor any way of seeing what was on the top of the mound. They walked around it only to find more boulevard on the other side, and then, as it was late, prudently went back to the hotel through the same street by which they had come.

"You're not very strong at finding the way, Cousin Angela; neither am I. Distances are so deceptive by night, and everything looks so differently. I do not dare to let you get too far away from that charming room that is waiting for us."

They discovered next morning the true state of the case. The hotel in which they were stopping was in the lower city, which was an outgrowth of the old fortified city on the hill, and laid out after the uninteresting pattern of a gridiron, with the boulevards, formerly the old moat, surrounding it on four sides. The ancient cité is not visible from any place on the walk they had taken the previous evening.

"Letters! Letters!" cried Margot. "Something to

make up for our disappointment and the portcullis!"
She entered the room and, turning on the light, began to look over her bundle of correspondence. She was so absorbed in one lengthy epistle that she did not answer when Angela said:

"Georgina expects us day after to-morrow. She says our time will be up then and she has engaged our rooms for that date. I shan't stir, even if there's nothing to see here; we are too comfortable, and I mean to do some writing. Would you like to go on to-morrow?"

Margot, who had retired to the other side of the room, let the long letter she was reading fall on the floor.

"To-morrow? To-morrow? Please, Cousin Angela, don't go before Monday."

While she was still speaking a knock came on the lofty, shaky double door, which was followed by the entrance of the black-eyed, smiling chambermaid, Clotilde. From the rolling, slipping pronunciation of her tongue to the quick, graceful gesticulations of her hands, from the alertness of her small body and the constant shrug of the shoulders to the lifting of the eyebrows, everything in Clotilde denoted the native of the Midi.

"The ladies are going to-morrow?"

"No, indeed," quickly answered Margot.

"*Bon, c'est bon!*" There was a suspicious sound of *g* at the end of *bong*. "To-morrow will be market day and that is gay, but alas! on the next day we will have our elections, and that will be '*bieng triste*,'"

Carcasonne 247

"Why '*triste*'? What is there sad about the election?" asked Angela, with interest.

"Ah, Madame! It is sad because the candidates are all democrats. Social democrats! When the elections are made, if these men are elected all the churches in France will be closed up; that is, unless in other *pays de la France* the people are more fortunate than we poor ones in Carcasonne." She sighed deeply.

"Who told you that, Clotilde?"

"*Mais, Madame!* All the world knows! Did not these miserables come here and take the list of all the treasures in our church. We made a riot! *Mais, c'etait bieng une emeute! Madame la Comtesse de C*——, *Madame la Baronne de D*——, all of us who are *elēves du couvent* were there, but the dragoons came and *une scene terrible* occurred. Nobody was hurt, *mais, comment on a criée!* Ah, what a noise! The wretched creatures! They wrote down on paper everything there was in the church."

"Did they steal anything, or take anything away?"

"*Non! non, Madame;* they did not dare! You must go to-morrow and see the treasures they counted. All the great silver hearts, the beautiful gifts and ex-voto tablets presented in gratitude to the Virgin for her miracles! We have also a miraculous Virgin here. The deputies by this time have read all those lists and, *sans doute*, each has chosen what they liked best; and if the elections go wrong for us they will put all these rich objects in their pockets."

"Then let us hope it will go right," said Angela. But Clotilde was in a despondent mood, and holding up high her shrugged shoulders, went off shaking her head.

The following morning the cousins were roused at a very early hour by the noise in the square outside their window. Loud voices and rattling carts heralded the coming of the market folk. Robinson, very much excited, instantly mounted a windowsill so broad that it could have accommodated a Saint Bernard dog with comfort; consequently this small Boston terrier walked up and down like a lion and stared out at the scene below with an interest which betrayed itself by his low mutterings and half-suppressed barks.

" Here is what our cheap restaurants always label as ' Unsurpassed Coffee,' " said Margot, smacking her lips. Clotilde had spread a very dainty breakfast table for them. " After all, I think women understand chamber work in its refinement better than all our Jeans have done," went on Margot, looking at Clotilde.

" Don't be ungrateful to those who were so good to us."

" And the honey of the country," proudly interrupted the little servant maid.

Angela quickly took her hands out of the wash basin and hurried to do justice to what to her was the most welcome meal of the day. She grew so emphatic in her praise of the delicately brown rolls, the rich-coloured coffee, the pats of fresh butter and golden honey, served them on delicate china, with snowy linen and a dewy rose at each plate, that Robinson leaped down from his place of observation, attracted by the enthusiastic tone of voice, expecting to find a feast of

Carcasonne 249

liver and beef bones; when his mistress offered him dry bread he retired disgusted to resume his watch of the market.

"Clotilde can tell us, I am sure, how to find the *cité*." Clotilde at once broke forth with delighted directions and ejaculations which convinced them that for wonder, for beauty, for *superbe point de vue* nothing on earth could equal the *cité*.

"Be sure that we take the guide book, Cousin Angela."

"I can't to-day; it's down at the very bottom of my trunk, and I am not going to unpack anything but the basket until to-morrow. Then I shall get books and manuscripts all out."

The market was a sea of white caps when they stepped out of the hotel door. The cousins threaded their way among the booths and passed the vendors under the arcades, through which they went into *La Grande Rue*.

"When we come back from our walk it will be just as lively here as it is now, probably more amusing," said Angela, seeing that Margot was inclined to linger.

The peasants who come to buy from the more distant villages had not yet arrived, and many of the peddlers under the covered arches were only beginning to spread their wares.

"Where do you suppose the entrancing Carcasonne of the picture books has hidden itself? The *Rue de la République*, *Liberté* and *Carnot*, all those dull names of new France, do not suit me in this place at all."

"At least they have kept the name of *Grande Rue*

for this narrow street, which ought to be called *La Petite Rue*. That has a flavour of antiquity. I suppose it was very big for olden times. A splendid, wide thoroughfare for this Carcasonne of the plain."

They entered a prosperous-looking book shop which lay on their path, and bought from a pile of historical matter Viollet-le-Duc's monograph on Carcasonne, from which they absorbed much technical and, to them, incomprehensible matter, together with some few entertaining facts of history, upon which Angela Victoria pounced with delight. Not sufficiently self-confident to be convinced that notwithstanding Clotilde's careful directions she was perhaps leading Margot astray by turning in a direction diametrically opposed to what she had been told, Angela stopped to ask the way of a woman sitting in front of her shop door.

"*Oui, oui, Madame,*" declared the woman with interest. "Continue by this street and pass over *La Square Gambetta* and you will come to the bridge; there you can see *la cité.*"

Margot laughed. "I knew we should strike Gambetta somewhere. I suppose that square, as they call it, once had some delightful queer old name full of suggestion which the ardent republican soul of modern France has pushed away into obscurity to honour a politician. Why is it republics are never artistic? They never *are!* "

Angela Victoria nodded her head wisely. She had no answer for that theory. He thoughts were occupied with dreams of the past. She fancied herself crowned with a high, pointed headdress with a floating veil, long, flowing sleeves, a troublesome train, pointed shoes, and a shining girdle hanging from her slender waist, as she picked her way through the mud of a *Rue du Chat qui Saut*. She would surely have been lovely to look upon in that costume, but, romantic as she was, the modern Angela Victoria had a strong affection for the bathtub, and therefore little genuine sympathy with the habits of the age to which she wished to belong; indeed, she was disturbed in her dreams at this moment by the disgust she suddenly felt for the swift-flowing open gutters of the *Grande Rue*.

Robinson had quite different sentiments on the subjects. He had no leanings toward the romantic past, but he could not be kept out of the gutter. Margot was forced to stop and lecture him on his common, low tastes.

"Aren't you ashamed of yourself! And you from Boston! If you can't keep away from these muddy French dogs, or if you stop again to play in the water, I will hang you on the leash!"

Robinson, very much hurt, came promptly to heel.

In Carcasonne every inhabitant owns one and sometimes two dogs; these are perfectly good-natured, harmless canines, who enjoy life while lying in the middle of the street or playing in a lazy way with one another. Robinson was overcome with the ignominy he would endure if he were hanged on a string in the presence of all these free creatures to whom he had just been boasting of his travelling experiences.

"Look at that lazy black dog. I don't suppose he would move even if an automobile came along." Margot shook her finger at her pet; Robinson understood perfectly these inconsequential remarks and felt sorry for himself; but he loved his kind; the sidewalk was not many inches wide, so, while he pretended repentance, he slily walked into the clean water of the flowing gutter and then jumped back close to his owner before she saw him, rejecting all the advances made him by those dogs with whom he longed to frisk.

The Cité is fully a mile from the Hôtel Bernard. The cousins saw it first from the old bridge, looking up to where it crowns the hill through the soft, glowing, warm sunshine of that southern spring morning. The walls and towers took on shades of pink, purple, blue and yellow in that golden atmosphere. The place seemed like a vision of the past, a mirage of the Middle Ages. The inequality of the land on which this fortress was built adds infinite grace to the Cité as it rises above the steep banks of vivid green turf. The ramparts undulate with the rise and fall of the heights and hollows of the ground, and as they gazed upon it the bristling slate tops of the many towers stood shiningly silhouetted against the brilliant blue sky. The air was balmy and fragrant, and the snow lingering on the distant Black Mountains sent no sharp, cutting blast toward Carcasonne. The river, swollen by the rain, swirled through the arches of the ancient bridge, *Le Vieux Pont*, built in 1184, and in one of the niches above the massive spurs the two cousins seated themselves on the broad parapet, struck with the beauty of the magic fortress which seemed so unreal that they feared it might vanish at any moment; the painted plaster walls and tiled roofs of the houses of the *bourg* clustered near the river below the rampart was a mass of pink, red, and dull violet colour. The leisurely peasant driving his slow-going, sleek horse, clad in its great horned collar, passed by them over the bridge on the way to market and brought colour into the scene.

These great collars, which constitute almost the entire harness used upon the draft animals of the Midi, are frequently very expensive affairs. The horns are made of stuffed leather of different colours and most ingeniously sewed together like a piece of patchwork by leather thongs in place of thread. The drivers add to the artistic effect by hanging on these horns the light sacking they use as blankets for their animals, when this is not in use. The effect is extremely quaint, graceful and picturesque.

The climb to the Cité through the ill-paved streets of the bourg and then up the steep road below the mound on which the citadel is built and which leads to the chief entrance of the walls, *La Porte Narbonnaise*, was easier for Robinson than for anyone else in the party. He raced up the steep embankments and tumbled down again, galloped up the road and rushed back, just to show what a simple matter it was to storm an ascent.

The cousins toiled up slowly, stopping to rest in a tiny park without the fortified gate. They then passed over a stone bridge and through a zigzag passage which crooked itself between the two great twin towers of the Porte, and entered upon a deserted street lined with ancient houses, low, solid structures covered with plaster, fronting on a narrow, mounting way paved with cobbles and silent as the tomb.

The sound of their footsteps reverberated in the echoing streets. Robinson ran ahead quietly on velvet paws, occasionally stopping suddenly and pointing with his blunt little muzzle thrust forward and one paw in the air. In the deep doorways leading between the thick walls into the houses nobody came or went.

"Do you suppose nobody lives here or that everybody ran away with the mediæval armies?" whispered Angela. Somehow it did not seem quite proper to talk out loud and boldly.

"It is very melancholy," whispered Margot. "I am glad we brought Robinson. Perhaps he will unearth a cat."

They went on ascending, always ascending, through twisting passages hardly fit to dignify by the name of street; the irregular byways of a citadel.

All at once Angela stopped and held up her hand. Her ear had caught a sound.

"Listen!" she said impressively.

A strange buzzing noise, which somehow seemed familiar to her but which she could not at that moment place, floated down from behind the blinds shielding a queer old twelfth-century casement. Margot, who was somewhat behind, hastened up and stood looking at her cousin, with the vague, wondering expression on her face.

Whirr-whirr-whirr-whirr!

Margot listened a second and burst out laughing.

Carcasonne

"Why, Cousin Angela! don't you know a sewing machine when you hear one?"

The spell was broken. The dead were awake and stitching busily, but not a living creature did they see until they came out in front of the Château, where they spied a shabby, solitary French soldier loafing on the entrance bridge.

"It seems after all that we are not the only live thing in this town with a ghost sewing machine to keep us company," said Margot.

The soldier stirred into life for a minute at the sight of the ladies and the dog, and then leaned back against the parapet, resuming his stony attitude and looking bored to death.

The Château at Carcasonne, a fortress within a fortress, is now, like many others in France, used as a magazine. Its towers and crenelated ramparts stand surrounded by a moat awaiting an enemy which never comes to attack it. The open space fronting the Château is sun-baked and dusty, strewn with great blocks of stone left lying there when the repairs were made upon the city walls. A few rough patches of coarse grass grow in tufts near the solid, simple dwellings which surround this open place.

"Let us hurry on," exclaimed Margot. "I am afraid I shall become petrified myself. The soul has gone out of this place and left the shell. Can't we find somebody to talk to?"

They speedily discovered such an individual in a guide lingering at the *Porte de l'Aude*, who was not only ready but anxious to talk. It was his business.

Visitors were rare at this season, and rarer still on market mornings. Two attractive women whose eyes sparkled with enthusiasm and curiosity, and who hung breathless on the wisdom he shovelled out to them, accompanied by a small dog, who flattered him by his confident attentions, did not fall to this man's share every day.

As Margot afterward told Mr. Hardy, this learned personage began at the very bottom of the walls and worked up through hundreds of years of history in La Cité to the flourishing garden he himself had planted with success close beside the ramparts. He was a marvel of learning in archæology, and seemed intimately acquainted with all the Gauls, Romans, Visigoths, Saracens and French who had built these defences. Angela Victoria listened carefully and attentively with a view to her book; but alas! she remembered none of it when the time came to use it. Margot drew him out because she liked to hear his rich southern accent. She didn't care and didn't know anything about the shape of the towers, and she never found out whether it was the Saracens or the Visigoths who built the square ones.

The Cité of Carcasonne is surrounded by two lines of defences. The outer wall with its rounded bastions has no towers and stands much lower on the hillside than the inner ramparts. It looks far beneath them, and while walking around the inner circle the eye is unobstructed and roves off across the broad valley to the indistinct, dark form of the Black Mountains silhouetted against the horizon. Inside the ramparts the silent

Carcasonne

little crowded city shrinks away from the wall. The monarch of the Middle Ages took the wise precaution of forbidding buildings to be built close to the walls of fortresses.

"They all passed by here, these nations," meaning the lists he had just poured into their ears, "and each one of them added to the strength of the citadel. We are here in the path to Spain and Italy. We were assaulted, besieged and taken again and again, until the time of Philippe-le-Hardi, who finally encased the Cité of Carcasonne in a formidable cuirass of stone and we settled down to the tranquil life of a sentinel quiet at his post."

"Richard Hardy," whispered Margot in Angela's ear, "isn't in it with this man for reincarnation. I judge from the little sketch he has given us that he has lived several thousand years without stopping."

Angela suppressed a wild desire to giggle; but fortunately the man was so absorbed in his subject that he continued without noticing. "Do you know what our Cité was called? Non? It was called the impregnable '*Pucelle de Languedoc*,' *mais oui, Mesdames.*" Nobody had disputed him.

"Carcasonne has suffered much. Did you see the bust of *La Dame Carcas* as you came through *La Porte Narbonnaise?* You thought it was a battered old saint, hein? *Mais non, Mesdames!*" he laughed disdainfully. "*Pensez donc!* That old woman, a heathen, a Saracen, kept the city and defended it against Charlemagne!" Angela and Margot expressed proper surprise.

"What! This great big place! and only one woman!" Margot could not control her incredulity.

"*Ah dame!* I don't believe it was very big then. Like the Château now, perhaps, but anyway for years, *oui, Mesdames, pour des années*, the great emperor besieged it. One by one the soldiers of the garrison perished, all the women and children died but *la vielle femme Carcas*. She ran from tower to tower, *bien vite, bien vite;* let fly a javelin here, loosed an arrow there, and made the besiegers believe there was a strong force within. The soldiers tried to reduce the place by famine, but the clever old woman crushed any hopes of this by throwing out a pig fattened with corn. In despair the army was getting ready to retreat when a great miracle occurred. One of the towers bowed to Charlemagne, rendering him homage as Emperor of the West, and the old woman surrendered."

"I don't wonder," said Margot. "She must have been in a hurry to get out."

"*Ma foi, oui,*" laughed the guide. "I wouldn't have stayed there myself."

"That was the time when he was not around," whispered Margot again, and this time Angela laughed outright. The guide, thinking it was at his wit, joined heartily in the merriment.

"Does no one live in this city?" Angela asked the guide. "Is it not inhabited?"

"*Mais si, mais si!* Certainly the Cité is full of people, but they are all labourers and they are at work to-day or at the market. That is why it is so still. But it is long ago since a high officer, a viceregent for the

Carcasonne

king, lived in the Château, and these houses sheltered gay nobles. Now all the rich live in *La Ville Basse*, where the ladies are undoubtedly stopping."

They did not lose this chance to ask this repository of wise information something about the lower city.

"It is not so new," he said. "When Simon de Montford, who fought the Albigenses, captured the Cité from the heretics in 1096 he promised them honourable terms, but no sooner did he get inside the walls than he hanged all the knights and robbed the citizens of everything. With nothing but their shirts and breeches he sent the men into exile. After these poor wreches had wandered about for seven years in misery, St. Louis yielded to the prayers of the good Bishop Randolphe, and the king permitted them to come back on condition that they would settle far from the fortress on the opposite side of the river. That is how *La Ville Basse* was built. It was formerly surrounded by walls, but now boulevards occupy that ground and the road is where *les lices* (the place, Mesdames, between the two walls) formerly ran."

Before they had mounted the first tower Angela renounced her attempt to keep on a hat. "Does the wind always blow up here?"

"Always!" the man calmly said. "There are some ladies who cannot walk around the inner ramparts as you have done."

It was a long time since he had known such interested tourists, and he poured out all the knowledge he had ever acquired for their benefit. He showed them the wooden gallery which had been restored on one of the towers as it was in the time when archers shot down their arrows upon the attacking forces through the floor, themselves shielded from any projectiles. He pointed out to them the remains of the iron supports for the pulleys with which the great beams were lifted and forced into the openings left in the masonry. He told them how swiftly the carpenters worked, and was as wise in the matter of the constructing of galleries as if he had worked on them himself. Perhaps he had. He described with terrifying exactness how the defenders poured down burning oil and hot lead on the assailants, and then suddenly announced:

"Here we are, ladies, at the Cathedral St. Nazaire, which the great Bishop Randolphe founded. If you wish to enter I will wait outside for you and conduct you later to the exit by the *Porte de l'Aude*. It is the easiest way to leave the Cité."

"I shall be glad to go somewhere and sit down," said Margot. "I feel as if I had been upstairs, downstairs, and through my lady's tower quite often enough for one morning."

"I saw nothing to suggest ladies," said Angela, "but I shall be glad, too, to rest in the quiet of this delightful cathedral."

On the rugged walls of this fortress-church the lichen-clothed gargoyles looked down with comical grimaces on the upturned faces of the cousins.

"Isn't this the queerest, most delightful, romantic, enchanting, solemn old church you ever saw!"

Angela laughed. "You have snatched all the adjectives but noble, so I will add that one. Can't you

THE CITÉ OF CARCASSONNE

ON THE RAMPARTS

FROM THE BRIDGE AT THE PORTE DE L'AUDE

fancy these old gargoyles talking to one another every moonlight night and telling stories of the bloodshed and pillage they had witnessed in the twelfth century to the restored bits which have been put up later?"

"Yes, and interlarding their remarks with 'Before the nun who used to be in your place fell away,' or 'When the monkey you somewhat resemble was still beside me.' I believe those hoary, old moss-grown creatures up there, with their ears and noses damaged by the wear and tear of centuries, are horribly naughty to the newcomers and tell them monstrous lies."

The cousins left these strange carved creatures to their own peculiar doings and pushed through a low leather door into a flood of jewelled sunshine, which made the interior of the church radiant with light, and dignified its austere loveliness and beautified, if such a thing were possible, the marvellous Gothic choir forming the arms and top of the cross which stretched along under tall glass windows. The high altar is in the centre, with three chapels on either side raised above the transept by three long steps extending quite across the church. These chapels are divided from one another only by tall, graceful, springing arches. There is marvellous thirteenth-century stained glass in the long windows, and this end of the church is all illumined by the glory of their splendid colouring.

"What a gem!" cried Margot. Her very dearth of adjectives proved her enthusiastic appreciation.

It is a martial-looking church, notwithstanding the glory of colour lent by the brilliant windows. The severity of the stonework probably excited the masons to embellish every capital and cornice with highly amusing little figures calculated to distract the attention of the holiest canon from his Latin missal.

"What a love of contrast and what complex natures these old church builders must have had!" said Angela.

"They made killingly funny figures!" exclaimed Margot, "and it must have been a great joke to them when they carved their best friend's face on one of those absurd little animals."

"I'll venture to say the friend did not like it! But there he is, to amuse us long after his very name has been forgotten."

The exuberance of this fancy, of all these grotesque caricatures, this riot of sculpture, is doubly interesting against the stern severity of the simple stone arches and columns which dignify this church.

"I wonder if Richard ever came here?" whispered Angela Victoria.

"No, I don't think he has ever been in this part of France. I wish he was here now."

"I mean Richard Cœur de Lion," said Angela with dignity.

"Oh!" exclaimed Margot, "I thought you meant Richard Hardy."

The sexton showed them about, pointing out the tombs of the good bishops by whose efforts this noble church was built, and, murmuring a prayer of gratitude that it had been their blessed privilege to enter it, the cousins passed out again into the open air. The guide was waiting for them on the outside, trying to interest

Carcasonne

Robinson, who refused to be consoled for the absence of his mistress.

The man led them through a postern gate out among the defences of the barbicon and showed them the steep way leading down to the little town below.

"It grows more and more interesting every minute," said Margot.

"I will come here to-morrow and write. Never have I seen a spot more fascinating than this empty citadel, deserted by its garrison. *Il est bon quelquefois de rever du passé.*"

"Perhaps, if you tried very hard, you might see a Visigoth, or would you prefer a Moor? Here's a small boy, now, who is black enough for any Saracen, and he has a red sash on, too."

"He is a Catalan. The guide just told me with expressions of disdain that La Cité is full of them."

"Why doesn't he like the poor creatures? They do seem poor!"

"The only reason I could get out of him was that they can't speak French."

Down in the trenches, where blood had watered the soil during the crusades against the Albigenses and in the very place where the rising ground made it easy for Simon de Montfort to effect a breach and rush in with his followers; where, in the fiercest of fights, he had captured Trencavel, the lord of Carcasonne, afterward to condemn him to ignominy and death in one of his own towers, a flock of sheep guarded by a faithful dog was peacefully feeding as the guide led Angela and Margot through this spot on their way to the *porte* below.

The lively aspect of *La Ville Basse* was a warm contrast to the cold, deserted solitude of the lonely coronet of towers they had left behind on the other side of the bridge. Aged voters gathered around the placards of vivid orange, yellow and blue which were posted on the walls along the boulevards, and in rich patois discussed with ample gestures the coming election.

The cousins stopped to read what was printed on these violent-hued bulletins and to learn thereby something of the gentle art of vituperation. Each one of the posters was devoted to the praise of a favourite candidate and to setting forth with vehement condemnation the principles and character of his rival.

A small boy in a cook's apron and cap, the *marchand de berlingots*, was shaking his rattle to proclaim his wares and then diving down into the bottom of a huge, drum-like box to fish out with the dignity of a superior tradesman, for a crowd of clamouring youngsters, some of the appetising cakes he had for sale.

The smaller cafés were full of vivacious peasants talking excitedly at their *déjeuner*. The Place Carnot was a confusion of flowers, fruits and attractive-looking vegetables; while in the market place near the entrance to the hotel people were surging to and fro, collecting in goups around the pedlars, who tried to outdo one another by their cries.

The din of La Ville Basse was as great a contrast to the silence of La Cité they had left as was its gaiety to the quiet sadness of the deserted mediæval fortress.

When they went in to the dining-room of the hotel

it was crowded with numerous guests, who may have been travelling salesmen or prosperous vine cultivators from the country surrounding Carcasonne, but the main topic of conversation with one and all of them was the election, and through the hubbub of voices the names of the rival candidates were the only words distinguishable. The waiters flew around the tables serving a breakfast which it was no insult to call a sumptuous dinner. The rich, rolling accent of Provençe was heard on all sides. Robinson, who smuggled himself in with his mistress, cautiously protruded his bullet-like head from under the table to sniff at a tiny, rat-like dog, all bells and furbelows, who belonged to a remarkable looking woman with suspiciously glowing auburn hair. This lady ate most of her meal by picking tit-bits with her own fork out of the plates of her two escorts, and appeared to find it impossible to get along at all without the aid of the table to support for her elbows. She picked her miniature terrier up and, without even the ceremony of a glance, stuck the unfortunate little doggie behind her in the chair, where the wretched little prisoner remained in a most uncomfortable position looking down through the bars with a mortified expression in answer to Robinson's unconcealed surprise. This lady was leading actress of Carcasonne, a second Sara Bernhardt, in the eyes of herself and Clotilde, from whom Margot gathered this valuable piece of gossip. Bijou, the terrier, had appeared on the boards in a more conspicuous position than he occupied in the dining-room, and was a popular favourite.

Margot had never seen a provincial market day, and

to Angela's remembrances the one which she had witnessed in Poitiers appeared sad and sober compared to the surging movement and gaiety of Carcasonne. The pavement of the open square was adorned with the same motley heaps of ribbon, only, where at Poitiers there had been molehills, here there were mountains.

Enticing earthenware cooking utensils looked their most attractive, spread out on a brilliant red cloth. Margot hovered above the display with longing eyes. "I should like to take a dozen of those *casseroles* and *bouillotes* home; cooked in that rich brown, glazed lining, with the rough, snowy exterior, the poorest food would turn to ambrosia or whatever it was the gods used to eat."

"We'll buy a few specimens, anyway," said unresisting Angela, who at once burdened herself with a bulky parcel to be tucked away at some future time in a shawl-strap or perhaps broken on the journey. Fakirs were selling Waterbury watches, to which they ascribed most wonderful qualities, and getting rid of them as rapidly as they held them up, while beating a drum, as Margot observed, "to drown the tick of the watch."

Two dark-eyed individuals, each of whom wore on his curly Semitic head a tall red fez, were selling "*pour un rien* cutlery of the Orient"—made in France. These poor men's voices had degenerated into a mere harsh croak through their overloud shouting in praise of their wares.

Pots, pans, jewelry conveniently cheap, clothing for both sexes, dainty frilled caps made of the sheerest muslin for coquettish peasant women, postal cards, toys

Carcasonne

for Bébé and little Philippe, piles of embroidered felt slippers, filled booth after booth and did not lack purchasers.

"There is meat, poultry, eggs and cheese enough here to stock a fortress for a month! And all so fresh and clean!" said Margot, coming out after a visit to the covered market.

Angela had meantime been trying to talk with a woman selling delicious sweetmeats; she had selected some delicately candied quince and asked the price. "*Ung sou*," the peasant answered with a bright smile. Angela praised her wares, but the conversation was not proceeding very rapidly. The old woman was clearly not at home in the French tongue. To her purchaser's many questions she answered sweetly: "*Oui, Madame*," without variation.

Margot listened a moment to the halting conversation, and putting a sweetmeat between her white teeth, said:

"*Rachachiminaya!*"

It was the only word of Provençal she knew, but it broke the ice. The woman put her hands on her hips and roared with laughter, then pretending to pull away Margot's hands from her mouth, she offered her a piece of chocolate, shaking with glee.

"*Voicic ung vrai rachachiminaya.*" ("Here is a true chimney sweep!")

"That is a most useful word, Margot, as a solitary inroad into a language," said Angela. "Where did you learn it?"

"From my nurse. It may not be practical, but I

liked the sound and never could remember any of the more serviceable phrases she tried to teach me."

The green, orange, blue and red election posters, which proclaimed Monsieur S. an honourable, truthful, patriotic man, and Messieurs C., D., E., and F. all discredited and proven corrupters of political morals, were more popular than ribbons or the less novel market commodities, and were surrounded by changing groups of peasants, mostly women. The woman cannot vote in France, but she has ever been a strong power in that land, where her clear commercial instinct has placed her in an almost equal position with man. She takes a more violent interest in politics, knows less about them, and is more inconsequent than any of her sisters in foreign lands. The old women who could not read, and there are still many in the Midi, were gathering what knowledge was dispensed to them by the better schooled members of the younger generation and lamenting at the same moment that they benefited by its results, that compulsory education has brought liberal views to France. The army was in great disfavour with these aged agitators. As the cousins paused near an excited group around a placard, one of the withered old countrywomen turned to a passing soldier, a harmless youth, himself the son of a peasant, and, shaking her fist, called out to him with vehement gesture:

"*On va me prendre mon Dieu! Voila bien la liberté que vous m'avez donné!*" (They are taking my God from me. Behold the liberty you have given me!)

This phrase sounded very fine, but the old woman had actually not the remotest idea of what she was talk-

Carcasonne

ing about. As for the poor young soldier lad, he looked surprised and disconcerted.

The cousins left the noisy market and strolled into some of the attractive shops lining the streets. They wandered gradually out to the little *Jardin des Plantes*, where the *diligences*, innocent of paint and varnish, stood waiting to take back their loads of peasants to Aigues Vives or Prieux. These antiquated conveyances are decayed *Omnibuses des Chemins de Fer* worn out with usage in Paris, which have been rusticated and are laden down with funny imperials and seats on the top to hold peasants, instead of the heavy trunks of the transatlantic traveller. The fat, lazy horses, much too sleek for duty, slept with their noses in a feed bag while awaiting their owners or purchasers. In the saddlers' shops of this part of the town an endless variety of the cleverly made beautiful leather-horned horse collars were exposed for sale.

Margot patronised not one but half a dozen *patisseries*, buying cakes in each. "I simply cannot resist them, Cousin Angela," she said. "We will have Clotilde make us some tea. We will all sit on the broad window seat, and what I don't eat, Robinson can have."

When they got back to the hotel Clotilde frowned upon the idea of tea and recommended coffee. "Seriously, tea is only fit for invalids," she said; therefore, not being quite sure what variety of herb she would brew them for tea, they decided in favour of coffee. The window looked out into the arcade, where business was still brisk enough to entertain them. Almost directly under them a lad of decidedly Israelitish cast of countenance was selling coarse lace curtains whose beauty he displayed by holding them aloft on his yardstick, and then draping these luxuries gracefully back with its aid into folds. He was shrieking himself hoarse crying in a sing-song fashion: "*Trois sous le mètre!*"

A fixed, gentle smile on his countenance never relaxed for an instant; he threw its sunny beam on a crowd of small boys who stood like stone images staring in front of him, and won by its warm sweetness the favour of the peasant women, who bargained furiously for his wares. In a race of tradespeople he was the tradesman *par excellence*. His piping treble was drowned occasionally by the deep bass tones of another member of his nation who stood at a short distance and with vehement, eloquent gestures swore that the curtains *he* sold were infinitely superior, and only a few centimes dearer. The whole performance was a comedy, and sharp as French peasants usually are, they were completely fooled on this occasion. When the boy called out his price, the older man would leave his wares and stride over to the boy, if the female crowd displayed any uncertainty in buying, and, standing before the lad, he would lift his shoulders and both his hands with an inimitable gesture of immense surprise, calling upon high heaven in stentorian tones to witness that: "*Trois sous le mètre! Trois sous! Jamais je n'ai vu ça!*" (Three sous a metre! Only three sous—never have I heard of such a thing!) a remark which never failed in its effect.

Margot and Angela were so amused and interested by this farce that they forgot their *goûter*, and so Robinson got most of the cake and some of the coffee. The curtains sold so fast that more had to be secretly brought over from the other man's table. Although a competitor in public, in private the gentleman was evidently the father of the family.

In less than half an hour the new supply thus obtained having vanished, a sister from another part of the arcade brought her curtains into the field, and the cousins, quite as delighted as though they were to profit by the results, finally saw the reunited family, pretended rivalry thrown to the winds, go off with empty hampers but plenty of money, each munching a cake and congratulating one another on the profits of their Sabbath day.

The market began to break up. The booths were cleared away and a policeman appeared commanding a small company of old crones armed with brooms, the street cleaning department of Carcasonne, whom he marshalled about with such severity that in an incredibly short time the only sign of the busy throng remaining was a great green-covered carrier's cart to which the tiniest donkey ever seen was attached, who, finding himself alone, gave voice to his loneliness in melancholy song. When they came out from dinner the moonlight poured into the courtyard, and Angela Victoria hurried Margot to the bridge as soon as she finised her coffee to see the Cité in the full effulgence of that clear, brilliant southern moon. A liquid flood of silver bathed the tower-crowned hill, around them was silence, and the citadel looked still more mysterious and unearthly in the white light.

There is some soft quality in the moon ray which

opens the heart and unfolds the confidence. Margot sat looking down into the water while Angela gazed up at the ghostly fortress.

"I never used to care much for moonlight, but now I adore it. Don't you, Cousin Angela?"

"No, dear; not always. It is too sad."

"Oh, Cousin Angela, then you were never in love! You would never speak that way if you had been!"

"What makes you say that? What do you know about love?"

"I know all about it. I am in love now. *Horribly* in love!"

Angela tried, not very successfully, to laugh at her.

"You didn't suspect it, did you, Cousin Angela?"

The vision of Richard Hardy's face rose before her eyes. She was silent.

Margot, full of her all-absorbing topic, went on quickly. "I have been in love for a year."

"No wonder she will never be parted from Robinson; it was at that time he gave her the dog," thought Angela.

"I think it will come out all right now. Mamma had other plans for me; but I believe she is beginning to give in. Poor Mamma! She wants me to marry a young Frenchman. But I can't please her this time. That's why I begged to come with you. I didn't want to have any more fuss about him. Now you know half of my secret, and when something happens you shall be the first to know it all. Oh, I *am* so happy!

See, even the moon is laughing!" She was very vague in her confidences, but Angela asked no further questions.

"Dear child, I wish you all the happiness possible on earth."

Margot, her mind flying off after a dearer person, did not hear the slight note of despondency in her cousin's tones, but she demurred when, with a last long look at the sleeping fortress, Angela Victoria left her seat on the parapet and said:

"Let us go back. I have promised myself to do a whole chapter of my book to-night! You can tell the moon love stories from the window."

Margot put her arm around her cousin's waist and, ignoring the last remark, said: "And you will read all your work to me, won't you? I have always longed to be the very first to listen to a celebrated book. You are sure to write well. You are such a dear."

Although popularity in literature does not always follow exactly the lines Margot ascribed to it, Angela Victoria accepted the prophecy with becoming modesty and her usual hopefulness.

"I do hope people will like it," she answered thoughtfully.

The electric light quite chased the more reduced rays of the moon out of the contracted highways and byways of the lower city. The streets were lively with swarms of people.

In the window of an antique shop a lovely old comb brought forth a flood of enthusiastic adjectives from Margot's ready tongue.

"You shall have it," said her cousin, "for your engagement present." She entered and asked the price. It was expensive.

"I haven't the money with me to-night, but I will come and get it to-morrow," she told the shopkeeper. Margot blushed.

"You mustn't give it to me too soon, Cousin Angela. I'm not officially engaged yet. It might bring bad luck!"

"I shan't bring you bad luck, dear. I could not bear it. You shall have the comb to wear in your dark hair when you bring your lover to be congratulated," said Angela as they reached the hotel.

To the surprise of the waiter lounging before the entrance, Margot stooped down and gave her cousin a kiss on each cheek.

Later in the evening Margot, in a soft pink negligée, her own and Angela's pillows stuffed behind her back, sat on the bed with her knees drawn up, absorbing knowledge from "La Guide Joanne"; from "Viollet-le-Duc's" learned pamphlet on "La Cité de Carcasonne" and Hare's "Southwestern France," and repeating:

"I do like to read these books after I have seen the places."

Angela had cleared away the roomy writing table and was unlocking her trunk.

"Georgina was right about luggage. She is so clever. She says we all need so little. I haven't even seen this trunk since we left Brive, and I have not wanted one of the things I packed into it there."

Margot laughed. "I thought the contents were principally brass."

Carcasonne

" Shame on you! I only bought two pieces."

Angela shook out the clothing she had wrapped around the jugs.

" They are not dented anywhere, but oh!——"

She rummaged excitedly in the bottom of the trunk, then sat down in a heap on the floor. Margot jumped up, overcome with amazement.

" What is the matter, Cousin Angela? "

" Oh, what shall I do! I have lost all my note books and my money! I must have left it all in Brive! The portfolio with my express checks and everything! Perhaps someone has stolen them out of my trunk. What shall I do, what *shall* I do? " She struggled up on her knees, with wild despair in her eyes. " Every cent I have or expect to have for the next three months, my whole income, has disappeared! What *will* Georgina say? "

Even in this terrible crisis, the fear of Georgina's just indignation was uppermost in her mind.

Now thoroughly aroused, Margot bounded to the aid of her excited cousin. Robinson rose anxiously from his corner and joined the group. Pushing Angela aside, the young girl began carefully to take everything out of the small trunk, to shake every pair of gloves, look into the shoes, while Angela still sat a picture of unhappy melancholy.

" Where did you put the checks? What did the thing look like they were in? "

" They were all in a black, flat case," Angela stammered. " I can't remember where I put that."

" Think hard, Cousin Angela, where was it you cashed your last check? "

"I drew some money at Argenton." They both sat silently meditating for a few minutes. At last Margot said: "Well, we won't let Cousin Georgina know! I will telegraph to mamma for money at once!" And then Angela's memory suddenly awakened.

"Oh, I remember *now!*" she cried. "I put that case, together with my pencils, my note book and some thin writing pads, in a leather box your mother once gave me. I must have left it all in Brive!"

To her surprise Margot burst out in a fit of laughter.

"Found at last, but far away!" she exclaimed. "Don't you remember, you dear, vague thing, that you gave me several packages to put away. You wanted to get that brass stuff into your trunk."

"Oh, how could I have been so stupid as to forget! I am losing all the small wits I ever had! How glad I am it's not lost! Do give me the letter case at once."

"I wish I could," sheepishly murmured Margot, "but I gave it and the contents of the entire box to Mr. Hardy to put in his big bag. I found I could not squeeze it in among my own things.

"Ah!" It was a genuine note of despair that sounded again in Angela's voice. "We are just as badly off as before. How can we get the checks?"

"That is easy enough. We can telegraph him to-morrow. I know where he is. He will send it at once, and we shall get it on Monday and be away from here on the day Cousin Georgina commanded us to go." Angela's face looked so sad that Margot tried some nonsense to bring back her smiles. "Only wait with your book until we get off on that wedding journey, you

Carcasonne

and I and Dickey! Oh, *then* you can write! It will be so much more interesting, and you can read the manuscript to us every day. We can go on as leisurely as we choose, and not be obliged to flash through the country to catch up with Cousin Georgina as we have been doing these last few days."

Angela tried her best to enter into the spirit of Margot's humour. " Oh, but then I couldn't see half as much! When I get in an automobile I only want to go —go—go—all the time." She was thinking of that ride from Poitiers to Le Blanc. "I can't write to-night, of course; I have no paper now. But fortunately, for me, all the shops in France do not close on Sunday, so I can buy what I need to-morrow." She sighed without reason.

Not only do the good people of Carcasonne open their shops, but on Sunday the market was as lively as on the previous day. Angela Victoria, after passing a very uneasy night, looked out early upon the square. The fakirs and the curtain sellers were absent, probably enjoying a delightful Sunday on their profits of the day before; and the grey stones were no longer brightened by piles of gay ribbons; but other merchants had taken their places. Where the curtains were sold the day before an old cobbler sat busily in a booth tapping away with the implements of his trade at a good stock of worn shoes. Early as it was, a well-dressed young woman was pacing slowly up and down under the arcade with the skirt of her smart frock lifted very high to display a pair of clumsy, grey felt shoes, and awaken if possible a desire in the hearts of the women who passed to buy a pair of the same sort from a rich store heaped upon an adjacent table.

Clotilde lingered over the breakfast table and talked despondently about the result of the election until it was time for the cousins to go out. While she was chattering, Margot stole quietly downstairs and sent a telegram, then told Angela not to worry, that everything was right, so when they went out that dear, easygoing lady bought a generous pad for immediate use in her novitiate as an authoress. The cousins seated themselves in the pretty little park now called the Square Gambetta, which probably had formerly some delicious romantic name. It is opposite the combined schoolhouse and museum, which on that day was being used for the polls. More of the showy placards had been posted for election purposes during the night. Every available space on walls and public buildings was covered with them. Before the *bureau d'election* on either side of the wide door, and stretching across the gravel path between the houses and the trees of the boulevard, sat six men, all very quietly and orderly on six rush-bottomed chairs. They solemnly presented every voter who passed them going into the polls with a slip of paper bearing the name of some certain candidate. Of those who ran this gauntlet, a few took all the slips; others took one or two; the others rejected all the proffered tickets. These slips had no bearing upon the election beyond suggesting a name. A constant stream of peasants in their glossy Sunday blouses, workingmen in their best clothes, and shopkeepers passed in and out to vote. Near by a solitary and very magnificent *gendarme* lingered; a crowd of boys and women, which increased as the people came from church to swell the throng, stopped before the *bureau* under the trees and lingered a while; but except for one loud-talking group gathered about the bootblack stand at the street corner, none of the political excitement the cousins hoped to see exhibited itself.

Some few of the voters went to the placards and read the cutting accusations and high recommendations set forth by each candidate in his own peculiar and vehement style. A couple of gaudy soldiers in uniform and several black-robed priests gave colour to the crowd. One eager fisherman on his way to the river laden with net and rod passed by without a glance. What cared he for Republicans, Royalists or Church party when the fish were waiting to bite?

On the park bench they had taken, two old ladies sat beside the cousins. These dear old persons lamented bitterly over the frightful disasters they had been told awaited the church. Margot and Angela endeavoured to dispel the despair in their souls, by judicious praise of the churches in the Ville Basse, and nearly banished the election and the terrors predicted for France from the old ladies' minds. To divert their minds, Angela asked them questions about La Cité, bringing to light the astonishing statement that although one of them had been born here in Carcasonne never had she been to the La Cité in her life; while the second considered it only a show place for tourists.

"I have climbed there once or twice with visitors from Toulouse," said the more enterprising one of the two, "but it is a long way even in a carriage, *et je n'aime pas voyager.*"

The old ladies could find no beauty in fortified walls and towers. "It is all right for foreigners; but *pour nous autres*, what do we want of such sights? La Ville Basse is much more beautiful."

After luncheon Angela left Margot writing letters, and, armed with her splendid new note book, ample enough to hold all the thoughts she could jot down in a week, with a pencil and penknife, she prepared to pass a delicious afternoon somewhere among the heights in the old fortress.

"Please take Robinson, he's no bother; he will play about while you write, and later I will join you if you can tell me where to find you? Shall you be inside or outside of the ramparts?"

"Neither. I shall be in the trenches between the two, on the oldest part of the wall I can find, where, protected from the wind, I can look over the wide valley and gain inspiration from the beauty of the landscape and the wonderful circling walls above me."

"In some romantic corner where you can peep out through the openings where the archers shot their arrows? Never mind; I'll find you, and after you have written enough we'll hunt up the old guide of yesterday and see some more of that delicious cathedral. Good inspiration! Be sure and dedicate this chapter to me."

The citadel was more silent and deserted when Angela Victoria reached it than it had been the previous afternoon. The inhabitants of the crowded little town were all down in the street at the foot of the hill, where

CARCASSONNE

AN OLD COUPLE OF MARKET-FOLK   A POLITICAL DISCUSSION
A PROUD DONKEY

she passed walls as thickly decorated with gay election placards as were those of the town on the other bank of the river. The names of the candidates alone were different; the crude green, blue, yellow, pink and purple colours were just the same.

Angela had her thoughts filled with Margot and her love affair. She was oppressed by a feeling of misery and loneliness she tried in vain to throw off as she climbed the paved way of the ancient barbican to the Porte de l'Aude. Her feet were so heavy that Robinson had raced up and down four times before she was half way to the top. Bored by vain attempts to hurry his companion's footsteps, the little dog crouched like a rabbit on a stone waiting for her, and looking so comical that he succeeded in reviving her spirits and forcing her to join him in a race to the top. When they reached the walls they saw crowded on the lower step of a gloomy postern gate two baby children, the Sunday garrison of La Cité, who had been left by their parents to play with a dirty but beloved doll. Angela found directly opposite them a comfortable spot which she thought would call forth her literary inspiration. She seated herself in a sheltered angle of the bastion, while Robinson, disgusted at her desertion, cautiously approached and smelled the doll, to be greeted with cries of combined glee and terror by the babies.

Where the sentinels of olden times paced the outer defences and looked over the wide country for approaching enemies, the wall has a raised shelf on the inner side, enabling the archers to spring up and discharge their arrows at an advancing foe through the crenelations in the outer wall. Angela Victoria, safe from the wind in one of these corners, with a step at her feet and a wall at her back and a round peephole through which she could look out far over the golden distance, opened her immaculate note book, examined her pencil, smiled quietly to herself as she thought of the single line she had written that night in Saumur. Nothing so commonplace would she jot down now. She glanced over the landscape again where shining in the clear valley she could see from her watch tower the many-coloured roofs of new Carcasonne, and then thought a moment intently. But she must write! She would write! And almost unconsciously while Robinson was engaged in an attack and retreat, his small, short barks mingling with the now hilarious cries of the babies, her pencil traced some deliciously poetical words. They came readily. She read them carefully over. They were lovely; the ideas were unusual, but they had a ring which was too familiar. Again she read them, and suddenly discovered that they really belonged to some author whom she could not at that moment place; either Symons or Robert Louis Stevenson. She had only pulled her literary efforts out of the storehouse of her memory; again she tried to concentrate her thoughts, but her mind refused to leave Margot and Richard. The girl was so youthful! Why had she not chosen a younger husband? She remembered how she had ignored the conventionalities, and accused herself bitterly of having failed in her duty by allowing him to travel with them. "Propinquity, propinquity is always so dangerous," was what Georgina said. And Angela had forgotten this wise saying, because she, forsooth, took pleasure in Richard's society. With an attempt at regretfulness, she secretly confessed this crime to herself. She became very enraged at him; the idea that he had deceived her, used her as a convenience—how, she did not know—but she was sure he had used her as a convenience, incensed her very much. She could not blame Margot, but Mr. Hardy was old enough to know better. He had treated her very inconsiderately. It was extremely cruel. She began to feel very sorry for herself. She wished above all things that they had never met him. To be sure he was agreeable and useful and she could not altogether hate him; she had done wrong, but how, she did not know, for even Georgina could not have considered three or four days a very long time to permit a man who had a perfect right to go wherever he chose, to remain in their company. Still, she was responsible in a way for the girl's conduct; and if she could live the last week over, she would behave much more wisely, she was sure. How indignant Georgina would be! It was evident Margot's parents disapproved of the match, otherwise why was her engagement not announced? Angela had a vague, guilty sense of having made some serious blunder. She went on, growing more and more indignant. She was angry with herself, but she was much more angry with Richard Hardy.

At this point of her uneasy meditation Robinson, whose playing with the babies had consisted in approaching as nearly as was safe to the much-desired dollie and then being warded off from his prey by four sturdy little feet, suddenly stopped his attack and gave vent to a perfect shower of sharp barks, shook his little frame and danced past Angela out behind the wall onto the barbican.

Angela peered around the corner without rising, expecting to see Margot, but to her horror she beheld Richard Hardy's tall figure advancing upon her. Her first impulse was to rise and fly, but surprise chained her to the spot; there was no escape. With Robinson leaping about him begging to be noticed, Richard strode forward to where she sat, greeting her with a smile. He held aloft her flat portfolio containing the checks.

"I knew Robinson would help me find you. Good doggie. Margot told me you were up here somewhere, so I took my chance. I really came to bring you this." He gave her the purse, which she took without a word. "I hope you've not worried about it; I thought it held some of Margot's nonsense, and I looked inside the cover for the first time last night to see if it was worth sending her by mail. Then I realised how important it would be to you, and started this morning by the first train I could get."

"You got the telegram?"

"I got no telegram; I started too early, although Margot says you sent one."

"It was Margot who sent it," Angela said, with dignity. "It was very stupid of me to put that box in her care." Her head began to swim. "I am so careless—Georgina—I was afraid it had been stolen—I was horribly worried!" How confused and stupid she felt!

"That is why I insisted upon bringing it up here to you at once instead of leaving it with Margot at the hotel. She told me I would find you somewhere in this fortress of silence." He looked around and seemed inclined to sit down beside her, but she gave him no encouragement. " Are these tiny guardians the only men-at-arms left? How majestic the deserted old place looks! Is it waiting for its garrison to wake up from the dead and stir the echoes of these grey walls with trumpet and drum?" Angela hardly heard him.

"It was so kind of you——" she began to murmur. "There was no necessity for you to hurry and travel here on my account. You could have posted this case."

He smiled. " And left you without money! You see, I had looked inside. That is how I happened to know the case was not Margot's; your name was on the checks. Had I waited to send it you might have had worry and inconvenience. I would never wish to cause you either."

She looked up to thank him, but before she had opened her lips he put up his hands, as if to ward off her gratitude. Instead, he laughed gently, and, looking down into her eyes, said:

"I will confess my selfish soul to you! I did this all for my own sake. I was glad of any excuse to come back; in fact, I was longing for one, and searching for something that would bring me here without displeasing you. Never have I spent such happy days in my life as those I passed last week."

Angela Victoria's heart stood still for a minute. A sharp pain pierced it like a knife. Was he, too, going to confide in her? She tremblingly waited for what might follow.

"Now that I've brought you back your money may I not claim a reward?" He smiled down on her pleadingly. "Please don't send me off again!"

Angela struggled to her feet. She said, with a start, half stammering, half sobbing: "Oh!—I must—I can't—I ought not—I really cannot—it would not be right! I am very sorry we travelled with you! Oh, no, I don't mean just that! I thank you so much for bringing my money! It was so good of you!—I am very grateful, but I cannot let you stay now—I really must not!"

She sank down again on the stone step. Never had poor dear Angela Victoria been more explosive in her life; never more vague in expression; never more erratic in speech. Her heart was beating, her face flushed crimson. She felt she was a coward. Although no tears fell, the moisture was very near her eyelids. This was the climax of a train of unconscious mental anxiety started by Margot's confidences of the previous evening.

Richard Hardy stood overcome with surprise. His face was very serious. For a few minutes he did not speak.

Angela watched the shadow from a cloud over the "Tour de la Justice." How gloomy the battered old tower looked!

When he spoke he seemed to be muttering to himself, but she heard him perfectly. "I did not know you disliked me so much."

His tone excited her to reply. Her words came faster and faster, but her phrases were more involved than before.

"I do!—I mean—oh, no! Oh, please don't think I dislike you—it is not for that reason! I wish you every kind of good wish—I enjoyed—having you with us—but I cannot, I ought not—I will not let you stay now. It is not right," she said, with a sudden spurt. Poor Angela was trying to copy the dignity of Georgina; she drew herself up and looked severe. Richard continued to gaze down at her with an inscrutable expression in his eyes.

"Not right?" he asked, slowly. He seemed about to speak again, then to change his mind. She was silent. He turned away abruptly, lifting his hat.

"Very well, since you command me I will go," and he had passed the rampart and was half down the Barbican road before she could think of anything to say. Robinson left the babies and raced after Richard, following for a short distance, but in obedience to a sharp "Go back!" he returned dejectedly and lay down at Angela's feet.

Angela almost mechanically stepped up again on to the rampart, and kneeling down, leaned out between the crenelations and gazed after Hardy until he disappeared amid the red-roofed houses of the lower street. She rested her head in her hands.

Georgina was right! She was not fit to travel alone. What a tangle she had made of everything! At that moment she was suffering physical agony; her head felt light; her eyes hot and stinging, and she wanted

288   *A Spring Fortnight in France*

to cry. Tears did not come readily. With all her sentimental temperament Angela Victoria was not one of those who weep.

She continued to stare down at the road for fully five minutes; then her duties as a chaperon, her responsibility to Margot's mother, her awe of Georgina's anger suddenly possessed her mind; and suspecting Richard Hardy would go straight to Margot and that Margot would ignore those conventionalities which had so suddenly become important to Angela, she quickly took up her recovered portfolio, which had dropped unheeded on the stones, and started down the hill at such a furious pace that Robinson, believing he was in for a game of romps, behaved in his most riotous manner.

Her new note book, with its beautiful borrowed sentiment, had slipped from her lap on seeing Richard, and lies to this day in a crevice of the old Cité of Carcasonne.

She reached the bridge in an incredibly short time, but Hardy's stalwart form had vanished; over the Square Gambetta she hurried, and then down the Grande Rue. Hardy was nowhere within sight on the long, straight street. The crowd of loungers looked at her in amazement as she rushed by. She began to walk a trifle slower, feeling encouraged. He could not be in the hotel; he had not had time to get there. Perhaps he had lost his way. Angela Victoria so often lost the way herself that she suspected every one else of the same weakness. When she finally entered the hotel her manner was so excited that the waiter, who was wiling away his time by gently waving a watering pot to and

Carcasonne 289

fro over the courtyard foliage, stopped his labour and stared at her in surprise.

"Has any gentleman been here to ask for Mademoiselle?"

"No, Madame, not recently. A gentleman came nearly an hour ago. I called Mademoiselle and he drank coffee on the terrace while he talked. They sat there, Madame." He pointed out a certain table as if it were of the greatest importance. He scented mystery and romance and felt compelled to quiet madame's mind. She grew anxious.

After she hurried rapidly into the house he still stood shaking his head, and a senseless stream poured from the watering pot he held suspended in midair.

Margot rose to meet her cousin when she entered the room.

"Well, Cousin Angela," she began, gaily; but her face fell when she saw the cloud on that lady's countenance. Her cousin, usually so joyous, looked positively glum.

"Why! Have you come back so soon? I thought you and Richard would be climbing towers and enthusing about a medley of history, romance and other wonderful things. I was coming by and by to join you, and bring a whole pound of cakes to eat by myself while you drivelled about the Middle Ages and Richard Cœur de Lion. You saw him, I know, for you've got the portfolio there in your hand. He didn't think it was funny at all that you should be left without money. He was mad because I laughed. He gave me a frightful scolding for having entrusted the stupid old package to his honest care. Is he downstairs? I'll go down and make him apologise to me at once for his words. Where did you leave him?"

A great light broke over Margot's mental vision.

"Oh, Cousin Angela! Did you send him away? Why did you do it? Poor Richard! He wanted to stay. He promised to stop if you would let him." She stopped short, alarmed at her cousin's pallor. "What is the matter, dear? You look ill. What has happened?"

Angela sank down on the bed.

"I think the sun has made my head ache. I will lie down a while."

Margot, forgetful of all else in her sympathy, immediately kneeled down and pulled off her cousin's shoes; she then helped her to undress, brought a loose gown, shook up the pillows and darkened the room in an incredibly short time.

"I am so sorry! Poor darling! Now keep perfectly still and I am sure you will sleep it off. We will take ourselves off, Robinson and I, and you must rest until we come back for tea."

Margot wondered what had happened; her suspicions were aroused, but she was wise enough to ask nothing. She gathered up the letters she had been writing, clapped on her Panama hat and went quickly out, followed by her little brown companion.

The genial waiter, still at his task of trickling a few drops of moisture over the foliage, gazed admiringly as the young girl passed out into the street; he remarked to Clotilde, who stood looking over the balcony:

"*Bien jolie! Bien chic, celui la!*" and went on nodding his brown head for a few minutes, like a Dresden china mandarin. He admired the young "American mees" with all the fervour of his *méridional* nature.

Left alone, Angela's head throbbed and burned worse than ever. Sleep was impossible. She tossed from side to side on the pillow; all her hopeful, sanguine nature was overcast and engulfed by a deep sense of despondency which prevented her from thinking sanely. Her thoughts went whirling round in her head, regret and satisfaction chasing one another in a perfectly inconsequential manner. She knew she had not said the right thing to Richard Hardy. To Margot she had not spoken as decidedly as she should. The expression of the man's eyes haunted her. When he asked to be permitted to stay, was it possible that her presence had vanished from his consciousness and that he was looking through her at Margot, his lovely young sweetheart? He had plunged his gaze into hers in a most peculiar manner. She felt a warm wave of emotion surging over her and sat upright, only to throw herself down again in confusion and misery. Self-accusing truth filled her with shame. She had sent him away because she could not bear to see lovers' happiness. "You are jealous!" cried the loud voice of conscience.

Poor, gentle Angela! The tumult of thought would not be stilled until it wore itself out, and then, her temperament asserting itself, she began to find consolation in that sanguine imagination which had stood her in such good stead through so many other trials. Tears came to her eyes; they soothed her spirit and brought sleep to her tired brain.

Meanwhile, to the only other hotel that Carcasonne boasted the interested Margot bent her way, wondering what could have happened, and where Richard Hardy had disappeared. She was told by the manager that no English-speaking gentleman had been seen there. She then made her way to the railway station, where the gallant *chef de gare* cheerfully and readily gave her much information he would have withheld from a less attractive maiden.

"*Oui, oui*—a tall handsome Englishman!" The chef remembered him well. He arrived with the train from Marseilles, left his baggage *en consigne* and then returned in less than three hours to take a ticket back to the place from which he had come. The gentleman had waited at the station, marching up and down the platform all the time. "*Le train vient de partir.*" He has just gone. "A very long journey to take twice in one day!" exclaimed the interested official. He, too, had suspicions.

Discouraged, and her curiosity but half satisfied, Margot walked slowly back to the boulevard, now gay with the promenading Sunday afternoon crowd. She sought out a bench, and with Robinson beside her made a picture under the trees that merited more than the usual admiring glances the men of the Midi shoot from under their dark eyelashes at such fair women.

Margot noticed none of them; her thoughts were galloping back and forth and busy with the question of what could have happened between Richard and

Cousin Angela. He had run away so suddenly, and she, clearly, was so much disturbed. Margot could come to no conclusion, so she rose, saying to her little doggie: "Never mind, Robinson; together we will make it all right."

At five o'clock, when she peeped cautiously into the bedroom door, her cousin's eyes were slowly opening. The storm had passed, the usual sunny light again shone in their depths. Margot darted out, gave an order to Clotilde, who was in waiting, and then flashed back again.

"Don't you move! You look so much better. You have quite a colour. I will drag the table up to the bedside, and Clotilde shall bring us some of that wonderful tea she wouldn't let us have yesterday. We will try it. Perhaps it won't be bad. She consents, for, being an invalid, she thinks you have a right to it to-day. Look at these cakes! Robinson and I bought them. Don't they look good, and awfully rich? You needn't shake your head; they won't hurt you a bit. It was the hot sun made your head ache. It was so vivid at noon, and your hat was too heavy. It is awfully becoming to you, and the most stylish creation I have seen this year, as Madame Virginie always says, but it weighs a ton. When we go out again I will lend you one I have in my trunk. You will look like an angel in it. After tea I am going to take you for a drive. I have ordered the carriage; the air to-day is heavenly. A lady who sat down beside me just now on the boulevard told me that in Paris it is beastly cold and that everyone is hovering over the fire. Poor mamma, she hates the dampness! I don't believe she is having half as good a time as we are!"

Margot gave her cousin no chance to talk, but rattled on without mentioning their vanished visitor, while they drank their tea, and good tea it proved to be.

Refreshed, Angela rose, and they drove out over the smooth roads among the perfumed hedges, past rolling fields splashed with the red of countless scarlet poppies. They went as far as Pennautier, where a château famed in troubadour annals interested and diverted Angela's mind. The driver took them the tour around the boulevard, the pride of La Ville Basse de Carcasonne. He insisted on their admiring the prefecture and the fine houses hidden in deep gardens, and to his infinite satisfaction they pretended not to have seen them before. He directed their particular attention to some of the ancient bastions of the wall, now enjoying a peaceful old age as blooming gardens. "They deserve garlands after all their victories. *C'est que nous avons dans la Ville Basse aussi des antiquities.*"

The cafés were merry with gay family parties. The citizens were still awaiting the news of the election returns. The *cocher* confided to them that he was a radical, a republican. He said he had no party prejudices. If the candidate had suited him he would have voted with the socialists. "*Quesque ça me fait a moi!*"

He was as anti-clerical as Clotilde was pious, and dismissed the idea of the church party with a vigorous shake of the head and a wide flourish of his whip.

"*Ce sont des can-cans de femme, si Mesdames me pardonnes.*"

Carcasonne

Like the driver of the omnibus, he carried an automobile horn and punctuated his remarks by a loud fanfare. He blew a mighty blast after this last remark and wheeled into the hotel courtyard.

Angela Victoria's spirits were completely revived by the amusement she had enjoyed, and the driver went off chuckling at the generous *pour-boire* Margot pressed into his hand.

Clotilde's face wore a very gloomy expression when she came up later with the hot water. She prophesied a dreadful fate for France, and with slow, despairing gestures announced that the election was "*ci qu'il a de plus mauvaise*," which did not prevent her from coming into their room later to watch *la marche aux flambeaux* and listen with enthusiasm to the strident music with which the winning party celebrated their victory while marching around the town with torches and banners.

Quiet at last settled over the little town. The procession was over; the lights were out. Margot slept, and Angela Victoria tried to calm her nerves by reconstructing castles and filling them with kings, knights, troubadours and fair ladies. But the images of her fancy all rolled themselves into one form. A tall, substantial figure stood obstinately before her and looked down through the night into her wide open eyes with an expression she could not fathom.

"I have spent three of the happiest days of my life—but I will go if you wish it!" the ghostly visitor repeated again and again.

Could anything be wrong? Could she be mistaken?

Was it possible Richard did not love Margot? Hopeful thoughts rushed through Angela's brain, to perish in the darkness. Life seems very hard in the blackness of the night. Every chance gleam of gladness the future may hold goes out with the light. To-morrow they would go to Arles. She sighed. Then on to Tarascon. She would like to skip that; but Margot had insisted on seeing the city of her beloved Tartarin, and she, too, had been so enthusiastic, braving Georgina's wrath, that she dared not pass it now. Perhaps they might hurry on from there and speed along the *littoral* without stopping the night at Marseilles. She felt absurdly indifferent and tired. Margot had been so uncommunicative about her plans and about Richard that she wondered with a shudder if he could be waiting for them in San Remo. She thought of Georgina with an unusual access of affectionate longing. How good it would be to get under her sister's protecting wing again!

The pleasure in the sunny plains of Provençe, the sky, the brilliant sea, the charm of the warm, captivating cities which Angela Victoria had so enthusiastically anticipated, changed to dread.

"Spring into summer!" she muttered to herself. "Spring has turned into winter, and a winter that will never end."

Forty times that night she wished she had never come, and as many times she confessed unwillingly to herself that never had she been happier than on this journey. As the day began to dawn and the birds in the courtyard to twitter, a wave of hopefulness, perfectly senseless, foolish hopefulness, but a hopefulness essentially characteristic of Angela Victoria, crept into her heart. Her nature responded to the light. She felt happy, and she slept.

Chapter X

ARLES

"COUSIN ANGELA, it is nearly ten o'clock! I could not bear to wake you before. Robinson and I have made all the necessary arrangements for leaving. I have done all the packing. Nothing will be left behind this time. All you have to do is to eat this honey, smell these roses, drink your coffee, and then get up and draw some money with your recovered checks."

" May I not dress first and have a little bread and butter with my honey? "

" I will graciously permit all these wishes to be granted. You look blooming this morning, dearest, and we have plenty of time. We do not leave for an hour or more."

As the easy-going train rolled slowly on, bearing the cousins toward the south, the grim mountains, grey and bare, soon shut away the deserted fortress of La Cité from their lingering gaze. Fertile fields and a country sparsely sprinkled with olive trees spread away at the base of the sterile rocky elevations, but soon the train passed this stern strip of country, and leaving the Black Mountains behind, flew straight on into the heart of summer. The vine stalks near Carcasonne, which showed but a shimmer of green on the bare wood, grew like Jack's beanstalk into tall and full-leaved vine-

Arles

yards after they had left Narbonne basking in the warm sunshine as they passed it.

At Cette, with its curving beach and white glistening houses, the travellers saw for the first time the birdlike boats, with their pointed sails fluttering out of the bay into the shimmering, deep, violet-blue water of the poetic Mediterranean.

Full-blown roses hung heavy as they climbed above the open-arched granges, and stolid oxen stood placid before great waggons piled high with hay. Peasant women with gaudy headgear and men with dull red handkerchiefs about their waists worked industriously in the great flat vineyards, labouring unceasingly to destroy the countless enemies lying in wait to injure the wine crop, as they must.

The little cabins, built of cornstalks, like the fairytale houses, and the cottages of the "*garde barrière*," half open, save for a thatching of the same straw, afforded admirable trellises for white-flowered vines. Wild roses bloomed beside the line of the railway, and the small groves of fragile olive trees added a dusky splash of shadow to the juicy green of the vineyards and the great flaunting red masses of the poppies.

As they neared Montpellier, palms and exotic flowers waved in the gardens of the private villas along the white road. The poplar had vanished from the landscape to give its place to the dark ilex standing stiff, strong and sombre in the radiant, smiling scene. A mosquito, as debonnaire and light-hearted as those careless foes of humanity are wont to be, ventured singing into the carriage to be snapped at by Robinson, and done

300 *A Spring Fortnight in France*

to death between Margot's quicker palms. The trains of horses meandering into Montpellier wore more bells and swinging red tassels on their harness than at Carcasonne, while agile little donkeys were dressed with collars and horns which were marvels of gay leather work.

The cousins bought little baskets of strawberries nestling in dewy leaves, as a substitute for cakes and "tea," and bestowed the small bottle of red wine they had found in their luncheon box on the grateful fruit peddler at the station.

"*Je vous remerciez bien, Mesdames.* Are you sure you do not want it for *goûter?* It is not bad," she declared, damning with faint praise. Angela bought two more baskets for the fabulous price of fifteen centimes each, while Margot and Robinson were stretching their legs up and down the platform.

After Montpellier, vineyards, flowers, and palms, and the white light of Provençe resolved themselves all at once into dull stretches of marshlands and watery flats. A line runs from the junction at Lunel, down through this green morass, to Aigues-Mortes, a sadder, more ghostlike, and as strong a fortress as that of Carcasonne, without the charm of location or the same glorious and far-reaching memories into the past.

Aigues-Mortes, dead almost before it lived, was built for the Crusaders by St. Louis, who, having no port from which to embark for the Holy Land, purchased from the monks a tower standing here among the fishermen's huts. It was never any nearer the sea than

ARLES

A BULL FIGHT IN THE ARENA

Arles 301

a canal could bring it, but the king sailed his ships up to the quay still in existence. Philippe the Bold made a great fortress of the place, and in the unhealthy air scores of Crusaders on their way to Jerusalem lingered and died. The sad little town, built inside the great mediæval fortifications, the most perfect now in existence, was kept well away from the walls by the royal builders. To its small, symmetrical streets have been added no new structures. Like an aged person, it has shrunken into a sad, wrinkled little city, melancholy and withered. As Figuier says in " Le Gardien de la Carmague," " Forgotten by the ages and the world, Aigues-Mortes presents the rare and curious picture of a French city which has been left behind by the centuries."

The tragedy of Aigues-Mortes was its capture from the Burgundians by the troops of King Charles VII. in 1421. Such a wholesale massacre then took place that the corpses were thrown in heaps in a tower, and covered with masses of salt. La Tour des Bourgundians, at the southwest angle of the wall, owes its name to this wholesale burial. The canals, which formerly brought vessels of considerable size to the place where the great iron rings, still visible, were hung in the wall to fasten their chains, are now filled up, otherwise, to quote from Hare, the shore near Aigues-Mortes has changed less than any other part of the delta of the Rhone.

A soft, pink, warm sunset glow spread over the walls of the great Roman amphitheatre, which, seen from the car window, announced to the cousins that they had arrived at the station of Arles.

Every characteristic of the Midi was more evident here than at Carcasonne; the crowds in the numberless cafés were gayer, the streets were narrower, the foliage duller and dustier, and the sensation of warmth, intensity and summer life more pronounced.

"They actually have to have switches in these narrow streets, so the waggons can pass one another," exclaimed Margot, when the omnibus driver drew up to wait, where there was a broadening curve in the contracted thoroughfare.

The Place du Forum, despite its pompous name and the Roman pillars still visible in the wall of the Hôtel du Nord, is as bourgeois and homely as a village common.

Shaded by broad-spreading trees, surrounded by cafés and small hotels, adorned by the usual kiosk, the starting place of a miniature tramway, it has still managed to preserve a most intimate, genial air.

"The genius of the South!" enthusiastically exclaimed Angela Victoria, who really knew nothing about it, but thought that sounded literary.

From the windows of their room they could look into green branches where a chorus of birds practised an evening song, each little chorister trying to out-trill the other.

After a long day in the train and a lunch-basket *déjeuner*, the healthy appetites of the two cousins cried out for food at an earlier hour than they usually chose for dinner.

"Garlic or no garlic, I must eat *saucisson d'Arles* in the land of its birth."

Margot at the dinner table was balancing a piece of this noted *hors d'œuvre* on her fork, when a great Russian wolf hound walked into the dining-room waving his splendid plume-like tail with indescribable dignity. Margot's eyes followed the handsome creature as he made his way to a table occupied by officers at the extreme end of the room.

A gentleman in civilian's dress, who was sitting with his back toward the cousins, turned to pat the dog, who had been ordered out by its master.

Margot dropped the sausage and stared. She leaned quickly across the table and whispered excitedly to Angela.

"There is the Vicomte de Solanges! What can he be doing here! I hope he won't see me!"

But he had seen her. Turning quite around in his chair to laugh at the injured way in which Borzoi Ivan Ivanovitch made his exit, he caught her eye and rose at once to greet her, followed by the envious glances of his friends.

She introduced him to her cousin.

"How fortunate that I have met you here. I came from Paris yesterday on regimental business. I hardly hoped for such pleasure as this. May I call upon the ladies after dinner?"

"Certainly," answered Angela, "but our salon will be the bench before the door. The trees invite us so cordially to come and rest out under them."

"Perhaps I can persuade you to drink your coffee

at the café there on the square. It will be amusing, and the coffee is good."

Angela Victoria, to whom his invitation was addressed, consented, and he returned to his friends, who overwhelmed him with questions which he took small pains to answer.

" He seems a very nice type of young Frenchman."

" He is," answered Margot, " earnest, wholesome and ambitious in his profession. He is the very best sort of a chap. I have known him long enough to be sure of that. Mamma is anxious to have me marry him, but I don't think he wants to marry me, even if I felt as she does about it."

Angela wondered more and more what turn things would take now.

After dinner they strolled across to the little café, Robinson and the Borzoi, side by side, creating a great deal of merriment by the contrast in size, but common dignity of manner. The master of the hound, an elderly colonel and a family connection of the Vicomte de Solanges, accompanied them.

While drinking their coffee Margot gave an amusing account of her *impressions de voyage*, and listened delightedly to the news of her sister Constance's great success as a society belle.

It was then proposed to look at the Roman ruins, and see the moon rise above the noble arches of the amphitheatre.

" Little as now remains of Latin splendour, that little is worth coming far to see," said the Colonel enthusiastically.

Arles

There is something so mysterious, so appealing to the imagination, so exciting to the fancy in seeing a place for the first time in the dark that Angela at once consented to the plan. In the tender twilight which preceded the moonrise, the *Place de la République* appeared majestic, the buildings splendid; the narrow streets seemed lined with palaces and the auditorium of the Roman theatre filled with silver-robed spirits. They left the cafés of the boulevard, with their merry patrons and glaring lights, and entered the little park, above which, on rising ground, are the ruined arches of the former splendid entrance to a theatre built by Augustus. There was a solemnity about the lonely twin columns rearing themselves among the ruins, and the silver half light exaggerated the dignity of the surroundings and shrouded the decayed splendour with mystery. Margot cared little to linger, however, as Roman ruins made but a vague appeal to her just then, so they went on quickly and entered a small dark street, stumbled over cobbles which were a torture to the feet, and suddenly the noble arches of the amphitheatre were before them.

"We must get inside into the arena and watch the moon peep in at us first through the upper arches, then look over the top, and flood the whole place with light. It is the most wonderful sight in Arles." The officer sent off a small boy to fetch the keeper from an adjoining house, and a franc unlocked the gates.

"Do not try to mount. It is not safe in the dark, Mesdames, Messieurs!" cautioned the *gardien*.

They had no wish to climb the dark, uncertain stairways. The great ring opened before them and the moon was nearly ready to show her beauty.

The dogs frolicked in the sawdust, playing at bull baiting, and the antics of the long-limbed, lithe hound, opposed to the alert evasion of the little terrier, moved the officer to a thrilling description of the harmless bull fights which delight Arles every Sunday during the summer months.

With picturesque gesture and Southern fluency he described the sport of which he was plainly an ardent amateur. A bull "*pas trop sauvage*" is ushered into the ring with music and drums, and then excited by bold young men, who wave bright handkerchiefs in the animal's face, and jump from the ring over the encircling wooden fence, against which Angela was leaning at that moment, whenever the prancing bull plunges after them. The sport consists in snatching off a rosette fastened between the bull's horns. The winner is given a large prize in money, and the youths of Arles become very adroit at the game. There is rarely an accident, and the bulls enjoy it so much that they have frequently to be driven out of the ring.

The gay crowds and beautiful women, the dashes of gaudy colour against the grey stones, the wonderful tints of the sky showing through the open arcades, ah, that was something to see! And the cries, the laughter! Angela Victoria's vivid imagination pictured it perfectly. She responded to the enthusiasm of the description, and almost jumped over the fence herself when Borzoi leaped toward her; then the moon suddenly appeared through one of the arches before her and shot a clear ray across the arena down on Margot and the Vicomte de Solanges. The Colonel had turned to see the lighted arcades at his back; in the fervour of his bull-fight souvenirs and Angela's attentive interest, he had not even noticed that the two younger members of the party had wandered away.

Angela now stared with wondering eyes. Was Margot a flirt? She was so full of gay, light spirits. You never can tell about these girls. She certainly had confessed to being in love, and Angela had suspected——

Her fascinated gaze was fastened on the couple. He was speaking earnestly, she was smiling radiantly, and suddenly he bent down and kissed the hand she offered him. It all happened in a second. The Colonel did not even notice that she had not turned as he did. Her heart gave a leap and almost choked her. She could not tell whether she felt gladness or sorrow. Poor Richard! but perhaps——

"Perhaps what?" asked the blurred moon, and at the same moment Margot's voice, with a happy, new note in it, sounded at her elbow. She had slipped her hand through her cousin's arm.

"Isn't this too enchantingly, entrancingly lovely! I suppose you are seeing all kinds of Roman ghosts in flowing togas and veiled heads filling these seats, and applauding every time a lion eats up a martyr."

The Colonel bowed respectfully to Angela.

"If I have caused Madame to wish to see the Greek-eyed Arlesiennes, with dark silken dress and dainty fichu, the soft black hair crowned with a tiny cap of rich lace and broad ribbon; if I have persuaded her how well worth while it would be to stop over until next Sunday to see the first bull fight, I shall be very happy." He looked at the lady with beseeching glances, so Margot declared later. " Ah, Madame, the excitement, the amusement! the cries! the cheering for the handsome bull fighters! Ah, Mesdames, you will remain until next Sunday!" He joined his hands in an attitude of prayer, and looked very playfully at Margot.

" By next Sunday we shall be with my mother and sister and Cousin Georgina," she said, smiling at Angela with mischief in her eye. Then she turned a glance on the young Vicomte, which puzzled and annoyed her cousin so much that at once she said:

" We must go back to the hotel. The moon has done all she can for us. She has lighted her lantern and made this scene so captivating that it will enchain my memory forever."

So out under the broad and mysterious solemnity of the arches they passed through patches of moonlight, that was almost golden in its radiance, and then under dark purple shadow again back through the narrow streets to the electric lights and laughter of the Place du Forum.

" I shall be gone before you are up to-morrow morning, ladies, so allow me to thank you for your company this evening, and to say ' *au revoir*,' " remarked M. de Solanges. "If you need a guide to-morrow," he laughed, " M. Colonel will be here. He is a passionate lover of Provençe, of Mistral, of Daudet, and of all the curiosities of Arles——"

"——who is happy to offer his services."

"*Au revoir! Au revoir!*"

Said Margot to the Vicomte: "You may take my love to my mother and sister, and I will send down to the office to-night a letter for you to put in your pocket."

The adieux had been spoken, and, as the cousins mounted the staircase, the young girl cried with a mock tragic air:

"Another secret! Another secret! I have three now! How I wish I could tell you one of them! I shall burst if another comes my way! *Arrive! Arrive! Viens*, Robinson! I must whisper them all into your ear, or I shall die before morning."

She kissed Angela Victoria rapturously, and dashed into her own room, leaving her poor cousin to pass another troubled night.

A letter from Georgina came up on the breakfast tray: "I had engaged your room, and now I shall expect you on Friday without fail. I am getting very tired of waiting for you. I cannot imagine why you have lingered so long by the way and overstayed the time you set yourself for the length of the journey. I can always calculate better. Caroline [who was Margot's mother] has written that she and Constance want to join us here. She writes that she is tired of the cold and wet, and that Constance has been so gay she needs a rest. Her husband is coming over from America by the Southern route to meet her here."

Angela had just reached this point in the epistle, when Margot, looking fresh, rosy, and adorably pretty in one of those deliciously simple negligées that the Parisian needle-woman knows how to devise for the young and lovely, came in, her eyes full of happiness, her hands full of letters.

"We have an invitation from Marseilles, Cousin Angela. No stupid hotel for us there! A villa on the Corniche! Mamma says I may go. I know you will be glad to accompany me." She bent down to kiss her cousin good-morning, looking, meanwhile, very mischievous.

"What are you talking about, dear? Who is it you know in Marseilles?"

"I know Mrs. Hardy. She has taken a villa for a few months, to be there with her husband. He has some sort of shipping interests which force him to remain there. I ought to know all about it—but I don't."

"Mrs. Hardy!" Angela felt as if she were shrieking. "Have I been travelling round with a married man who has never once mentioned his wife!"

The scene in La Cité de Carcasonne rose before her eyes with renewed horror, and nearly blinded her.

Margot threw her hands up behind her head and went off into peals of laughter.

"You dearest, properest, foolishest cousin, it isn't Richard Hardy who is married. It is his brother. This Mrs. Hardy is his sister-in-law."

Angela Victoria flushed scarlet, and a little, awkward, confused smile stole over her face.

ARLES—THE ALISCAMPS

A GALLO-ROMAN SARCOPHAGUS
THE CHAPEL AT THE ENTRANCE

ALLÉE OF THE TOMBS

Arles 311

"Do forgive me for teasing, but I am so happy this morning that I am silly! just silly!" she leaned her elbows on the table and bent over toward Angela.

"Now, you are going to hear all my secrets! I have permission to let you into my garden of joy!"

She took her letters from the table, and, holding them like playing cards in her hands, laid them down again one by one, as she counted them off:

"Mamma has written one. Constance has written one. Mrs. Hardy has written one. And——" she clasped the last envelope fervently to her heart, while her eyes shot forth flames of pleasure, "Dick has written to say all is right!"

Angela Victoria, inwardly quaking with nervous excitement, listened quietly.

"Here is the first and most important secret! I am engaged; number two, Constance is engaged; number three, mamma is in ecstasy, and last, but greatest of all, Mrs. Hardy is just crazy about me as a daughter-in-law. So Dick says, and he must know. She wants you to come and approve of her son. He knows all about you, you dearest little thing!"

And Margot executed a manœuvre which was partly war dance and partly embrace, and succeeded completely in dragging her cousin out of her chair.

Her son! So Cœur-de-Lion was only *Uncle* Dick!

"Sit down, you wild girl, and tell me all the news! I know nothing about Constance, or why you flirted so outrageously with Mr. Hardy."

"Constance is easily disposed of. You saw her future husband last night; he has been in love with her for a long time. He only liked me, although mamma imagined he wanted to marry me—that is why Constance and mamma are coming down to meet us. They want to get out of Paris until the engagement is announced. That will be when papa comes." Then she blurted out: "How can you say I flirted with Uncle Dick! He knew all about my engagement with Dick II. That is why he joined us, and I wanted him to fall in love with you, but you treated him so coldly and acted all the time as if you wanted him to go away." She paused. "I don't believe we shall see him in Marseilles. I am awfully sorry."

Life had many happy days in store for Angela Victoria and Margot, but the memory of that day spent in Arles held its place through long years as one of the brightest days on earth. Margot knew why she was happy, but her cousin could find no reasonable excuse for the light-hearted mood that so completely possessed her soul. Perhaps it was the brilliancy of the glowing sun shining into every crevice of a city still stately with the monuments of a past civilisation—for Arles is older than Rome.

The cousins first bent their steps toward the Aliscamps, a spot the early Christians of Roman Gaul believed to be the holiest earth in which to lay their dead. They went across the boulevard and down a long lane, from whence they turned into the avenue shadowed by quivering aspen leaves, which leads to the Church of St. Honorat. The way is lined by empty stone sarcophagi, where, in rude blocks hollowed out of great pieces of granite, a past race had been interred.

Arles

Margot, in her trim white clothing, and Angela, in the grey gown she had despised so unreasonably in Saumur, walked joyously down among the tombs, happy in the bright, warm air, and in listening to the trilling song of the birds, who found happy homes in the great stone coffins prepared for long-departed Gallo-Romans.

The keeper of the church was waiting outside the gate for them when they came up.

"Good-morning, Mesdames. You did well to come early. It will be warm to-day."

"What an enchanting spot this is!"

"*N'est pas, Mademoiselle?*" He opened the gate under the fine archway for them to enter the courtyard of the church. "There are but few of the splendid monuments left; they have been stolen, sold, scattered through all the great museums of the world, and the railroad has ruined the place—all but the Avenue. It was there the finest tombs, the sculptured sarcophagi, were placed in early times. Yes, Mesdames, from all over the world came the bodies of Christians to be interred here, for Christ himself appeared and blessed the old pagan burying ground, and the devil had no power over the bodies placed in this earth. When the railroad was built, the men, in digging, came upon tier after tier of the Gallo-Roman stone coffins you see outside on the Avenue. Here are thousands of them still in the earth, for in the early Christian days it was only necessary to embark a body on the Rhone with money for burial, and it was brought here to rest near the tomb of St. Trophime. There were

once nineteen churches, served by the monks of
St. Victor, where now there are but ruins and tombs.
I often think, Madame, of all the tears that have been
shed here, and all the despair buried here, and wonder
how the birds can sing so joyously all the day through
in these trees and the roses climb over every inch of
these banks."

He was a poetic philosopher, but Nature cares little
for the anguish which in her wisdom she knows to be
futile, and the present visitors could not believe in
sorrow that bright morning. It seemed as far away
from them as the dead of the ancient Aliscamps.

The place was almost impossible to leave, it was
so beautiful in the vibrant sunshine. Margot sat upon
a rudely carved sarcophagus, and diverted the old
man's thoughts into more vital channels by asking
him about the lovely women of Arles.

There was a theme which fired his pride of country!
The dead and their tombs were forgotten in the eloquence of a pæan of praise sung to the soft, velvety,
dark orbs, the perfect features, the ivory skins, and
the grace and charm of the Arlesienne, but it ended
with an invective against that enemy to beauty, which
had likewise been the enemy of Aliscamps.

"*Mais le chemin de fer!* It will ruin all that! The
employees, ugly men from the North, are marrying our
prettiest girls, and the type will vanish as did the wonders of these fields," and he mournfully made a sweeping gesture over the country near the street of tombs,
through which an engine was slowly puffing along.

Considering that the glory of Aliscamps had be-

A CORNER IN ARLES

Arles

gun to wane in 1152, the railroad, built only in 1848, cannot have been altogether responsible for its utter decay.

"Do you know Mistral, the great poet of Provençe, the author of 'Mireille'? "

Margot did not, but Angela loved the warm notes of the poet of the ardent South. "*Je chant au soleil*," she quoted. (I sing in the sunshine.)

He nodded with approval. "Madame knows and she must go from here to the Musée Arlaten. You will see there one of our Arlesienne beauties, *et une bien belle je vous en réponds*. There is a collection of curiosities of the province founded by our great poet, his cradle and pictures of his Mireille."

It was just the sort of museum for these two, so they left the loquacious old fellow with infinite regret, and through the palpitating shadows thrown across the sunlit path by the rustling leaves, they returned lingeringly along the lane of empty tombs to the boulevard. There they hailed a cab.

"The sample I got of these Gallo-Roman cobblestones last night makes my very feet curl up inside my shoes," declared Margot. "There will be no more walking in Arles for me!"

They chose their driver because he was smiling, and his horse because it was fresh and well-kept. Their judgment proved good: the driver smiled all day, turning every moment round on his box to show them his beaming countenance, and impart to them all he knew and whatever he could invent concerning the history of his native place. The horse trotted so bravely that by noon they had been all over the city. Both, childish enough in their tastes and always intensely entertained by all the local interests of whatever city they visited, the cousins were delighted with the museum, where the noted beauty, who fully deserved the title, left them to their own devices, after persuading them each to buy a " *cigale* " pin, emblem of the poet's device " *Je chante au soleil.*"

Dolls, dressed in the costume of the country, local scenes which these manikins illustrated, were the sort of sights Angela Victoria loved. They gave her a peep into the habits of the people. Margot shared her cousin's pleasure.

" Why haven't they these museums in every city? "

" Because they have no Mistral," said Angela decidedly, and after a pause she added, " and because, perhaps, such collections do not interest everybody. Georgina wouldn't like this, I'm sure. It is what she calls clutter."

The interested driver then whisked them away to a mediocre gallery of local paintings, which only received a weak tribute from their inartistic souls. The picture of the artist's daughter, Mademoiselle Réattu, was the only thing Margot looked at, and Angela spent her interest on the old house, once belonging to the Knights of Malta. It took them no more than ten minutes to see what they liked best in the archæological museum, a rapid process, which sadly disappointed their smiling driver, who had persuaded Robinson to sit on the box beside him when they went in, and expected to wait and play with the little dog at least half an

Arles

hour, but he was appeased by their long absence in the enchanting cloisters of Saint-Trophime, that great church standing out so rough and unfinished on "La Place de la République."

Here another ancient citizen of Arles showed them around these wonderfully beautiful arcades of the twelfth century. He pointed out, with pride and pleasure, each separate figure, every perfect detail to these visitors whose admiration was not stinted, while the play of the sunlight through the arches, the atmosphere brimming with golden atoms, the incomparable beauty of the romanesque galleries awakened all the enthusiasm their guardian could desire, and his warm thanks at their departure were called forth more by their interest than the liberal fee which they bestowed.

"*On est comme ça en Provence.*" As they again entered the fiacre, the driver stood up and waved his arm widely over the square. It was a magnificent gesture.

"Behold! *Voila!* The obelisk from the Arenes! Egyptian! There is no other like it in France!"

Then away he galloped his nag up the narrowest of narrow streets to the theatre. The rich-coloured African marble columns, touched by the sun, glowed with splendid tints of colour which had been hidden in the moonlight. The driver pointed out with his whiphandle the *exact* spot where the Venus of Arles had been found. It is now in the Louvre. He almost told them that he had seen it discovered, and as 1683 was the year in which it was dug up, his statements were both received with a trifle of incredulity by his hearers. In the amphitheatre they climbed to the outer uppermost circle of seats by the restored staircase they had been forbidden the night before, and tried to imagine the place with the two hundred and twelve houses which the guide told them had existed among these ruins in the beginning of the century. Angela and Margot looked down into the Arena and laughed over the events of the night before. It was such a good place for confidence that they sat nearly an hour, while Margot poured out the entire history of her love affair, which, with the sole exception of her mother's feeble objection, was a most unromantic tale. The driver waiting without was content with the attention they had bestowed on the pride of Arles.

" *On viendra bien loin voir ça! Un merveille té?* " and cracked his whip at the gay horse, who, off in a flash, stopped short whenever his master pulled up and gave vent to a " *Voila!* " thus denoting the church of St. Mary Major on the site of a temple of Vesta, St. Cesaire, the oldest church in Arles, and the chapel of La Madeleine, an interesting bit of romanesque architecture. They halted before La Maison des Saints.

" Here the apostles, St. Paul and St. Jacques, came to visit St. Trophime. *Il y a longtemps de ça!* " he said, shrugging his shoulders, but leaning down with elbow on the box seat and nodding his head sagely, first at the little house and then at the cousins.

" It looks just like all these other old houses! " said the unsentimental Margot, but Angela Victoria could not agree with her. Off again dashed the gay horse;

Arles

this time to the quay, where they saw the Palace of Constantine, that son of Maxentius and Fausta, who was born in Arles. Nothing now remains but a great, rough fragment of a Roman tower.

The driver nearly went into spasms of enthusiasm over the old wall, but, when he found that they infinitely preferred looking at the great stream of the Rhone, and watching the picturesque groups lounging about the quay, much better than the massive bit of wall which once sheltered Visigoth, Ostrogoth, Francs, and even a Roman emperor, he did not frown on them at all, as they feared he would. His ardour cooled and his explosive expressions of "*C'est magnifique*," etc., instantly collapsed when he found they met with no response, and, turning his sprightly steed onto the broad highway beside the river, he exclaimed:

"*Moi, aussi, j'aime beaucoup mieux le mouvement que ces vieux pierres.*" (I, too, love gaiety much better than these old stones.)

"What a good time we are having!" exclaimed Margot. "Can you imagine a better guide than this!"

He suited Angela perfectly. He never once asked them to get out and examine anything unless they chose.

Dumas, somewhere in his writings, says that Arles is a tomb, but the tomb of a people and a civilisation, a tomb to be compared to those in which the barbarians interred their gold, their arms, and their gods. And, amid all these buried treasures, with a redundancy of youth, life, and light hearts, the cousins, merry and happy, drove back to enjoy a good *déjeuner*, to which they brought healthy appetites, after dismissing the *cocher*, of whom they felt they had made a friend for life.

"I hope you did not tell M. de Solanges that I was not really '*Madame*,'" said Angela, as they sat over their luncheon; "he might wonder, otherwise, that I was permitted to undertake the duties of chaperon."

"Not a bit of it! I'll leave that to mamma. She will think it is a huge joke on Cousin Georgina's sense of the proprieties. Didn't you notice that he addressed you as '*Madame*' up to the very last moment?"

"Georgina will not be surprised. I told her I should assume that title."

"I know the gallant M. le Colonel thinks you are a widow. I saw him looking at you with more than interested eyes."

"Please, Margot! I entreat you not to make me uncomfortable."

Margot giggled. "I won't! Because if he asks us to go anywhere, or to see anything worth seeing, I want to go—'Madame.'" She added the title with emphasis.

After *déjeuner* they went out to sit on a green bench before the hotel door, beside the columns of the old forum built into the wall, and were watching Robinson gulp down his dinner, while they laughed at his greediness, when the Colonel appeared before them.

"And has Madame seen Arles thoroughly?" he asked with interest.

ARLES

THE CLOISTER OF S. TROPHIME

Arles

The cousins both answered eagerly that they had enjoyed a perfect morning.

"So you have been driving all over this lively sun-bathed city with one of those perfect cicerones, a good fiacre coachman. This afternoon, if you will permit, I should like to show you a great contrast—a strange, melancholy city which is dead. Will you allow me to conduct you along an admirable road in my small motor car? It is not grand, but it is good, and in an hour we can be at Les Baux, one of the weirdest sights in this part of the country."

"Oh, do let us go, Cousin Angela! You love old ruins, and we could not pass the afternoon more delightfully."

Persuasion was not needed; Angela Victoria was ready to consent almost before her cousin spoke, and it was not long before they were running out of the city in a small, but perfectly comfortable, machine.

"This is the road to Tarascon," the Colonel told them.

"Where we expect to go to-morrow."

"To meet Tartarin?" asked the Colonel. "He is always there, if you can only manage to meet him. He is in Arles, too. He is everywhere in our country, because you know, '*En France, tout le monde est un peu de Tarascon.*"

"Darling old thing! He is *my* hero!" said Margot, with so much fervour that the Colonel, who was old enough to be her father, gaily docked his cap, pretending he took the epithet for himself.

They soon left the main highway and by a detour

into a rougher country, but on an equally good road, came upon the ruins of a noted abbey.

"This is Mont Majour," said the Colonel. "We cannot pass it."

"When Cousin Angela motors, she never stops unless she falls off the side of the world!" laughed Margot. The Colonel looked puzzled, while Angela Victoria shook her finger at Margot and jumped out before the officer got a chance to help her.

Mont Majour has justly been named one of the most enchanting, romantic spots in France; the old abbey has a deep, dark serried wood on one side, and a sheer precipice that falls down to the plain on the other. The palatial monastery buildings are now in ruins, but the magnificent church, with its splendid cloister, the remains of a great tower and a noble gateway, still show high above the tops of the trees from the gorge below. Two very fine Gothic tombs remain.

The place where Mont Majour stands was once an island, and in those days connected with Arles by a causeway. Here St. Trophime lived as a hermit, and a stairway still exists which winds down the rock, amid masses of laburnum, to the curious little cell where he used to shrive his penitents. Three of these small cells are built side by side; in the outer one the sinners waited, praying, before their confessions, on a stone bench; in the second, where a tiny window communicated with the cell beyond, they made their confessions; in the third, the holy man lived.

An interesting chapel, built in the sixth century, where the saint performed his offices, still exists.

Arles

"All we have seen here belongs to the dead past, but it is dignified and somewhat preserved in spite of its decay, but Les Baux, to which I am taking you, is much more remarkable. It is a city of princes, over which a sorcerer has waved his wand, crying, 'Crumble and fall and cease to be.'"

They went on by the road that turns off at Fonteville, and here a ghostly barren collection of broken structures, ready to slide off the side of a hill, silhouetted against a deep blue sky, met their gaze. It was all that remains of the great principality and citadel of Les Baux, as strange as the unearthly hill cities of Africa, as desolate as Pompeii.

For an hour the party wandered through the silent streets of the crumbling burgh in the wake of a guide. This ruined city was, in the days of its glory, the apotheosis of all the rock dwellings in France. Châteaux, mansions, churches, and a great hospital were here carved out of the living stone in a tufa so soft that in many cases it crumbled at the foundations, and the towers, belfries, walls, and chimneys sunk slowly down, so that now, years after their fall, they still lean against the stronger dwellings as dead forest trees lean against the live oaks. In some cases the mason's art aided nature in the building, and mansions were begun by carving the rock and then finished by great blocks of stone brought from the near-by quarries.

Les Baux remembers a glorious past, but now its only inhabitants are a few poor peasant vine growers. Its history begins as far back as in the time of the Gauls. When Provençe was overrun by the invading

Saracens this citadel became a refuge for the country folk who flocked in from the neighbourhood for protection. Its importance increased in the tenth century, and by the beginning of the twelfth the seigneurs of Baux with proud confidence traced their ancestry back to one of the three Magi and bowed before no monarch on the earth. They owned seventy-nine burghs and great castles and immense stretches of territory in Provençe and elsewhere among the southern countries. "The lords of Les Baux in their heyday were patterns of great feudal nobles. They warred incessantly with the counts of Provençe, with the archbishops and the burghers of Arles. Crusading, pillaging, betraying, spending their substance on the sword and buying it back again by deeds of valour or imperial acts of favour, they tuned troubadour harps, presided at Courts of Love, and filled a long page in the history of Southern France with their deeds. The Les Baux were very superstitious. In the fulness of their prosperity they restricted the number of their dependent towns to seventy-nine, because these numbers in combination were supposed to be a good omen to their house.

Berral Les Baux, Seigneur of Marseilles, was one day starting on a journey with his whole force to Avignon. He met an old woman herb-gathering at dawn and said: "Mother, hast thou seen a crow or other bird?" "Yea," answered the crone, pointing. "There is one on the trunk of that dead willow." Berral counted upon his fingers the day of the year, and turning his whole troop, rode back whence he had come.

With troubadours of name and note these lords had

Arles

many dealings, but not always to their own advantage, as the following story testifies: When the Baux and Berengers were struggling for the countship of Provençe, Raymond Berenger, by his wife's counsel, went, attended by troubadours, to meet the Emperor Frederick at Milan. There he sued for the investiture and ratification of Provençe, while his troubadours sang and charmed the Emperor. Frederick, for the joy he had in hearing them, granted Berenger the sovereignty. Hearing thereof, the lords of Baux came down in wrath with the clangour of armed men. But music had already gained the day, and where the Phœbus of Provençe had shone the Æolus of storm-shaken Les Baux was powerless. Another time, when Blacas, a knight of Provençe, died, the great Sordello chanted one of his most fiery hymns, bidding the princes of Christendom flock around and eat the heart of their dead lord. "Let Raboude Des Baux," sang the bard, with a sarcasm that is clearly meant, but at this distance unintelligible, "take also a good piece, for she is fair and good and truly virtuous; let her keep it well who knows so well to husband her own weal." But poets were not always adverse to the house of Baux. Fouquet, the beautiful and gentle melodist, whom Dante placed in Paradise, served Adelaisie, wife of Berald, with a long constancy of unhappy love, and wrote upon her death an entrancing poem, known as "The Complaint of Berald Des Baux for Adelaisie." Guillaume de Cabestan loved Berangere Des Baux, and was so loved by her that she gave him a philter to drink, whereupon he sickened and went mad. Many more noted troubadours are cited as having frequented the Castle of Les Baux, and among the members of the princely house itself are several poets.

" Some of them were renowned for their beauty. We hear of a Cécile called Passe Rose, because of her exceeding loveliness. Also of an unhappy François, who, after passing eighteen years in prison, yet won the grace and love of Joan of Naples by his charms. But the real temper of this fierce tribe was not shown among troubadours, but in the courts of love and beauty. The stern and barren rock from which they sprang and the comet of their scutcheon are the true symbols of their nature. History records no end of their ravages and slaughters. It is a tedious catalogue of blood—how one prince put to fire and sword the whole town of Courtbezon; how another was stabbed in prison by his wife; how a third besieged the castle of his niece, and sought to undermine her chamber, knowing her the while to be in childbirth; how a fourth was flayed alive outside the walls of Avignon. There is nothing terrible, splendid and savage belonging to feudal history of which an example may not be found in the annals of Les Baux, as narrated by their chronicler, Jules Canouge."—J. A. Symonds.

The desolation, the ruin of this once splendid town, is a fitting grave to the makers of such history.

The road is cut through houses, splendidly carved chimney pieces, which recall the opulence of the former inhabitants, overhanging the path to the castle. Many of the dwellings are embellished with splendid Renaissance sculpture, but are now walled up like tombs, while

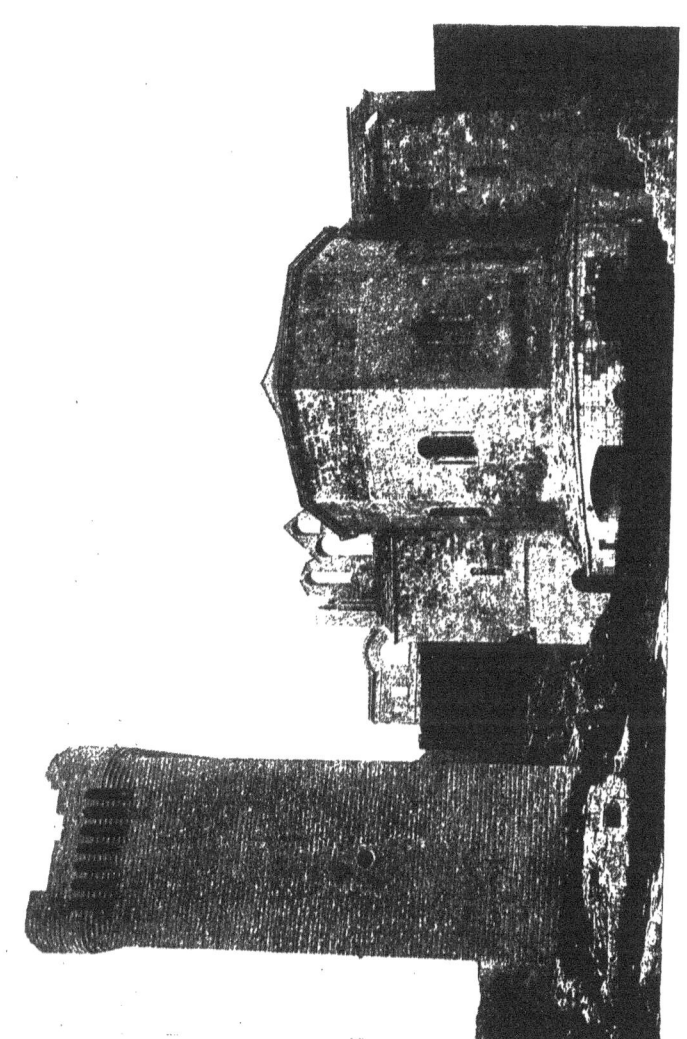

THE RUINS OF MONT-MAJOUR

others stand open to the sky, and among the walls the lizards flash in and out in the brilliant sunshine. There is a church, once dedicated to St. Andrew, which has crumbled to its very foundation. Vaulted halls, wherein splendid festivities once were held, gape on one side to the air and allow the passer to marvel at their decayed splendour. A few olive growers now inhabit this ghostly place, once the home of the richest, greatest nobles in Provençe. A splendid panorama spreads out to the view from the terrace in front of the church, and from the only thing which now remains of the château, a little vaulted chapel, the whole weird and fantastic mass of the roofless city lies at the feet of the sightseer. The cousins, standing there, looked far beyond this pile of desolation to the Mediterranean, thirty miles distant, over the strange country of La Crau, with its gleaming rivers and shining lakes.

The Colonel pointed out to them the glistening line, like a streak of silver quivering on the horizon. "That is the sea," he said.

"Where we shall be to-morrow," replied Margot, joyously, with a ring of expectancy in her voice.

Down again through the fantastic, jagged ruins, and then over a stretch of down, they passed on their way to the motor car.

Said M. le Colonel: "There is not always truth in the old saying that it is good to build on a rock. Look at these dwellings; they are built on *ce qu'il y a de plus de rocher*, and yet they have crumbled away like sand."

"That may be true, but the rock foundation is still here, and dreary enough it is!" The varying colours of an afternoon sky in Provençe changed the landscape through which they were speeding back to Arles to the semblance of a picture done in mother-of-pearl.

That evening, as the cousins were parting for the night, Margot said: " Oh, I hope Uncle Dick will be in Marseilles when we get there; don't you?"

" No, indeed; I do not want to see him!"

" Not want to see him? Oh, Cousin Angela; I'm so horribly disappointed! I hoped you would marry him! He must have fallen in love with you!"

" Don't talk such nonsense."

" But I'm sure of it, Cousin Angela! No man ever looks at a woman as he looked at you, when your eyes were turned away, of course, unless he's in love with her. I caught him at it heaps of times. Oh, please, Cousin Angela, please love him for my sake!"

" Go to bed, you silly girl, and dream of your own affairs of the heart. Mine are of no importance."

Georgina and Angela differed as much in their characteristics as it was possible, considering that the two sisters had many sympathies in common and were in many points extremely congenial. At home Georgina went about everything in the calmest and most methodical manner; while Angela, lively, sensitive, and almost always happy, was extremely erratic and uncertain in her habits. When travelling, Georgina asked questions unceasingly, but with such an air of interest and such grace of manner that everyone cheerfully gave her all the information at their command. Angela was more timid and somewhat shy, and, being vague and dreamy, got into countless difficulties simply because she was so easily diverted from her course by every new emotion that came upon her and every unexpected incident that crossed her path. In the matter of admirers, neither of the sisters had failed to attract a goodly number of the male sex; but while Georgina had only dismissed her suitors after critically and sternly looking over their qualifications, Angela never realised that any man was in love with her until she was surprised into a refusal.

Chapter XI

TARASCON

MARGOT was awake the next morning before she heard the birds; but not before the denizens of the little southern city were stirring.

If Arles merits the reproach of "*une tombe*" hurled at it by Dumas, and which M. le Colonel had repeated with vehemence the day previous, it is a very lively tomb from sunrise to sunrise, thought Margot, as she leaned out to look at the passers. "Nobody ever sleeps in France when they should!" Although it was only at rare intervals that the young lady herself had been sleepless enough to confirm this opinion, many tourists will agree with her.

It was far too early for Margot to hope that her cousin would be awake, or to expect a cup of coffee; but hearing the cheery voice of the porter, who was sweeping the apology of a sidewalk adorning the front of the hotel, and who was beguiling the dulness of his task by joking with the passing market women, she dressed slowly, packed her luggage and went down. She was greeted with a rare welcome by the sweeper, who went off at once and brought her coffee.

She took her slender meal in the bright morning air, where above her head in the nests among the fresh green leaves of the thick shining foliage of the great trees

Tarascon

the belated birds were preparing for their day's work. The papa-birds, who had been out hunting that imprudent early worm, came home and vied with one another in song. The big Borzoi appeared with the Colonel's servant, and Robinson, who, notwithstanding the presence of a tramway, was as secure from harm as he would have been in the depths of a forest, was left to play with his long-legged comrade while his owner went to wake her cousin.

They were to take a very early train, so Angela came down to have her coffee likewise before the door. The cordial hostess presented them with a pretty souvenir of Arles, regretted their departure, their trunks were brought down, the omnibus filled with their numerous parcels, and away went the swaying, rakish, rattling little vehicle on a mad career through the irregular, narrow streets, the foot passengers fleeing at its approach to the miniature sidewalk, not wide enough to afford a good foothold, and blotted against the houses, laughing and rallying the driver as he pretended to flick them with his whip.

Angela Victoria counted their packages, to which a few more had been added in Arles, and were numerous enough to cause them to be mistaken for travelling Belgians.

"What will Georgina say when she sees all these bundles and boxes!" she said in despair to Margot, when she was tying them up before starting.

"She won't see them unless we choose to let her. I will buy a basket in Marseilles and dump them all in together. How many are there, seven?"

"Yes; not quite one for each city we've visited."

"I don't care. I adore travelling with you, Cousin Angela; you don't care how we go or what we do. Mamma would have been very cross if I had asked her to go to some place where we would have to come over the same line again, as we shall do this afternoon."

"So would Georgina," thought Angela to herself, but she didn't say it. "We can't very well help coming back, if we turn our faces northward when we ought, as orderly tourists, to keep on going toward the south. I shall be glad for my own sake to pass through Arles again and see the amphitheatre."

"It will seem just like coming home when we see it. I feel as if we have lived a year in every place we've been to."

They were such adaptable tourists that they had lived themselves into the life of each town in twenty-four hours, even though they remained deplorably ignorant of some of the most noted curiosities that the usual sightseer adores.

The train took them from Arles to Tarascon so rapidly that a lady in the corner who was telling her beads to put herself to sleep hardly got forty winks before the guard threw open the door and called on them to "*Descendez.*"

Margot sent off a lengthy telegram as soon as they were out of the station. It cost her fully one franc and a half, and, being written in English, excited the operator's inquisitiveness so much that he could hardly be restrained from insisting upon the translation. Such a long and expensive message from *une jeune dame*

Tarascon

charmante to a gentleman! By some means he found out what a part of it meant before he despatched it.

"*Un rendezvous!*" he thought with glee, and clicked it off at once.

It was still early in the day. A few cats were sunning themselves on the boulevard at Tarascon; some babies were playing in the soft sand, but there was no excitement except that caused by naughty Robinson, who insisted upon behaving in a very unruly manner, stiffening out his legs and bawling at the cats; refusing to come on when called and finally becoming so totally lost to all sense of obedience that he met with the effective and disgraceful punishment of being fastened onto a leash. His intimacy with the Borzoi had completely demoralised him.

Margot looked about and at once settled upon a house which she declared must have been the home of the great Tartarin. To her Daudet's hero was a real personage.

"I know this is the place, Cousin Angela; isn't this the third house on the *grande route,* and see what funny sorts of plants are in the garden, and what a great *grille* there is!"

Angela was not nearly as familiar with Tartarin of Tarascon and his doings, so minutely described by the witty Daudet, as she was with the deeds and private life of Richard Cœur de Lion, who has not now a historian worth quoting and about whom few know the truth.

Alas for Margot! the villa she picked out was not on the left, as it should have been, but on the right, and the queer growth she flattened her nose up against the railings to see was only the result of neglect. Roses, syringas, dwarf fig trees and vines were all fighting for place in a garden white with the dust of a dusty boulevard. The cousins strolled down into a narrow street, where under arcades built beneath the houses the market had sprawled itself all over the place. It was swarming with purchasers bargaining, buying, crying, and gesticulating; all noisy, all gay, all intensely *méridionale*.

"Every householder in Tarascon is here!" said Margot. "Isn't it delightful and amusing! How I love these people! But the cobbles are worse than in Arles. I must, I simply must, walk around the narrow streets where Tartarin used to creep like an Indian on the warpath every evening when he went to the *Cercle*." So, with the luckless Robinson in tow, like a prisoner, they hobbled painfully over the cruel pavements, turning and twisting corners and stumbling along through the narrow streets, until both, nearly lamed and very tired, turned on to another boulevard which, although picturesque, was exceedingly domestic in its character. The family washing of all Tarascon hung in long lines between the trunks of the fine trees, unblushingly waving in the breeze in front of some pretentious large houses enclosed in lovely gardens.

"Perhaps Tartarin lived here!" said Angela, a trifle maliciously. "This Boulevard *Intime* is quite as original as the delicious hero of Daudet's romance."

"Tarascon has ways of its own. I am sure this is a thing we can find nowhere else in France."

TARASCON

THE DOMESTIC BOULEVARD   THE MARKET PLACE

Margot shook her head sadly, and a melancholy horse, slowly dragging an equally sad fiacre, passing at the same moment, she immediately hailed the man and jumped in.

"I've done my duty, and hobbled in Tartarin's footsteps until my suffering feet shriek aloud for mercy. We will ride the rest of the way," and both horse and coachman, gathering courage from patronage, started up gaily, and off they went down between the lines of waving laundry to the Château of King Réné.

This massive, imposing castle is now a prison. It had one very sanguinary episode in its history, a bloody page which the gentle King Réné would have shuddered to foresee. The Revolution being over and Napoleon, who had reigned in France, banished from the empire he usurped, during the Hundred Days, Tarascon went mad with reaction. From the top of these château towers men, children, old men and women were cast ruthlessly down to perish on the rocks below; the slaughter was so great that after this wholesale season of murder the waters of the Rhone were clogged with floating corpses. The Duchess d'Abrantes gives a most horrible and vivid picture of this terrible period in her memoirs.

The big gateway and dignified aspect of the castle awakened in Margot's breast visions of romance which took quite a different form from those dreamy longings in which her cousin so often indulged.

"Think of housing miserable old felons in such an interesting place! I think they should have instead deposed kings and queens and poor knights and ladies, all pensioned by a rich republican government and ordered to walk around with crowns and look royal."

"My dear Margot!" exclaimed the horrified Angela. "What put such an extraordinary idea into your head?"

"Well, you see, my dear Cousin Angela, I can't whistle up ghosts as readily as you can, and I have always wanted to see some really royal personages, with their courtiers, walking around on castellated walls."

"In other words, you would like to have a sort of human antique museum established in every old castle."

"Well, not exactly. I can't express my idea very clearly, but I know what I mean. Old Paris, which they had at the time of the Exposition, was what put the idea into my head just now, I enjoyed it so much. I could realise then just how things looked in olden times. Why couldn't decayed tragedians and comedians be given good homes in old castles on condition they would dress in character? It would add so much to sightseeing; besides, it would make me want to study history."

Angela laughed heartily; but in her soul she thought herself it wouldn't be a bad scheme, although she could close her eyes and see knights and damozels at any hour of the day. She only said:

"They would all want to play the part of royal personages or they wouldn't stay. I am told that is the way with actors."

The view of the château from the long bridge over the road is less beautiful and more severe than from the land side. It rises sheer, a great yellow pile, from the rocks on the river bank. The suspension bridge was once carried away by that raging wind of the south, the furious mistral. Daudet does not let pass this incident in his incomparable tale. He sends Tartarin to Africa before he has ever ventured across the bridge between Tarascon and Beaucaire.

"The Rhone is so broad at that point, *ma foi! vous comprenez!*—Tartarin de Tarascon prefers the solid earth."

"He was just like the old ladies in Carcasonne who never went to La Cité," said Margot.

The Château of Beaucaire is a splendid ruin, still haughty in sleep, dreaming of its former grandeur. It looks down from a height across the Rhone on its rival, the more lowly castle of Tarascon. At the foot of the sheer rock on which its beetling towers stand are nestled the red-roofed houses of the little town, half-hidden in foliage.

"Everything is gold and turquoise to-day," said Margot, as they drove over the suspension bridge and looked back at Tarascon. No shade of blue known to artist or jeweller was lacking in the water and the sky. The young green of the trees which cover the islands in the river shone as though each leaf had a rim of burnished gold. The Castle of King Réné and the jagged ruins of Beaucaire, under the influence of the brilliant summer sun, looked like polished vermeille.

They left their carriage and wandered round through the old ruins until at last they came out under the shadow of a great tower and looked down on the glorious landscape spread out at their feet; the mighty river, the old town of Tarascon, looking most picturesque and full of colour, and Margot, perching herself where she could look about at castle and town, glanced mischievously into her cousin's face, as Angela leaned dreamily gazing about at the romantic old castle, then drew out of her pocket a book, from which she took a slip of paper and began to read aloud:

"Gone is mediæval glory, though we cherish still the story
   Of the deeds of knightly valour, which the modern heart expands.
 Would that with those gallant drubbings had gone also daily tubbings,
   That those knights and dainty ladies had seen fit to wash their hands."

"Oh, Margot!" said Angela, horrified. She had been meantime off mind-chasing after Aucassin and Nicolette, the ideal lovers of Beaucaire. "Where did you get that sacrilegious rhyme?"

"Be careful how you criticise, for I would have you know that this fine poem, which gives me infinite delight and satisfaction, was written right here at Beaucaire by no less a personage than the great Thomas Janvier, a real lover of the Midi."

"Stop, stop!" cried Angela, as Margot attempted to read more; "you are chasing away my choicest dreams of love."

Margot at once closed her memorandum book ostentatiously and sprang up.

"You have shut me up. Just speak to me of love in that tone, and the wit of even Thomas Janvier goes

TARASCON

MARGOT AND ROBINSON ON THE QUAY
THE TARASQUE LED FORTH

THE TARASQUE
TARASCON FROM BEAUCAIRE

Tarascon 339

back into seclusion—for the time being," she added, softly. "Let's talk about those other people. Who were they? The lovers, I mean."

"You shall have the poem about them. It was written in old Provençal, I believe, but I have a translation by Andrew Lang. I will give it to you to bind in one book with the witty bit you have in your hand, and then you can read them alternately to keep your wits balanced."

"Cousin Angela Victoria! I think you are the one who needs to keep her wits balanced! You are letting Robinson chew up your glove!"

Sure enough, the little brown doggie, not interested in lovers, and still less in washings, had stretched his neck, and the absentminded Angela had bestowed upon him one of her gloves, which he was enjoying hugely, having no bone. Robinson knew it was time for luncheon.

"He's so awfully naughty to-day! I don't know what to do with him, he's so bad," said his mistress, looking at him with the fondest affection. "He must be getting tired of travelling."

They got into the fiacre and went back over the sunny bridge, rejoicing in the warmth. They had not yet seen the church, which the guide book declared was worthy of a visit.

"We've almost come to the end of our journey," said Angela Victoria, with a sigh, "and we mustn't miss anything that Georgina will ask us about."

Margot made a grimace, and then, when she saw that on the face of the Church of St. Marthe, above the sumptuous portal that some vandals had painted in yellow and red letters a foot or more long, "*Liberté Égalité, Fraternité,*" she positively refused to go in, and told the *cocher* to "drive on." Even the tomb of a king could not tempt her. Amiable Angela Victoria allowed the young lady to have her own way, and they drove about in the light and air until it was time for *déjeuner* at the Hôtel des Empereurs. Here in the solid old inn, centuries old, spotlessly clean, where the thick walls occupy more space than the rooms, they ate a good luncheon; Robinson and some gaudy cavalry officers being the only other guests.

"We still have an hour to wait here before train time," said Margot. "Let's go shopping. You need some gloves."

"I wouldn't stumble over those petrified mole-hills again," said Angela, looking down at her shoes, "for all the gloves in the world."

Margot tried to tease her. "But we haven't seen enough to put in your book."

Angela winced. Her illusions about her ability as an ideal traveller had been swept away effectually. They had died in the glowing air of the South. Her literary aspirations had ended at Carcasonne. "I don't care anything about the book! And I will not walk on those pavements. If you can find a shop on the boulevard you can go in and buy me some gloves. I will sit in the sunshine under the trees outside and wait. The boulevard sand is soft to my lacerated feet; they will bear nothing else, and the boulevard is on our way to the train."

"*Va pour le boulevard!* We have oceans of time, and I see a Grand Bazar in the distance."

They strolled slowly down the broad dusty walk under the trees, passing numerous cafés, deserted at this hour; at last they reached the shop, which was on a corner very near the house Margot insisted upon believing had been Tartarin's.

" I wonder what they are going to do with all those stones piled up there? " asked Margot. " I hope they are not going to ruin our garden and build up some horrid new shop."

Angela looked around. Tarascon had exhibited to her unobservant eyes no violent signs of improvements or activity in the building line. Even the Grand Bazar appeared to have inherited its shelter from some building erected in the last century and modernised only by a great sign and a promiscuous assortment of articles which overflowed onto tables spread before the door.

With Margot's usual habit of exaggeration, she had converted some bags of mortar, a little mountain of sand and a piled-up heap of stones, with which for the last six months Tarascon had been preparing to restore the curbing along the boulevard, into a six-story building.

Margot looked on the array of articles exhibited by the keepers of the Grand Bazar with the eager delight of a young American who is anxious to spend her money.

"I see lots of things I want, Cousin Angela," she said. " You sit down there on the bench, if you don't want to come into the shop, and I will buy your gloves."

Under the trees was the bench indicated, and thereon sat a very old man sunning himself while he smoked.

Angela took her place beside him, and he at once politely removed his pipe. She begged him to continue smoking, and he smilingly bowed his thanks and immediately asked her if she was a stranger in Tarascon. She told him that she was and that she had come because it was the home of Tartarin. He laughed merrily and shook his head.

"*Ce coquin de Daudet!* At first we of Tarascon were very much incensed at his nonsense, but he has sent us more tourists than Beaucaire, King Réné and Ste. Marthe all together." Angela was preparing a reply when Margot dived out of the shop in a hurry, driving Robinson.

"Oh, Cousin Angela; please hold Robinson! He's hunting all over the place for rats and upsetting things right and left." She left him and went back toward the shop, and then suddenly turned round, calling over her shoulder: "Keep a watch out for automobiles!"

Angela did not understand at all what this last mysterious injunction meant. She supposed the warning concerned Robinson, and as the little doggie sat dejectedly down beside her she put her foot on his strap to hold him there. Robinson turned his melancholy gaze toward the bazar and watched his mistress disappear into the door of the place where his instinct told him there were numerous rats to be slaughtered.

The old man looked at the comical little dog with a highly amused expression in his eyes.

"He is very funny, *très drôle!* A true little Tarasque!" Robinson did not appear insulted at all, and yet the Tarasque is the reverse of beauty.

"You do not know the Tarasque?" the old gentleman asked.

Upon her negative reply he told her the story. The Tarasque is a mythical beast who grew out of a legend. Provençe does not hesitate to claim as pilgrims to its shores all the near friends of our Saviour who left Jerusalem after His crucifixion. One of these, Ste. Marthe, a sister of Mary Magdalen, chanced to wander up the Rhone as far as Tarascon. Here she found weeping and wailing and gnashing of teeth. A horrible dragon, whose chief diet was young children, roared and belched forth fire and smoke and lived in a most inconvenient proximity to the town. There was in those days no mighty hunter like Tartarin, no troupe of *chasseurs de casquette* to demolish him. If any of these heroes went out against the monster he ate them up so effectually that they have not survived in history. St. George was far away, but Ste. Marthe, a gentle, weak lady, who must have passed by that time the first flush of youth, came to the relief of the countryside. As soon as she heard the wails and woes she went into the woods in search of the dreadful beast, exorcised and tamed him so completely that she returned to town leading him from his lair by a piece of blue ribbon—at least, so she is represented when the Tarasque is paraded once a year in her memory, at Tarascon, guided gently to the place where the procession starts by a young girl leading the horrible monster with a simple leash of that colour.

In remembrance of the sainte's somewhat disagreeable pet the Tarasconais fabricate each year a less dangerous monster of wicker and painted cloth.

"In my young days," said the old man, "we fellows used to get inside of the dragon and go sprinting all over the town, upsetting everyone who came in our way. Why, I nearly ran down——" he went off into chuckles of delight at his recollections. "Why, I nearly ran down my dear old wife. She was '*une jeune fille*' then—and—but where is your Tarasque?" he cried.

Angela looked down in alarm. Robinson had not only disappeared, but she heard the "chug-chug" of a motor approaching through the narrow street, coming, as it seemed to her unsophisticated ear, at a high rate of speed around the corner. Margot's injunction flashed into her mind. She started up, calling anxiously, "Robinson! Robinson!" His little brown body met her distracted gaze on the other side of the pile of stones. He was directly in the path of the auto, she imagined, and was straining violently to get himself free from some invisible fetter. The car was coming nearer, and Angela, never cautious, always recklessly impulsive and daring, because she did not stop to think, jumped forward without a moment's hesitation and tried to snatch the little doggie she loved. His leash had become entangled. Anyone else would have remembered and unhooked the fastening. Not so Angela Victoria. She threw herself on her knees and tugged at the leather strap.

There was a crash. A car twisted suddenly around.

Something happened which no one present was ever truly able to explain. It was all over in an instant after the old man spoke, but it seemed the tragedy of an hour. A man leaped from the car, jammed with its front wheels against the stones; Angela, paralysed, still clinging to Robinson, felt herself lifted and carried limp and fainting into the Grand Bazar. The driver flung himself out of the auto, the old man stood up and beat on the bench with his stick, shouting for a doctor; the clerks ran out of the shop, and a tumult of small boys appeared from no one knows where. Margot rushed out in the wake of the others, crying: "Oh! oh! What is it? Dick! Angela! Robinson!"

She was too excited to think, until her cousin, put gently in a chair near the door, staggered to her feet and dropped the dog. Richard Hardy tried to laugh it all off. "I did not expect to come upon you like this!" But his face was very pale, and Angela's smile was hardly merry.

Margot flew in and out of the bazar, talking excitedly in English and French. To Angela she reported:

"They have smashed something. Uncle Dick doesn't know yet what it is. Perhaps they can fix it up and get back to Marseilles, as they intended."

Robinson, perfectly subdued and knowing full well that his forbidden pursuit of rats had caused some dreadful disaster, hid discreetly under Angela's chair. This lady, who felt quite as ashamed of herself as the naughty little doggie, made a violent effort to recover her self-possession, and left the shop to join the rest of the party. She knew what Georgina would say; so she knew what Mr. Hardy must think. She did not dare to look at him while she made some silly attempt to excuse her stupidity. Young Richard, looking very much like his uncle, as he stood with his arm linked through Margot's, assured her that not much damage had been done.

"Uncle Richard is under the machine now! It was all his fault! We were going awfully slow and could have stopped all right, all right, if he had only left my hands alone. I don't know what could have struck Uncle Dick. I never knew him to interfere with my steering before!"

But something had been injured beyond repair. Mr. Hardy and a man who had arrived without warning from some unseen garage came around from where they had been crouching under the body of the car, examining springs and wheels, and reported that the auto would have to return ignominiously as freight.

The quartette of would-be motorists therefore had to pursue their journey to Marseilles in an overcrowded compartment of a train instead of gaily rolling along the fine roads in an automobile.

The accident, slight as it was, afforded Tarascon a theme of conversation for the rest of the week. The old gentleman went home, and with many "Ohs!" and "Ahs!" enlarged upon the affair with such picturesque eloquence and with such a wealth of hyperbole that his excited family would not let him go out alone again for days.

Stories fly with as lightning-like rapidity in Tarascon as they do in most small towns. Therefore, two young women, who, an hour after the accident, sat in the same carriage with Angela and her party, but were perfectly unconscious that their companions were the heroes of the occasion, were in a fever of anxiety about a terribly battered auto, as one of them described it, that had been wrecked in the streets of Tarascon.

"They say a man was hurt and a woman nearly killed! The wheels mounted that immense pile of stones near the hospital. *Tu sais!* those great stones that have been there since the winter. It was dreadful! The car hung in midair and all the bottom was bent into scallops by the sharp edges of the blocks." She gave her imagination free rein regarding the car; and although her friend knew that the injuries were quite as much exaggerated as the size of the pile of stones, she received the news with a shower of ejaculations: "*Aie! Oh, la, la!*"

Nobody contradicted the story-teller. Everybody listened respectfully, even Robinson, who tried to make himself very small and to look very meek in atonement for his part in the affair. He snuggled close to Richard, who stroked him gently nearly all the way to calm his little dog feelings.

Before they had run through the poppy-strewn land and had come to the bare limestone hills which, falling down into dusky olive groves, finally bathe their feet in the azure flood of the Mediterranean, young Richard and Margot had forgotten everything but their own happiness at being together again; and Angela Victoria was as serene as if she had never recklessly and foolishly thrown herself in the path of death. Richard Hardy was the only one of them all who seemed more grave and serious than the occasion demanded.

"Do you always travel round with all those packages, Margot?" asked young Dick. "You look like an express messenger."

"Then that's what you'll look like when we get out," said the happy young girl, "for I expect you to carry every single one of them."

"Why not give a few to Robinson?" laughed Dick.

"No, Robinson has to look after Cousin Angela now. She's proved how much she loves him."

"Too perilously!" murmured Uncle Richard. It was his only contribution to the conversation.

Mrs. Hardy, Dick's mother, was overcome with surprise when they arrived, tumbling out of a crowded fiacre instead of rolling up the driveway in a beautiful motor car.

After all had been explained she said to Angela: "You must stop here in Marseilles with me until the automobile is mended. The run along the Littoral from here to San Remo is so entrancing it would be a shame to lose it."

But Angela's pleasure in motoring was over for the present. She would like to have stopped there in that beautiful villa among the tropical plants in the luxuriant garden, with the wide blue sea at the foot of the terrace; but she did not dare. There were many things that disturbed her serenity, that combined to make her fear for her own happiness.

"I could not possibly disappoint my sister. She has waited for me so much longer than she intended. We must go to-morrow."

They had tea on the terrace, and sat long afterward watching the wonderful variations of the jewelled hues on the water, as the sun sank lower and lower. The desolate, protecting, embracing mountain whose grey mass rises above the Corniche road became glorified with the oblique rays of the great, golden sun. The glittering top of Notre Dame de la Garde shone like burnished gold, and the Château d'If floated like a bit of dull amethyst on the rainbow-hued water.

After tea, when Mrs. Hardy had gone into the house to make some arrangements about the morrow and Margot and young Dick had long since taken themselves off in a fiacre to town " to buy a hat Dick thought would be becoming to her," Angela, left alone, strolled down among the thick palms to the edge of the garden wall, there to stand and watch the opalescent water. The sun, growing larger and more vivid, was almost at the edge of the horizon, and the beauty of the scene grew bewildering to her soul, when she heard footsteps slowly crunching the gravel behind her.

Her heart began to beat violently. She wanted to fly, but she had not even the courage to turn. She would brave it out. She would be curt in her speech. She hardly had time to determine what she really would do when Richard Hardy stood beside her.

"How very wonderful is a splendid sunset after a dark, dark day!"

She looked up at him in surprise; it was not what

she expected. "But this has not been a dark day!" she exclaimed.

"It held one second so dark for me," he said, with great intensity, "that years will not be long enough for me to forget it." Then, talking very rapidly, he went on: "Oh, how could you risk your life so recklessly! You could not know what you were doing! You ought to be scolded like a naughty child, and I would like to tell you how I feel, if I had but the courage."

It was all so unlike what she expected that she looked up into his face coquettishly, with a little malicious smile, and said:

"Do you lack courage, Lion Heart?"

"I lack it so much, I am such a coward, that I let you drive me away from you at Carcasonne. My lion heart was not bold enough to ask you to give me back just a little of the love which had grown to be too strong for me to hide."

Motor cars coming upon her suddenly could never give Angela such a flood of indescribable terror as poured over her soul at that moment, standing in a halo of orange light above the calm sea. She did not know what to say or how to say it; insensate joy followed the terror, and just as the round, hot, red sun dipped into the water she turned and smiled at him.

Life was all brightness at that sunset hour!

Before Angela knew how it had happened, Richard put his hand under her chin, tipped back her head and kissed her squarely on the mouth. Angela Victoria, whose heart was as young and timid as her fresh spirit, shrank a little from this bold caress; but her lover put his strong arm more firmly around her, and drawing her to his side, pressed her head close against his heart.

"As long as I live I will love you and I will take care of you! You shall wreck no more automobiles! No more portfolios shall be lost! You shall travel when and how you like—with me, of course! And if you elect to write ten books, I will see that they are all published. And Robinson shall live with us on the fat of the land, for I owe him my happiness."

"Margot will never give up Robinson!"

"But you and I want the little doggie. Suppose we go in this moment and ask her to surrender him to us as a wedding present!"

So, with his daring arm still clasping her shoulder, he led her slowly through the thicket of palms and roses, up the steps into the salon of the villa, where Margot and Dick came storming in to receive them on their return from the shopping expedition. Angela Victoria cringed a little at Richard's bold embrace, and her face was diffused with a colour that made her look inexpressibly lovely.

"It was hard to get up so early and leave everyone and come off by train when we expected to bowl along the Littoral in a motor car!" Margot told Georgina, when, after the arrival in San Remo, they were drinking tea on the balcony of the Villa Mafalda. "But even from the train the coast is superb! The hills look like old, thick-skinned, crouching grey monsters come down to drink in the sea. There are funny little

A Spring Fortnight in France

towns built on the top of hills; there are gorges and plains and olive groves and oranges; and, of course, the great, changeable Mediterranean, with the fashionable villas in splendid gardens. The mountains were first grey, then green, then red; and the flowers! the flowers! Did you see them, Cousin Georgina? Or did you come by night?"

"Oh, I came quite another way, my dear," she answered. "But, Angela, how did your writing come on? Is it finished?" There was a tinge of sarcasm in Georgina's voice.

Angela Victoria's face grew crimson. She hesitated for a reply. But Margot answered glibly: "She hasn't got the book *quite* written, Cousin Georgina, but she's got a publisher waiting, and he's coming to fetch it *very* soon—in an automobile!"

Georgina looked astonished, puzzled, then grave. She understood.

"I see, Angela Victoria, that you are even less fitted to travel alone than I thought."

www.ingramcontent.com/pod-product-compliance
Lightning Source LLC
Chambersburg PA
CBHW020632230426
43665CB00008B/144